Alexander Wedderburn

Special report on the extent and character of food adulterations

Including state and other laws relating to foods and beverages

Alexander Wedderburn

Special report on the extent and character of food adulterations
Including state and other laws relating to foods and beverages

ISBN/EAN: 9783337200961

Printed in Europe, USA, Canada, Australia, Japan

Cover: Foto ©Andreas Hilbeck / pixelio.de

More available books at **www.hansebooks.com**

U.S. DEPARTMENT OF AGRICULTURE.

DIVISION OF CHEMISTRY.

BULLETIN   No. 32.

SPECIAL REPORT

ON THE

EXTENT AND CHARACTER

OF

FOOD ADULTERATIONS,

INCLUDING

STATE AND OTHER LAWS RELATING TO FOODS AND BEVERAGES,

BY

ALEX. J. WEDDERBURN,

SPECIAL AGENT.

PUBLISHED BY AUTHORITY OF THE SECRETARY OF AGRICULTURE.

WASHINGTON:
GOVERNMENT PRINTING OFFICE.
1892.

LETTER OF TRANSMITTAL.

U. S. DEPARTMENT OF AGRICULTURE
DIVISION OF CHEMISTRY,
December 9, 1891.

SIR: I have the honor to transmit for your approval the manuscript of Chemical Bulletin No. 32, being a popular report, by Mr. A. J. Wedderburn, on the adulteration of foods and drugs.

This report is a continuation of the work published in Bulletin No. 25 of the Division of Chemistry, and is designed to place in more popular form than the strictly scientific bulletins of the Division the information which we have collected in respect to the extent and character of food adulteration.

Respectfully,

H. W. WILEY,
Chemist.

Hon. J. M. RUSK,
Secretary.

LETTER OF SUBMITTAL.

ALEXANDRIA, VA., *October* 20, 1891.

SIR: I have the honor to submit herewith a special report upon the character and extent of food adulterations in the United States, prepared in compliance with the terms of my commission received from the Secretary of Agriculture March 4, 1891. Having been directed to prepare a report similar in character and scope to Bulletin No. 25 of the Division of Chemistry, I have carefully collated such new information upon the subject of food adulteration as is obtainable, and from the mass of valuable matter thus acquired have selected that which seems to be most important. In performing this work the effort has been made not to encroach upon the scientific phases of the subject, which are now receiving the attention of the division under your charge, and have already afforded such satisfactory results.

Very respectfully,

ALEX. J. WEDDERBURN,
Special Agent.

Dr. H. W. WILEY,
Chemist of the U. S. Department of Agriculture.

TABLE OF CONTENTS.

7

EXTENT AND CHARACTER OF FOOD ADULTERATIONS.

By Alex. J. Wedderburn.

THE EXTENT OF ADULTERATIONS.

The inquiry into the extent of the adulteration of food, drugs, and liquors, provided for by act of Congress, demands a report on the actual condition existing as to the adulteration of all articles taken into the human stomach, and that such report be sufficiently terse to be generally useful and at the same time so free from scientific statements and phrases as to make it available to the average reader. The object of Congress in making the appropriation in question was evidently to secure facts upon a subject of great importance, and one which is now agitating the public mind to an extent never before reached except upon a political question. Keeping this object in view, the attempt is made in this report to follow the character and scope of Bulletin No. 25. The correspondence had with leading men of all professions, especially with those engaged in investigating food adulteration and in manufacturing food products of various kinds, is thoroughly convincing as to the very general extent of the sophistication of the food, drug, and liquor supply.

No one can follow the varied and valuable reports made by the various State officers, in those States where laws exist (and a sufficient appropriation is made to execute them), without being convinced of the value to the State of such legislation. In previous bulletins issued by the Department, various laws upon this subject have been published, and herewith will be found some new laws recently enacted by other States, and which seem, in some respects, to cover the ground better than older laws. There will also be found numerous extracts from reports, letters, and other documents supplied by correspondents who have kindly assisted in the effort to procure facts worthy of consideration. These extracts have been classified and arranged under various headings, and will be found under their classifications in as short space as it is possible to present them. There is no mention herein of a subject that occupied considerable space in Bulletin No. 25, viz, the diseases of animals used for food, Congress having by legislative enactment eliminated the subject from discussion, at least for the present.

9

Only one question of importance connected with the cattle industry and the food supply remains to be considered, and that is "milk." This article of universal diet, and upon which the future generations depend for life, is shown conclusively to be extensively adulterated both with water and by feeding the animal producing it with unhealthy food, and using the product of diseased cows.

The scientific work performed in the Division of Chemistry of this Department, in its investigations into the various food adulterations, shows conclusively the actual extent and character of food adulterations, and should be carefully considered by all interested in the subject. That adulteration exists to a most alarming extent can not, from the evidence be doubted; that the character is generally fraudulent rather than dangerous seems to be also pretty well established.

The extent to which sophistication has been practiced and the utter recklessness and hard-heartedness of the adulterator are shown by numerous instances which have come to my attention where the food for animals, horses, and cows especially, have been adulterated, in some cases the products having been heavily weighted with sand and plaster. Comment on such action is needless.

Wholesome laws have succeeded in checking the commercial frauds, but it is generally conceded by all State officers engaged in the work that until national legislation supplements State laws, all such enactments will prove insufficient and unsatisfactory. The report from London shows that the anti-adulteration laws of Great Britain have almost entirely stopped the nefarious practice. The laws of New York, New Jersey, and Massachusetts, which have been fairly well enforced, have done much towards stopping the practice, or at least compelling the proper branding of the articles sold.

There is a general demand for remedial national legislation on this subject. No one, however, desires to prevent the legitimate manipulation of any article so long as it is branded properly; to ask more would be unjust, to ask less is to condone a felony and countenance a fraud.

THE CHARACTER OF ADULTERATIONS.

Fortunately the character of the adulterations used is generally harmless except from a financial standpoint. Were the case otherwise the damage done to the public health would be alarmingly great. While commercial frauds are the rule there are, as is proven, many cases where ill health and even death follow the use of articles poisoned with pigments, acids, tin, rancid oils, and other injurious commodities which are used to cheapen or add beauty to the article sold.

Polishing, powdering, watering, and adding such harmless ingredients as earth, cracker dust, peas, beans, starch, etc., are comparatively harmless, and would pass for honesty and uprightness when compared to the compositions above alluded to, and others, such as plaster of Paris,

soap stone, fusil oil, red ocher, fuller's earth, terra alba, and other ingredients of like character; but even these are less harmful than the
adulterations of drugs by which, as is shown, the very element of strength
upon which the physician relies to save life is often extracted, left out,
or diluted until it becomes a matter of grave doubt whether a prescription really contains what is ordered by the physician. When we call in a
physician and he prescribes certain drugs, it is our right to be able to
purchase them and not such spurious articles as dishonest manufacturers
and venders may palm off at their option. It is shown elsewhere that
laudanum, an article generally used to assuage suffering, has been sold
at a standard of 0 when the morphine should have reached 1.2 to 1.6.
It is also shown that in the fifty samples reported to the Pennsylvania
Pharmaceutical Society that there was a variation from 0 or even .03
to 1.19; the dose required in the one case to relieve pain would in the
other bring permanent and final relief.

The various decoctions, after being doctored with fusil oil, acids, ether,
chloroform, and other drugs usually sold for stimulants and beverages,
are undoubtedly the cause of many diseases and result not infrequently
in death. That they increase drunkenness is an admitted fact, impair-
ing the intellect and creating an unnatural thirst which leads the user
to greater excesses in his desire to destroy the effects of the poisons
taken into the system.

While this class of adulterations is certainly criminal, the commercial frauds are the most general, but result in less physical damage,
except in the case of milk adulteration; by this practice the nourish-
ment of the babe is abstracted, the helpless infant slowly starved,
and, when suffering from the pains of hunger, is made to keep quiet by
doses of injurious narcotics. To assume that such things are done
through lack of intelligence is asking too much of even the most charitable; it is simply done through a desire to accumulate money by unlawful and dishonest methods or to compete with some rival who is
cheating his customers. Hence it is thought necessary by most dealers
to join this army of knaves, self-preservation being the first law of nature.

COST OF ADULTERATION.

No reason exists for a change of the views expressed in Bulletin No.
25 as to the cost to the country of fraudulent adulterations; and, while
those figures have been attacked in certain quarters, still it is undoubtedly safe to estimate that at least 15 per cent of the entire food
product is adulterated in one form or another, the overwhelming proportion of which is sold under fraudulent brands.

Recent State laws are gradually rectifying this evil, but, as long as
the article is branded "pure" when it is "compounded," just so long
is the deception a fraud and the purchaser swindled. The American
Grocer adheres to its estimate of 2 per cent of adulterations, which

may hold good in New York, New Jersey, and Massachusetts, where good laws are tolerably well enforced;* no such figures will, however, answer for the entire country. Fifteen per cent, as stated in Bulletin 25, would be much nearer the mark, in which case the loss on food alone would reach nearly, if not quite, $700,000,000 annually. Whether this be true of food alone can only be determined by Government inspection and actual figures; but certainly when the adulteration of drugs and liquors is added the figures given are largely below the average.

LACK OF DEFINITION.

To define an adulteration one must first be able to define what the pure article is. This, in the absence of law and of regular formulas, is in many cases a matter most difficult. For example, in the case of all articles made from unestablished formulas, such as yeast powders, beers, patent medicines, etc., there can be no definition of purity; in the absence of such definition the attempt to define its adulterants is an extremely difficult, if not an impossible, undertaking. But when the manipulator in the pursuit of gain uses poisons, which upset digestion, impair the human constitution, and in many cases cause death, the matter becomes serious, and is too generally neglected. The use of such elements should be positively prohibited by law; in the absence of such legislation, the practice is carried on with impunity.

IS ADULTERATION UNIVERSAL?

The London Hospital, in discussing this subject, says:

Speaking from an experience of fifteen or twenty years, one medical man, at any rate, is able to say that he has not found his fellow men of the business class half so black as they have been painted. Wines, which are so commonly ordered for sick people, are seldom or never the poisons they are said to be, unless they are purchased at poison prices. The poor, who can not afford to pay for good wines and spirits, should leave such things entirely alone, if they can not procure them from charitable friends. An old-fashioned wine merchant admitted to the writer quite recently that poisonous wines and spirits are undoubtedly manufactured, but then they are manufactured because there is a demand for them on the part of people who can not afford to pay for bona fide wines and spirits. Those persons who can pay for genuine articles are just as sure of getting them honest and good as they are of getting honest and capable medical practice when they can offer reasonable fees for it. Exactly the same may be said of teas, coffees, cocoas, beef juices, infants' and invalids' foods, and their makers. All these things can be and are obtained of the highest order of excellence by people who are able and willing to pay for them according to their market value.

The above is doubtless true of America as well as of England, but, as stated elsewhere, the English laws have done much to mitigate the evil and protect the consumer.

It is a matter of less interest to the buyer to know that the article he

*The quotations herein made do not warrant such low figures, even for these favored localities.

buys is compounded or mixed than to know that it is properly branded. Few people suppose that a cheap article is as good as an expensive one, and many poor people, who are compelled to pay small prices, get poor goods.

Good prices, however, are no longer a guaranty of the excellence of those most important articles taken into the human system to relieve suffering and disease. It is plainly stated in New York State official reports that the cost apparently has had little to do with the quality of articles, as the poorest were often the highest in price, while the best were often sold at a low rate. All that can be learned from such testimony is that the practice of sophistication is general and sometimes, fortunately not often, dangerous. There can be no question as to the right of the buyer to get what he pays for. To delay, therefore, the enactment of laws which compel the proper branding of the food and drug supply is unjust to the many who are imposed upon by dealers selling inferior articles as good and pure ones.

The New England Grocer reports the case of George Valliere, of Fall River, Mass., charged with selling adulterated maple sirup, and says: " Here is a case where an innocent man may suffer for the sins of another. Let dealers be absolutely sure that the goods they sell are pure."

Cases of this kind are the ones which especially suggest the need of Federal legislation to protect the innocent dealer as well as his customer. The sirup in question came in original packages from an adjoining State, Vermont.

THE NECESSITY FOR INSPECTION.

All correspondents who have touched upon the subject unite in the opinion that the demand for national inspection is general and absolutely necessary. Among the replies received from New York will be found that of Mr. Thurber, one of the largest dealers in food supplies in the United States, and that of Mr. Barrett, editor of the New York Grocer, one of the most widely circulated and most popular journals in the interest of the food-supply trade, joins in the demand.

Dr. Chancellor, secretary of the Maryland State board of health, says:

Proper inspections, supported by honest merchants and citizens, can largely protect the community from the frauds and underselling of unprincipled adulterators here and everywhere, and to possess a reputation for honesty in this respect would be worth millions to the trade of the city of Baltimore.

The same writer remarks:

If a mad dog and nitroglycerin, though rarely present, are dangerous agencies, and as such require to be looked after, how much more important is it that we should take care of and protect from fraudulent adulteration the substances on which our existence depends. It can not be doubted that a fast advancing public opinion will, ere long, fully recognize the importance of health above any squeamish objections to a fancied disregard of " personal liberty " and property rights involved in the control of dangerous commodities.

As an example of the effect of inspection it may be noticed in the health report for the District of Columbia for 1890 that in the month of July, 1889, 648 dozen eggs were condemned. In August the number decreased to 90 dozen, and in September it fell off to one-fourth dozen, and since that date there has been none offered for sale. The same thing is noticeable in nearly all of the articles enumerated in the report.

The health department for the District of Columbia only four times in 1889 called on the courts, and in each instance the offenders were convicted and fined.

The saving estimated by Dr. Abbott in Massachusetts for 1886 was 5 per cent on $15,000,000, or $750,000. Such figures need no comment, and as they apply to all the States the necessity for protective laws is apparent.

In Massachusetts the average expense of collecting and analyzing for seven years ending in 1889 was $1.79 per sample. The increased purity of the food and drug products of the State show the cost to be comparatively infinitesimal, and the benefit of the greatest importance to the people of the State.

The percentage of adulteration found in the articles examined by the Massachusetts State board in 1886 was 36.9, while in 1884 it was over 60 per cent.

APPROPRIATIONS.

The following are some of the appropriations by the various States for 1890:

New York	$85,000
Massachusetts	95,000
Iowa	*20,000
Ohio	6,214

From the foregoing quotations it will be clearly seen that wherever efficient laws have been enacted, backed by sufficient appropriations to properly execute them, great good has resulted in interfering with the unlicensed trade in adulterated goods. Reputable merchants and manufacturers unite in urging general legislation backed by the State officials, most of whom in their reports complain of the lack of national laws and of inefficient laws or want of laws in adjoining States, which makes the enforcement of local laws much harder work, and in certain cases almost makes the law a dead letter.

Such laws as are enforced are giving satisfaction so general to consumers and to honest dealers that we find each year more rigid enforcement of the statutes, and that the field is gradually widening and additional territory is being covered, while in those States which have for the longest period been regulating the food supply we find amendments which greatly aid the inspectors in the performance of their work.

---

*Only half used.

All that is now lacking seems to be the enactment of a Federal law governing the interstate-commerce question, and misbranding (which is the greatest evil) will, at no distant day, become so rare that here, as in England, the fraudulent dealer will have ceased to ply his vocation to any injurious extent.

THE NECESSITY FOR LEGISLATION.

The necessity for legislation is proven by the existence of the fraud and the absolute impossibility of the States, by local inspections under local laws, to enforce a compliance with their regulations. The secretary of the State board of health of Maryland, Dr. C. W. Chanceller, one of the most distinguished sanitarians in the country, recently stated to me that in spite of the very excellent Maryland law (recently enacted and published herewith) he was unable to secure convictions under it, and that in his estimation a national law was the only remedy.

In New York and Massachusetts the health officers and inspectors have been more fortunate in their prosecutions, and numerous convictions have brought the offenders under some restraint.

The original-package decisions have added greatly to the trouble of enforcing State laws, and seem to demand of Congress some general legislation that will compel all products taken into the human system to be properly branded.

The unanimous opinion expressed by a large number of prominent State officials is that Congress should enact laws to protect the people against fraudulent branding of the supply of food.

The very general demand made by the leading agricultural and labor organizations of the country upon Congress for the passage of the pure-food bill, which came up for consideration during the last session of that body, indicate most unmistakably the feeling of the American people on the subject.

As a matter of convenience and reference the accompanying extracts, which are culled from the best sources of information attainable, are divided under appropriate headings.

A public acknowledgment of assistance rendered is due to the many gentlemen who so kindly and promptly responded to the requests for information. To enumerate their names would be impossible in the space at my command.

OPINIONS REGARDING THE NEED OF NATIONAL LEGISLATION RELATIVE TO FOOD ADULTERATION.

———

Replies to inquiries sent out were received from the following States: Alabama, California, Connecticut, Delaware, Florida, Idaho, Iowa, Illinois, Kentucky, Louisiana, Maine, Maryland, Massachusetts, Minnesota, Nevada, New Hampshire, New York, Ohio, Oregon, Pennsylvania, Rhode Island, Texas, Vermont, Virginia, and West Virginia, twenty-five in all.

The opinions expressed, as will be observed, unite in the belief that some relief should be secured to the people by national and State legislation. While the information received from some States has shown an absence of legislation on this subject, still the fact that so many States fail to provide proper laws to prevent misbranding the food supply is a matter of interest, especially when taken in connection with the earnest expression of competent, reliable, and efficient State officials who show that their greatest difficulties lie in this very fact, and in the lack of Federal legislation. It is to be regretted that no information has been received from certain other States, especially from Michigan, where good laws are in force and where the officials are actively and effectively engaged in enforcing them.

OPINIONS FROM STATE OFFICIALS.

In order to obtain expressions of opinion from those best qualified to speak upon the subject of a national anti-adulteration law, the proper officers of the various States, as far as their addresses could be obtained, were written to in regard to the matter. Their replies, which are given below, are worthy of perusal, and seem to indicate unmistakably the necessity for Congressional action, not only to aid honest manufacturers in carrying on a legitimate business, but also to enable State officers to enforce State laws:

COMMONWEALTH OF MASSACHUSETTS,
OFFICE OF STATE BOARD OF HEALTH,
13 *Beacon street, Boston, December 5, 1891.*

DEAR SIR: * * * A national law relative to food adulteration would certainly be very much to our advantage, since there are very many adulterated articles of food which come to us from foreign countries without restriction, the sale of which should be limited by law.

Yours, respectfully,

S. W. ABBOTT,
Secretary.

16

STATE OF MINNESOTA,
DAIRY AND FOOD DEPARTMENT,
St. Paul, December 11, 1891.

DEAR SIR: In reply to yours of a recent date, will say that the national Congress can not extend too much help to the several States in the matter of passing pure food laws and delegate to those States the right to pass such pure food laws as they may deem expedient and for the good of the people thereof.

I think a great work can be done in the several States through the State pure food departments and with the unrestricted rights of State legislatures to pass pure food laws for such departments to carry out and enforce for the prohibition or restriction of impure dairy and food products within the State borders. Our present interstate-commerce laws greatly interfere with the carrying out of many of our pure food laws. The interstate-commerce law and the courts seem to place impure foods on the same footing as pig iron or wool as far as the commerce between States go. An advanced step has been taken in the inspection of meats from a national standpoint, and I can not see why national law should in any way hamper the people's wishes in the matter of enforcing and passing pure food laws in their own States.

A. K. FINSETH,
Dairy and Food Commissioner.
Per J. A. LAWRENCE,
Assistant Dairy and Food Commissioner.

OFFICE OF NEW YORK STATE DAIRY COMMISSIONER,
Albany, December 16, 1891.

DEAR SIR: The dairy commissioner is not here and may not be for several days, hence I give you my opinion relative to the question you ask, namely: I believe that a general "anti-adulteration" law would be a good thing for all concerned. I believe it is always a wise thing to do the right thing, and I believe it is always the right thing to deal honestly. I do not see why dealers in commodities that are sold on the market for consumption have any more right to sell adulterated commodities than the purchaser of such commodities has to pay for them in counterfeit coins.

I believe that if some means could be devised whereby such dealing could be stopped or reduced to a minimum it would be not only a blessing to the people, but I believe that there are good reasons to anticipate that it would have a telling effect upon the health of the people of the country.

This is my personal opinion and not necessarily the views of the dairy commissioner of this State. Your communication will be laid before him when he returns; he may see fit to write you his views at that time.

Very respectfully, yours,

GEO. L. FLANDERS,
Assistant Dairy Commissioner.

OFFICE OF THE NEW YORK DAIRY COMMISSIONER,
Albany, January 21, 1892.

DEAR SIR: Your letter of the 10th ultimo has been laid before the dairy commissioner, together with reply to it by me on December 16. The dairy commissioner instructs me to say that he approves of the sentiments expressed in my letter, and he desires to add that Federal legislation may be such as to be a great benefit to us in this State in the enforcement of the statutes against imitation goods.

That one of the greatest needs now is, that some Federal legislation be enacted, such that we may be able to enforce the statutes upon our books without hindrance from the effects of the recent decisions of the Supreme Court of the United States in what is known as the original package cases.

Our laws in this State are aimed against not only adulteration, but goods in imitation or semblance of the pure or genuine article. Legislation that would help us most should be of such a character as to assist in enforcing laws along that line without necessarily bringing in the question of adulteration. That is to say, the laws may provide, as they should, against adulteration, but should not confine their operations to adulteration.

We find that goods are put upon the markets which are made in imitation or semblance of the genuine article, and well calculated to deceive the purchaser or consumer. Such goods may or may not be adulterated.

A law which confines itself to dealing with adulteration only would not reach this class.

Very respectfully, yours,

GEO. L. FLANDERS,
Assistant Dairy Commissioner.

———

TRENTON, N. J., *November 23, 1891.*

DEAR SIR: I sincerely hope Congress will adopt a suitable bill next winter to prevent adulteration and deception in food and drugs.

My time being limited to-day, I will take up your letter again and give you my humble views as to how a national law will benefit and assist the authorities in our State in the enforcement of her present laws on the subject.

I am, yours truly,

GEO. W. McGUIRE,
Dairy Commissioner.

———

OFFICE OF OHIO DAIRY AND FOOD COMMISSION,
Columbus, Ohio, December 3, 1891.

DEAR SIR: I was and am in favor of a bill similar to the Paddock bill. Will in the future write you more fully.

Truly, yours,

E. BETHEL.

———

OFFICE OF OREGON STATE FOOD COMMISSIONER,
Portland, Oregon, December 1, 1891.

DEAR SIR: I regard the manufacture of imitation foods, drinks, or medicines as frauds, and deny the power of any government to license a fraud. I believe that the Federal Government, as well as any of the States, have the right to prohibit the manufacture or sale of any article made in imitation of a pure article, it matters not under what name it is sold. The fact that it is made in imitation is fraud of itself.

The move put on foot to grant a State the right to prohibit the importation of articles from another State is plainly in direct violation of the Constitution of the United States. I don't believe that the Federal Government should pass any laws; let the State prohibit the making of all imitations. As regards butter imitations, the very fact that if the law requires the article (as our law does) to be "plainly marked, so as to establish its true character and distinguish it from pure articles," be strictly enforced, as our law is, stops the trade.

In 1885 I drove every pound out of our State inside of thirty days, and before I had been in office this time thirty days there were no butter imitations to be found.

Truly, yours,

W. W. BAKER,
Commissioner.

COMMONWEALTH OF PENNSYLVANIA,
STATE BOARD OF HEALTH,
Philadelphia, November 24, 1891.

DEAR SIR: Your favor of the 20th instant, in which you do me the honor to ask my opinion for your report as to the necessity and benefits of a national anti-adulteration law covering the interstate trade, is received. That we need stringent laws to prevent misbranding and injurious adulteration anyone who has taken the trouble to give any study to the subject can not fail to see. That it is unfortunate to have laws of different degrees of stringency and different scope of application in the several States is equally apparent.

If Congress could frame a law which would establish uniformity in regulation throughout the entire country the gain would be great. I am not enough of a lawyer to know exactly what constitutional objections might be raised against such an enactment, but it would seem to me that the result could be reached on the same line of procedure as that by which the interstate-commerce act was obtained.

Yours, very truly,

BENJN. LEE,
Secretary.

MADISON, WIS., *December* 4, 1891.

DEAR SIR: In my opinion too much can not be said to the end of securing national laws to control sophistication. State laws will never be so made that they can all be enforced without working hardship to manufacturers and dealers. Certain food standards will be fixed by one State and certain standards will be fixed in another. To have an effective law the same standard should obtain in all States. Then the maker or producer of foodstuffs can send one grade to all of his trade. Again, if national laws were in effect they would be a guide which all of the States would readily follow, and soon there would be a system uniform and just. I regret that I have not the time to follow this matter at length, but trust that you will do it for me. I am deeply interested in this matter, and none can more fully appreciate the discouragements that stand in the way of a single State or half dozen States to cope with this important question. We must have national legislation, and I firmly believe that it will come.

Very truly,

H. C. THOM.

Resolutions of the National Association of Food and Dairy Commsssioners.

The importance of a national law can not be more clearly shown than in the following expressions of the National Association of Food and Dairy Commissioners, adopted January 14, 1891.

Resolved, That it is the sense of this convention that Congress should at the earliest possible date enact such laws as will require that all dairy and other food products which enter into the commerce of this nation, both interstate and international, shall be true to name ; that all adulterations, imitations, or substitutions of or for any dairy or other food product shall be distinctly labeled as just what they are in all the commercial transactions into which they enter and over which Congress has control.

Resolved, That we respectfully ask of Congress such legislation as will secure to the several States proper police power, such as will enable them to protect their own citizens in the production of pure, healthful dairy and other food products, and against the importation and sale of fraudulent adulterations or imitations of such products, and of unsound and diseased meats, to which they are now exposed under the late famous "original package" decision of the Supreme Court; and to this end we most earnestly and respectfully ask that the Paddock bill, perfected by striking out the word "knowledge" in the fifth line of section 2 and in all other places where used in the same sense and connection, be speedily enacted into law, as also the pure-lard bill and the Hiscock bill.

The above resolution, so far as it related to the Paddock bill, was adopted.

Other reports—Arranged by States.

In Bulletin 25 the statement was made that the country had cause to be congratulated upon the character and ability of the gentlemen in charge of the sanitary and food inspectorships of the various States. Since that bulletin was issued the work of suppressing fraud in the food supply has been vigorously and in a measure successfully pushed. The same condition seems to exist now as at that time; the officers are careful, cool, and clear-headed in the prosecution of the delicate work assigned them, and in nearly every case where prosecutions have taken place convictions have followed. A merchant generally prefers to sell pure goods, but he is often deluded into selling impure ones because his competitor is doing the same thing, and the dishonest manufacturer paints in glowing terms the advantage and innocence of the deceit.

ALABAMA.

Dr. N. T. Lupton, State chemist, Auburn, writes: " I have no results of sufficient importance to report on the adulteration of food, drugs, and liquors."

CALIFORNIA.

J. Hoesch, secretary health department, San Francisco, writes : "We once in a while have an analysis of milk made; other than that nothing is done. If we find any food not fit for use, it is condemned by an inspector."

The great fight against adulterations in California came from the wine-growers. The State has special wine laws and a board of viticultural commissioners. The olive is fast becoming an important industry to this section, but as will be seen elsewhere the use of cotton seed and other vegetable oils as adulterants has so reduced the price that the olive orchards are being cut down to make room for more profitable crops. The State Grange has for several years warmly and earnestly advocated national legislation in favor of pure food.

CONNECTICUT.

From a pamphlet by A. L. Winton, of the Agricultural Experiment Station at New Haven, Conn., the following extract is taken :

The sale of adulterated foods in Connecticut has been carried on, as a rule, without restriction. We have, it is true, a general law " to prevent the adulteration of food and other articles," but it is practically a dead letter. While the special laws with reference to the sale of adulterated butter, molasses, and vinegar have been enforced and thereby much good has been accomplished, still other articles of food are grossly adulterated and the people find no protection.

The general adulteration law referred to empowers local boards of health to procure from dealers samples of suspected foods and drugs and have the same analyzed by one of the State chemists. In case a sample is found to be adulterated with "any deleterious or foreign ingredient" the certificate of the chemist to that effect shall be published in some paper and the cost both of the analysis and of publishing the certificate shall be paid by the seller. In all cases where samples are found to be pure the cost of analysis shall be paid by the city, borough, or town whose board of health caused the work to be done.

The principal reasons why this law has not been enforced are:

(1) Public opinion has not demanded it.

(2) It calls for the expenditure of funds from the treasuries of our cities, boroughs, and towns at the discretion of their several boards of health, and our municipalities have ever been loath to give their boards of health proper financial support.

(3) The State chemists are not equipped for making the analyses which the proper enforcement of the law would require. The food analyst should be thoroughly prepared to carry on a great variety of chemical and microscopical work.

The molasses and butter laws would likewise have failed to accomplish their purpose had not the experiment station at New Haven, in addition to the agricultural work for which it was originally designed, undertaken the analysis of the samples, in order that these laws might not become a dead letter like the general law regarding adulteration. The station is not, however, legally compelled to do this work. * * * In some measure the people in this State have profited by the work done elsewhere, chiefly in having their attention called to the subject. On the other hand, it is undoubtedly true that stringent laws in other States which drive adulterated foods out of their market drive them into ours. Adulteration is a profitable business and the opportunities offered in Connecticut are not neglected. Even where the best system for the suppression of fraud is in operation there are dealers who, especially when the chances for profit are great, are willing to run the risk of detection. Now that the people of Connecticut are being awakened to the importance of food adulteration laws, as was evinced by clauses inserted in the platform of both the leading political parties during the last State election, and in view of the extensive adulteration practiced in the other States, a better knowledge of the condition of the foods in our market seems desirable.

The evidence which has been produced, however, is sufficient to prove that the sale of adulterated foods is extensively carried on in the State, the material used being in some cases injurious to health, in others merely fraudulent. A subject of such importance deserves more of the attention of our lawmakers. While every effort is being made to secure the arrest and conviction of counterfeiters of money, the counterfeiters of foods, although standing no higher in the moral scale, usually go unpunished. This state of affairs will continue until a thorough system of food inspection is adopted. Adulteration laws properly enforced would not only save the public thousands of dollars every year, but the fines collected from offenders would go far toward defraying the extra expense incurred by the State.

DELAWARE.

Prof. C. L. Parry, chemist, Delaware College, Newark, Del., says: "I regret the work of this laboratory has not been on such subjects as to allow full answers to your questions."

The Delaware State Grange, like most all of the State Granges, passed resolutions demanding the passage of the pure food and pure lard bills.

FLORIDA.

Prof. Norman Robinson, State chemist, writes:

The only case of adulteration of which I have personal knowledge was a case in Sanford, Orange County, two years since, when a strong and probably "alcoholic strengthened" lager beer was sold under the name of "rice beer." The sale of the latter was permitted by the authorites; the sale of all "intoxicants" was, at the same time, strictly prohibited. Microscopic tests showed the entire absence of rice starch grains and the presence of barley and corn starch grains. My own conviction is that the beer contained "alcohol" which was the particular adulterant, and in this case was "poisonous or injurious."

The professor adds that his official duties do not require the examina- tion of food, drugs, and liquors, which are only examined incidentally.

ILLINOIS.

Dr. John H. Rauch, by direction of Governor Fifer, writes: "I regret to say that no systematic investigation has been made in this State with regard to the adulteration of food, drugs, or liquors."

Thanks are due Dr. Rauch for copies of synopsis of the laws of Illi- nois affecting health, and for the eighth annual report, in which he marks an account of the "Momence ptomaine" poisoning cases, which, how- ever, are not elsewhere referred to because the subject of live stock in- spection has already been acted upon by Congress.

Dr. Rauch says his board has several times investigated ice cream poisoning. In a few instances it was supposed to have been caused by the flavoring extract, but such was not the case.

Prof. Ed. H. Farrington, chemist, agricultural experiment station, writes: "During the year and a half that I have been in this State my attention has not been drawn to this subject. I believe a dairy com- missioner would be very helpful."

The following is taken from pages 64 and 65, Report State Board of Health, 1886:

FOOD SUPPLIES.

In general people must win and choose their own bread and meat; but it is too obvious to need argument, that the food supplies of cities must come from a distance, and the larger the city the greater the distance. In the long transportation decay begins its work and incipient diseases are engendered. Cupidity fearing loss conceals as best it can the damaged and tainted character of the meats and fruits it offers for sale, or tempts the poor, by a cheaper price, to buy and use its unwholesome viands. Adulteration comes to add its deceits and dangers in almost every dish which appears upon their tables. A thorough system of public inspection by competent, vigilant, well paid, and well watched inpectors may ward off much of the danger; but the remedy should begin back of that, in a well-chosen location of the abattoirs and slaughterhouses in a healthful situation, where the animals destined for slaughter may have ample yards and a supply of food and water, and where the meat may be free from tainted and germ-bearing air, and in the proper location and construction of the market houses, to allow them to be kept clean and sweet, free from all decay- ing animal or vegetable substances and from all taint of pollution and disease. The best food material may be spoiled in a few hours by the absorption of filth from a polluted and poison-loaded atmosphere. Cities must meet with due care the artificial condition which compels them to bring their food from such wide areas, or the ruined health and the scourging epidemic will surely punish their neglect.

The truth of these remarks will be generally admitted; but it is not the poor of large cities alone who are in danger; the well-to-do, and the inhabitants of rural towns and villages are liable to suffer also, as shown at Momence."

IDAHO.

Gov. Norman B. Willey, of Idaho, writes:

I regret to have no information to furnish you on the subject. The law of the State makes the offense a misdemeanor, but I can not learn that any punishment has ever been inflicted upon any person in connection with it. No complaint has been made to this office of unusual adulteration of food products or liquors, and no legislation has been undertaken.

IOWA.

Dr. J. F. Kennedy, Des Moines, secretary of the Iowa State board of health, says:

I am very much interested in your line of work, and wish we had some systematic inspections and examinations in this State.

At a later date, he writes:

We have no examiner of food and drinks in connection with our board, and hence no official reports. I have no personal knowledge on either of the above questions. Mr. Tupper, of Osage, Iowa, is our State dairy commissioner, and he can give you statistics relative to the purity of dairy products.

In another letter Dr. Kennedy says:

Unfortunately there are no provisions for investigations and hence no means of detecting adulterations. In consequence the law is, at least as far as any reported results are concerned, practically a dead letter. I presume some who know the prohibitions and penalties of the law are deterred thereby from resorting to such fraudulent methods as the law is designed to prevent.

KENTUCKY.

Dr. J. N. McCormick, secretary State board of health of Kentucky, writing from Bowling Green, says:

Your circular letter in regard to "adulteration of foods, drugs, and liquors," addressed to the governor, has been referred to this board for reply. Continued investigation in this State has developed the fact that the sale of adulterated food has been and is still extensively carried on. Our general laws upon the subject are practically valueless, although many municipalities are better protected by local regulations. This board has urged the passage of a bill prepared by the National Board of Trade upon the General Assembly, but its efforts in this direction have so far been unsuccessful. We hope to succeed better next winter.

LOUISIANA.

Prof. William C. Stubbs, State chemist, writes:

This station has recently made official examinations for the Chemical Division of the Agricultural Department, for the result of which reference to the report is made.

In his examination of molasses, honey, confectionery, etc., he found mainly glucose (starch and dextrin), and occasionally salts of tin, zinc, besides various coloring matters and terra alba in candies.

It will be seen that the salts of tin, zinc, and most coloring matters are poisonous. Terra alba (white earth) is certainly not wholesome, especially for children.

MASSACHUSETTS.

Reports furnished by Dr. Abbott, Boston, secretary to the board of health :

There were analyzed for the year ending September 30, 1889, 5,454 samples, being a greater number than any previous year except 1888, when under special legislation relative to oleomargarine the number was greater.

Food.

Number of samples analyzed	4,854
Samples found to be pure	3,213
Samples adulterated or not conforming to statutes	1,641
Percentage of adulteration	33.8
Number samples of milk analyzed	3,216
Above standard	1,971
Below standard or adulterated	1,248
Percentage of adulterations	38.7

Drugs.

Number analyzed	600
Of good quality	503
Not conforming to law	97
Percentage of adulterations	16.2
Total examinations of food and drugs	5,454
Good quality	3,716
Not conforming to statutes	1,738
Percentage of adulteration	31.9

The total examinations of food and drugs for the years enumerated show a marked decline in the percentage of adulteration, owing, doubtless, to the able State supervision and rigid inspections which are aided as far as possible by honest dealers and manufacturers. The inspection of 1884 shows the percentage of food products found to be adulterated was 60.3; since which time they have gradually been reduced until in 1889 they are only 33.8. In 1884 the percentage of milk adulterations was 69.1; in 1889 it was 41.9; in 1884 the percentage of drugs adulterated was 36.8, while in 1889 it was only 16.2.

Dr. Abbott reports 140 complaints for violation of the law, of which convictions were secured in 124 cases, the percentage of convictions being 88.5; 13 only were discharged, and 3 had not been acted upon.

In 1889, out of 53 prosecutions under the oleomargarine law in Massachusetts 47, or 89 per cent, were convicted.

A leading firm of millers' agents in Boston write:

Concerning wheat flour, would say that in twenty-five years' experience we never heard of but one case where adulteration with alum was charged, and that was a rumor, and if it was done it was to make bread show very white in baking.

The effect of such a flour on the system, especially young people who have not attained their growth, would be injurious.

Adulteration by white corn, ground fine, might be made and such has been done, but not of late years, since flour has been cheap. The effect of that would be not at all injurious, but would simply tend to decrease cost.

A prominent Boston packing house writes:

We have been offered a red coloring for tomatoes, but know nothing of its nature. Have never used it.

From several sources reports are heard of alum in flour, used to whiten, but a well-authenticated case of the use of this certainly injurious adulterant has not been found.

MARYLAND.

Governor Jackson says he "referred the matter to Dr. C. W. Chanceller, secretary of the State board of health, the board under the State laws having the power to enforce them.

Dr. Chancellor writes as follows:

I inclose herewith copy of the law passed by the general assembly, January session of 1890, in reference to the adulteration of food and drink. Since the passage of this act, I have had a large number of articles of food and drink examined, with the result that few of those, which admitted of adulteration or the adulteration of which was profitable, was entirely free from sophistication, and I can not, therefore, avoid the conclusion that adulteration widely prevails. Not only is the public health thus exposed to danger, and pecuniary fraud committed, but the public morality is tainted, and the commercial character of the country, no doubt, seriously lowered.

I may add that offenders against the adulteration laws of this State have, thus far, been treated in the courts in the most absurdly lenient fashion.

The following is taken from Dr. Chancellor's report for 1888, pages 36 and 37:

If our sugars manufactured here are all pure, our oleomargarine of the best, our vinegar all from high wines and cider, our beers and ales all they purport to be, our tinware all safe, our kerosene oil all up to the legal standard, our baking powders all good, our wines and spirituous liquors unadulterated and unmixed, and every one of our hair restorers and wall papers free from every dangerous ingredient, still there is need of competent inspectors to keep out the poisonous adulterated articles which are constantly liable to be brought here from other places.

B. B. Ross, of Baltimore, Md., reports baking powders and sirups as adulterated. He claims alum as the principal adulterant.

Some powders contain excess in starch filling, in 1 sample more than 50 per cent starch being found. Other food articles we have examined here have been free from presence of adulterations in appreciable quantities.

Messrs. W. P. Harvey & Co., Baltimore, truly say:

Everything has already been made public regarding the adulteration of lard. The merchants and handlers know all about it, but it is the great army of ignorant consumers who are deceived.

MINNESOTA.

A vigorous prosecution of the laws against dairy adulterations in Minnesota present a most satisfactory condition of the market, as they show an adulteration of only 7½ per cent. Of 20 samples of cheese none were adulterated, but 15 per cent proved to be below the legal standard of 40 per cent of fat to total solids. Only 5 per cent were skimmed cheese. The total average of cheeses examined were 45.17, while if all below the standard and the skim cheeses are left out the result is 50.91, or nearly 11 per cent above legal requirement, which speaks volumes for the effective enforcement of wholesome and judicious laws.

The report of the Dairy and Food Commissioner, Warren J. Ives, for 1889-'90 has in it much of value to the people of this State and the general public. The following extract is given:

As will be seen by reference to these reports, the inspection of the dairy and food products upon the market has been vigorously prosecuted. The results are such as to conclusively prove the benefits to the public resulting from the labors of the commission within the field included under the present laws with reference to dairy products; while some samples of milk are found that are below the legal standard, the cases of actual adulteration are rare. The samples of butter examined show that while there are plenty of samples of poor butter to be found, that but few butter substitutes are encountered upon our markets. The samples of cheese also prove to be uniformly pure and free from foreign fats.

BAKING POWDERS.

The statement has been repeatedly made that the law relative to the sale of alum baking powder was, to all intents and purposes, a dead letter, and since no prosecutions have been made under its provisions that it is totally without effect.

The aim and intent of the law was to secure to purchasers their right to a knowledge of what they were buying, and thus to enable them to protect themselves from misrepresentation and fraud. To this end it was prescribed that all alum baking powders state upon their labels "This baking powder contains alum." A conformity with this law is all that the Dairy and Food Commission seeks to secure, and their labors are proving successful, as shown by the following table taken from the report of the chemist. Since the publication of the former report there have been found 401 lots of alum baking powder on sale, of which 325 lots, or 81 per cent, have been found to be properly labeled, while only 76 lots, or 19 per cent, were without such distinguishing mark. That such a large portion of the alum powders of the market as found upon the shelves of the retailer should be those labeled in accordance with the law, which became operative only eight months ago, is surely a gratification to those having the enforcement of the law in charge, and plainly shows the wisdom of the methods employed in effecting such enforcement.

VINEGAR.

A large number of samples of vinegar have been examined, and are reported upon by the chemist. When the showing of the present is compared with that of former reports it becomes evident that the amount of vinegar that is manufactured and sold at wholesale which conforms in character and strength with the legal requirements is very largely increased, and that the manufacturers and wholesale dealers as a whole are endeavoring to supply an article that will pass inspection.

It becomes equally evident, as shown in the present report, that the retailer is largely responsible for the imposition and fraud which is still practiced. That such is the case is shown by the facts herein reported, that of a total of 163 colored vinegars examined 114 were represented to the inspector to be cider vinegar, while only 41 were found to be such upon analysis, and only 35 were found to be branded upon the barrel.

The law requires that all manufacturers and wholesale dealers in cider vinegar should brand the same as such, and that this provision is invariably carried out there can be no doubt. It is known by all intelligent dealers that vinegars otherwise branded do not represent the product of apple cider, and are not entitled to be sold as such. In consequence of these facts, in the future reports of the commission the plan of publishing the names of the retailers who persist in palming off colored low-wine vinegars as cider vinegars will be inaugurated in order that the public may be informed as to who the parties are who are thus imposing upon their customers.

In the same report, pp. 16 and 17, Prof. W. S. Eberman, chemist, makes the following report on vinegar and baking powders:

VINEGAR.

By referring to former reports from this department, it will be seen that the per cent of adulteration in vinegars is steadily on the decrease. Thirty-four per cent of the vinegar analyzed in the past four months was found to be adulterated. This report shows 29 samples of cider vinegar, 14 of white wine, 1 of orange, and 1 of maple vinegar; a total of 73 samples.

The temptation to adulterate and misrepresent comes through colored wine vinegar. The manufacturers and the wholesale dealers have worked well along the line of correcting the evil. The major portion brand and sell their goods according to the letter and spirit of the law. But many retail dealers take undue advantage of their customers, and instead of selling the pure cider vinegar, such as they call for, they palm off colored white wine. The deceptive practices of the retailer are being noted and in the long run will revert upon themselves.

BAKING POWDER.

In this connection I have to report 16 samples of baking powder received at the laboratory and analyzed. A marked improvement may be noticed so far as the general character of the baking powders found in the market is concerned. Only 2, or 12.5 per cent, were found to be adulterated or sold illegally. There is an evil, however, which is creeping in, and a practice among the manufacturers of baking powders that ought not to be countenanced, but receive the seal of condemnation. I refer to the blind label of the alum baking powders. Also, to their legerdemain in support of the use of alum in baking powders. As an illustration reference is made to an alum powder manufactured by the Phœnix Baking Powder Company, of Chicago, Ill. More especially is attention called to Nos. 70, 71, and 72 of the report, marked with a star.

The manufacturer of No. 70 states "that a small quantity of alum is necessary to retain strength of powder. Warranted healthful." Cream of tartar powders undergo a chemical change in baking which produces Rochella salts! What a marvelous statement for an intelligent manufacturer to make.

No. 71. "Alum adds strength but is not unwholesome or injurious."

No. 72. "It is free from potash alum and is not strictly an alum powder. We guarantee it to give perfect satisfaction."

Such jugglery would be tabooed by the veriest quack.

Prof. Charles W. Drew, of Minneapolis, reports to the Dairy and Food Commission the inspection of 1631 samples, of which 609 were analyzed with results showing:

	Samples.	Adulterated.	Percentage.
Milk	48	20	42
Baking powders	20	1	5
Vinegar	249	117	47
Lard	158	21	12
Ground coffee	10	10	100
Ground mustard	22	18	82

These vinegars mentioned above were not altogether below the standard, as only 48 per cent fell below the legal requirement, but the others were misrepresented as to quality and from what they were made.

The same authority says that out of 60 samples of confectionary examined he has failed to find a single case where terra alba existed, or any other article detrimental to health.

This report makes the first official mention that I have seen of the "manufactured coffee bean," which is being made in New Jersey and Philadelphia, and which the merchants are being induced to try. Dr. Drew says he has failed to find any of this spurious article in his bailiwick and that it is made of baked dough, pulverized coffee, etc.

Ground mustard is defined by Dr. Drew as the product of the crushing or grinding and sifting of the seed of the black or white mustard. In order to be considered pure it should be made from the seed in their natural condition without expression of the fixed oil and should be free from the adulterants, such as starch or flour and of coloring matter, such as tumeric, chrome yellow, or any of the coal-tar colors. The claim that mustard will not keep unless mixed with flour or starch or has the oil expressed is proven false by the fact that the best grades are those which are made from the natural seed.

MAINE.

Mr. A. G. Young, secretary to the governor of the State, writes:

The State board of health of Maine has done but very little indeed, or almost nothing, worth reporting in the way of investigation on the subject of adulteration of food, drugs, and liquors. Prof. Robinson, of Bowdoin College, a member of our board, has done something, and for a report of the little which he has done I have referred the matter to him, and I think you will hear from him before long.

Prof. Robinson writes from Augusta as follows:

I have made from time to time some analysis, but no systematic investigation. First as to food: Some three years ago I found that glucose was largely used to adulterate table sirup, but the examination of many samples through the past year has proved that less of it is now used. A year ago I made examination of many of the cheap candies sold in this town, but no poisonous adulterations were found. Starch and grape sugar were generally found. As to drinks, I have recently proved that most of the weak beers sold in the State contain salicylic acid in considerable amount. This is notably the case in a beer called "silica beer," which contains only about 1 per cent of alcohol.

NEW HAMPSHIRE.

N. J. Bacheller, secretary to the governor of New Hampshire, writes March 27:

We have no investigation on the subject of food, drugs, and liquors. A bill has been introduced into our legislature providing for such, which is quite likely to become a law.

NEVADA.

The State seems to be without law upon the subject, and no investigations have been made.

NEW JERSEY.

The work of protecting the people against fraud in their food products in the State of New Jersey has been vigorously pushed, and the different officers in charge of the work have been very energetic in the discharge of their duties. The report of the commissioner, George W. McGuire, for 1890 shows that the total examinations made by the State analyst were 2,186, of which 468 articles were found to have been adulterated. The summary is as follows:

Total percentage of adulteration........................... 21. 04
Percentage of drugs....................................... 40
Percentage of food 35. 6
Percentage of milk.. 8. 6

Below will be found extracts from Dr. McGuire's report. What he has to say upon the subject of drugs will be eagerly read by all interested parties.

FOOD

In our inspection of general food, we have found that most dealers show a readiness to conform to law. Most of the adulterated food products in our market are brought from outside of the State.

At its session the legislature enacted a law to protect dealers in food and drugs by warranty, valid only when received from persons residing within the State. It would be well, however, for all retailers to insist upon receiving the said warranty from wholesalers, whether within or without the State. By this much trouble to them would be avoided, besides showing their honesty of purpose.

The following is a copy of the enactment, also a form of the warranty which can be had at the office of the dairy commissioner:

CHAPTER XXXVI.

A SUPPLEMENT to an act entitled "An act to prevent the adulteration of food or drugs," approved March twenty-fifth, one thousand eight hundred and eighty-one, and the several supplements thereto.

Be it enacted by the senate and general assembly of the State of New Jersey, That any person accused before any court of selling, or offering for sale any article adulterated within the meaning of the act to which this is a supplement, and the supplement thereto, who shall prove that he procured such article under a warranty from any person or persons that reside within the State in the form, hereafter set forth, that said article was pure and unadulterated within the meaning of said acts, said person shall be discharged from prosecution: *Provided,* That such proof in defense shall be filed in court prior to the trial of such case.

SEC. 2. That no warranty shall be considered as within the meaning of this act unless in the form hereinafter given, and unless the article or articles warranted shall be specifically named and described in the body of said warranty; and no warranty shall be a defense if the person offering it shall have been notified, prior to the sale complained of, that the articles mentioned in said warranty are adulterated within the meaning of said acts.

SEC. 3. That any person uttering or giving a false warranty, or swearing falsely in relation thereto, shall be guilty of a misdemeanor, and on conviction thereof shall be punished by a fine of not more than five hundred dollars, or imprisonment at hard labor for not more than one year, at the discretion of the court.

SEC. 4. That the warranty herein provided for shall be in the form following, to wit:

WARRANTY.

It is hereby warranted that the following article or articles ———— are pure and unadulterated within the meaning of the acts of the legislature of the State of New Jersey regulating the sale of food or drugs. (Signature) ————

Dated at ———, this ——— day of ———, anno domini ——.

SEC. 5. That this act shall take effect immediately.

By a reference to the list of articles analyzed it will be noticed that the largest percentage of adulteration is in coffee, spices, vinegar, molasses, and jellies.

Ground coffee, as a rule, is always more or less adulterated, commonly with chicory, frequently with roasted beans, peas, cereals, etc.

In ready-package form it is largely adulterated, perhaps for the reason that the deception is less noticeable than in the bean. We have sometimes found such marked "coffee mixture," also "rye coffee." Whether this was intended to suggest "rio" to the purchaser can not be said. It was purely what it claimed to be, containing nothing more or less than roasted and ground rye.

During the early part of the year, and before my appointment, the market was flooded with bogus coffee, found to be nothing more than flour pressed into the shape and colored to the shade of the coffee berry. So well was it made to resemble the genuine article that when mixed with 50 per cent of coffee it was easily palmed off on the public for pure unadulterated coffee. Its sale was entirely suppressed by the former commissioner, Dr. Newton, whose full account of the transaction will be found in this report.

There is perhaps no commodity that carries a heavier weight of acception most unobservable to the casual buyer than spices, and no one receives the practical disadvantage of this more than the observing housewife. Grocers are often persuaded to buy goods of this character by the very flattering inducements offered them in the way of receiving valuable presents on bills of large amounts, etc. It is needless to say that this class of goods is always found to be of inferior quality.

The large percentage of adulteration in vinegar, as it is at present found on the market, is due no doubt to the more or less failure of the apple crop during the last two or three years. Of the 154 samples of this article purchased for cider vinegar 84 were found below the State standard of 4.50 per cent acetic acid, and 36 were not cider vinegar at all. The adulteration is by means of water, no foreign acids having been detected. The imitation cider vinegar is simply weak acetic acid colored.

There is no difficulty whatever for grocers to obtain pure cider vinegar, since responsible dealers will give a guaranty and the imitation is a fraud on those engaged in the manufacture of the genuine article.

The State standard is low as to per cent. No cider vinegar will fall as low, and when it reaches 3 per cent., as a number of samples show, there can be no doubt that water has been added. It is my intention during the coming year to proceed against this fraudulent traffic and compel more honest measures.

The cheap jellies, jams, and preserves so largely sold may all be classed as fraudulent, since very few of them contain a particle of the fruit under which name they are sold, being in nearly all cases simply apple pomace flavored and colored to imitate the fruit desired.

During the encampment of the national guard at Sea Girt we gave the food supply a thorough inspection and found it to be pure and wholesome. The milk, which was used in large quantities, was of a high grade.

DRUGS.

The examination of drugs has received a considerable share of our attention and expenditure, with what improvement in the same the figures below will show. Last year the adulteration in drugs was found to be 65 per cent. This year the average, as will be seen by the analyst's report, is 40 per cent, showing a marked improvement, brought about without resorting to prosecution, except in the latter part of the year, of which I shall speak further on.

Those figures do not represent the actual ratio of adulteration, but only of those drugs most liable to suspicion.

Our method has been to send warning notices to offending druggists that a repetition of an offense would be visited by a prosecution, and to learn how effectual this system would prove has been our object this year. On the whole it has proved satisfactory, as has been shown.

During the latter part of the year samples of certain drugs were collected by the inspectors, and on analysis were found so far below the United States Pharmacopœia standard of strength and purity that I proceeded against the offenders. Of these samples two were tincture opium, the average strength of which should be 6 grains of morphia to the ounce. One sample contained but 0.955 grains and the other 1.13 grains. At the trial the druggist claimed that the opium from which the tincture was made had been purchased from a reputable firm and that the tincture was made according to the formula of the United States Pharmacopœia. The analyses showed the opium used to have been previously exhausted, such as is known to the trade as "Boston opium." Precaution was taken to secure these samples on prescriptions, as the plea is often made by pharmacists that they keep two kinds of laudanum, one to be disposed of only on a physician's order, the other to sell in a commercial way, principally to persons addicted to the opium habit. The United States Pharmacopœia requires that tincture opium shall be made from the powdered drug of standard strength. This can be had from any reputable drug firm with the assay printed on the label and guaranteed, and how these experienced druggists could be so duped by this very reputable firm, or how, being so familiar with the true appearance of the finished tincture, they could dispense this liquid without a suspicion is one of those mysterious cases with which we occasionally meet. However this may be, a severe penalty should be imposed upon any pharmacist who is guilty, whether from incompetency or mercenary motives, of dispensing so debased an article when a human life may depend upon its action.

The cases above referred to are still pending in the courts.

The Pharmacopœia requires that tincture nux vomica shall contain 2 per cent dry extract. Four samples of this drug out of those collected were found to contain respectively 0.678, 0.712, 0.618, and 1.075 per cent. This discrepancy between the actual and required figures I considered sufficient to warrant legal prosecution. The claim made by two of the defendants before the trial was that their tincture had been prepared for a certain "standard" fluid extract, which they were led to believe would procure a United States Pharmacopœia tincture, but recognizing they had failed to meet the intent of the law, pleaded guilty to the charge and paid the costs of court, etc.

The manufacturers of the above preparations state that in order to meet the requirements of the law their fluid extract in future shall contain not only alkaloidal strength but shall possess the amount of dry extract required by law. No explanation was made by the other two defendants until the day of trial, when they stated that their tinctures had been made from a so-termed "normal liquid" having on the printed label a formula, which, by following, the manufacturers claim, a United Stated Pharmacopœia tincture would be obtained containing 25 per cent of alkaloids. The claim made by the proprietors of the article in question that a superior tincture can be had by adopting their formula, inasmuch as it contained the full alkaloidal strength of the drug, free from what they term its inert substance, led me to submit a few questions to a number of prominent physicians, chemists, and pharmacists as to the therapeutical value of the nonalkaloidal portions of nux vomica and whether or not a tincture containing 0.25 per cent alkaloids and 0.4 nonalkaloids would meet the intent and spirit of the United States Pharmacopœia.

The answers received were divided as to opinion, some indorsing the manufacturers' view, more opposing it on the ground that as no certain determination of the therapeutical value of the nonalkaloid portions of the drug had yet been made, it was unwise as well as unlawful to deviate from the pharmacopœial formula, and that a tincture such as referred to clearly does not meet the intent and spirit of the pharmacopœia. Be this as it may, it seems clear that the formulators of the prescribed method laid down in the United States Pharmacopœa for the preparation of tincture nux vomica must have recognized the therapeutical value of the extractive matter in the drug, and that it has a defined physiological action I believe most physicians will agree. Otherwise tincture nux vomica may as well be taken out of the medical books, and when the action of the drug is desired the physician can prescribe strychnia, which the druggist will find much more convenient to dispense.

The principle of having a definite strength for the most important drugs is undoubtedly a good one, and the publicity given to the above cases will in all probability result in good, since the United States Pharmacopœia is now in course of revision and the attention of those engaged in this work has been called to the fact that many of the most deadly poisons have no definite strength laid down.

While the United States Pharmacopœia is not only the standard text-book of the druggist, but also the legal guide by which he must be governed in this State in dispensing his officinal preparations, I shall endeavor to compel a compliance therewith.

NEW YORK.

Dr. Lewis Balch, Albany, secretary State board of health of New York, promptly complied with request to supply reports of his State. To show how varied and extensive the articles examined were found to be adulterated, the following extracts from these very able documents, under the heading of adulteration:

Prof. F. A. Hennessey, Saratoga Springs, N. Y., directs attention to an article in the American Journal of Pharmacy on "A new spice adulterant." This matter is more fully treated elsewhere.

Prof. G. C. Caldwell, professor of chemistry, Cornell, and public analyst, reports:

Coffee and tea (the adulterant in coffee is chicory); quinine pills and capsules—morphine pills and tablets; citrate of iron and quinine—tincture of opium. No adulterants used, but simply deficient in strength in case of portion of samples examined. The extent of those adulterations will be more fully treated in another part of this report in extracting from Prof. Caldwell's report to the New York State board.

The New York State board of health uses the following classifications (see pp. 451 and 452 of report for 1890):

Samples are classed as of good quality when they fulfill the requirements of the United States Pharmacopœia or fall below the same only in some trifling and unimportant respect; of fair quality if, while not fully up to the Pharmacopœial standard, they are evidently neither intentionally adulterated nor decidedly below such standard; and of inferior quality if clearly adulterated or falsified, lacking in any important constituent, deficient in strength from improper manufacture, partial or complete decomposition, or other causes, or containing an undue amount of impurity. In some cases, through ignorance or intent, a wrong article has been sold or some inferior article of a nature similar to that called for has been substituted, and such samples have been classed under the head, "Not as called for."

On page 455 of same report will be found the following summary of results of analyses made during the year:

Of the 532 samples examined, there were classed as of—

	No.	Per cent.
Good quality	233, or	43.8
Fair quality	54, or	10.2
Inferior quality	130, or	24.4
Not as called for	33, or	6.2
Excessive strength	24, or	4.5
Fictitious	58, or	10.9

Mr. F. B. Thurber, of New York, and one of the most active and earnest friends of national pure-food legislation, writes at some length, giving a description of the causes that have led up to the present pure-food agitation. He opposes " special," but warmly advocates "general" legislation. Among other things he says:

En passant I would call your attention to the valuable auxiliary you have in reputable manufacturers and dealers who, as you will see, have been trying to raise the standard of our food supply, and have already made strenuous efforts to this end. The result of their experience has been that they need official investigation and publicity to back them up, and then they can make headway against their unscrupulous competitors. But if a dealer in pure goods analyzes and exposes the character of a competitor's goods, the cry is at once raised of self-interest, and the exposure does not carry with it the same weight that an official examination and exposure would.

It will not need much effort on the part of the public officers if we can only get official investigation and publicity. The force of competition will do the rest. The heaviest penalty which an adulterator can have visited upon him is publicity, because it means failure to impose upon the public.

.   *   *   *   *   *   *

While there are some phases of the question that are only to be dealt with by State legislation, yet there is need of a national anti-adulteration law which will apply to interstate commerce. While there is no doubt but what the popular impression is largely exaggerated as to the percentage of adulteration in the food supply, that is, injuriously adulterated, still there is enough and more than enough that is a fraud upon the pocket to justify national legislation on this subject.

Mr. Barrett, editor of the American Grocer, in letters to the Department and to Mr. F. B. Thurber, makes some valuable suggestions, but which could not be carried out to the extent required unless much more liberal appropriations were made by Congress. The chemical division in charge of this work has, through its chief, Dr. Wiley, been engaged to a limited extent in investigations such as both Mr. Barrett and Mr. Thurber suggests, viz, in purchasing supplies of various food products on the open market in all parts of the country, and having them analyzed when purchased by the most eminent chemists to be found. Undoubtedly this should be done by Congress in every State of the Union, but when the investigation is made and the fraud proven, as is being done by the national and State investigations, what profits it unless restraints are put upon manufacturers and venders of this class of goods?

The canned-goods (to which both gentlemen especially refer) industry is one of great and increasing importance, and if there is no danger in them, certainly this great industry could do much to secure the passage of a general anti-adulteration law which would prove the fact to the world.

Mr. Barrett suggests the investigation of the nutritive value of artificial foods, such as oleomargarine and glucose. He adds : " I believe attention should be paid to the nutritive value of baking powders." In conclusion Mr. Barrett regrets the absence of American literature on the subject of adulterations, the greater portion of what " we have being a rehash of foreign works, and which are wholly inapplicable to the conditions existing here. The best work thus far has been done under the auspices of the Chemical Division of the Department of Agriculture, and embraced in the various bulletins issued by them." Mr. Barrett inclosed two valuable and interesting articles, one on adulterations and the other on the bills before Congress, from which extracts are made.

In the articles mentioned Mr. Barrett says :

It seems as if the interests of the consumer are made subordinate to those of producers and manufacturers. All that consumers demand is, that they shall be made acquainted with the true name and nature of all articles of food and drugs offered for sale, and they be left free to use whatever they choose, whether it is axle grease, butter, or oleomargarine. They want to know if baking powder contains cream of tartar or alum ; if salad oil is made from the olives or cotton seed. They also want a bill to prevent the misbranding of food and drugs and to prohibit absolutely the sale of all articles of food containing any poisonous substance or any article injurious to health. The German is fond of chicory, and there can be no reasonable objection to a mixture of coffee with chicory or with other harmless vegetable substances. And yet, unless these mixtures are sold for what they are, a fraud is perpetrated upon all who purchase.

A general act should contain an ironclad definition of adulteration covering every known manner of the sophistication, imitation, or adulteration of food and drugs, and be accompanied by a section providing that certain articles, mixtures, or compounds not prejudicial to health, and properly labeled as such, may be sold when permission is granted by the Department charged with the execution of the act.

Articles suspected of being adulterated should be analyzed by Government chemists, and when found injurious to health the result of the analysis should be made public, for publicity is one of the greatest of safeguards against the sale of adulterated food.

The bills now before Congress are loaded with details and some so burdened that their execution is impracticable. Experience has demonstrated that existing adulterations in ninety-nine cases out of one hundred are a crime against the purse and not against the person. Chemistry has given us many useful compounds which are nutritious and cheap. And yet the law* taxes these heavily merely to benefit a class. Such special legislation is obnoxious and against the spirit of our institutions. Let us have fair play and not a national act which imposes burdens upon a few, discredits valuable food products, and adds to the oppressions of taxation.

In his article on adulteration the writer says :

ADULTERATION.

Easy as it may seem to define the word adulteration satisfactorily, it is extremely difficult. The use of the word in connection with food conveys to the minds of the majority of consumers the idea of something that is prejudicial to health. With some the word adulteration is the synonym for poison. We appreciate the force of the statement made by a physician in discussing the subject, that "the villainies of diet are numerous." We recognize also that there is force in his declaration that "adulteration seems to be almost a characteristic of civilization." The legal definition, as found in the laws of New York and other States and in several of the bills pending in Congress, applies to every article sold for food or drink by man. In the case of food or drink, it declares an article adulterated within the meaning of this act—

---

* The writer evidently referred to a bill (presented in the Fiftieth Congress) which proposed taxing every article of food product, which was not even considered by the committee to which it was referred.

(1) If any substance or substances has or have been mixed with it so as to reduce or lower or injuriously affect its quality or strength.

(2) If any inferior or cheaper substance or substances have been substituted wholly or in part for the article.

(3) If any valuable constituent of the article has been wholly or in part abstracted.

(4) If it be an imitation of or sold under the name of another article.

(5) If it consist wholly or in part of a diseased or decomposed, or putrid or rotten, animal or vegetable substance, whether manufactured or not, or in the case of milk, if it is the produce of a diseased animal.

(6) If it be colored, or coated, or polished, or powdered, whereby damage is concealed, or it is made to appear better than it really is, or of greater value.

(7) If it contains any added poisonous ingredient or any ingredient which may render such article injurious to the health of a person consuming it:

The above is a broad, and comprehensive definition of what adulteration is at the present time, and if the laws against adulterated food and drink were enforced strictly on the lines of the above definition, it would work very great injury to the people and the manufacturers and dealers in food products. Therefore, very wisely, the law makes certain provisions as follows:

Provided, That the State board of health may, with the approval of the governor, from time to time declare certain articles or preparations to be exempt from the provisions of this act: *And provided further,* That the provisions of this act shall not apply to mixtures or compounds *recognized* as ordinary articles of food, provided that the same are not injurious to health and that the articles are distinctly labeled as a mixture, stating the components of the mixture.

Sec. 4. It shall be the duty of the State board of health to prepare and publish from time to time, lists of the articles, mixtures, or compounds declared to be exempt from the provisions of this act in accordance with the preceding section. The State board of health shall also from time to time fix the limits of variability permissible in any article of food or drug, or compound, the standard of which is not established by any national pharmacopœia.

The extent of food adulteration is by no means so great as it seems. Assuming that the minimum cost of feeding an individual is no more than the average cost of maintaining a pauper at a public institution, say $2 per week, we find that the sixty million people of the United States will consume not less than five thousand million dollars worth of food per annum. The question as to the integrity of the food supply becomes a very important one. All are agreed as to the declaration of one writer that "the prosperity of the nation depends upon the health and morals of its citizens; that the health and morals of the people depend largely upon the food they eat; that wholesome and palatable food is the first step; that good morals is conducive to business, skill in trade, and a healthy tone in literature." The question remains as to the extent of food adulteration. Fortunately, regarding this matter, we have a mass of evidence which when sifted proves conclusively that "practically there is no such thing as adulteration of articles of food as a sanitary question;" a belief which finds indorsement in all official reports on the subject.

Some recognize that there is a sanitary aspect to the subject, because facts demonstrate that the health of the people is put in peril by reason of impure meat, milk, and water. There is no doubt that these three cause more deaths in a year than are due directly or indirectly to the use of alcoholic stimulants.

Speaking of the pigments used by candy manufacturers, he continues: True, they are used in very minute quantities, but there is no doubt that the injection into the system of poisonous articles, even in doses very much more minute than a medicinal dose, is, in the long run, bound to work injury to the individual. Then we recognize that certain classes of people are fond of chicory in their coffee, and, it being harmless, is used as is other vegetable matter to make a mixture called coffee, but which often contains very little of the true article.

The use of baking powders as a matter of household convenience has come into general practice, and in order to make these it is necessary to introduce a neutral article, such as rice or starch, in order to prevent the premature action of the acid or soda. While these are perfectly legitimate they open the door for the fraudulent dealer to carry on his scheme of plunder.

Thus various difficulties are met. The moment that every consumer is made acquainted with the true name and nature of any article of food or drink offered for sale, he may be at liberty to use any sort of food or drink he pleases, but upon his own responsibility.

In one of Mr. Barret's letters he makes use of the following language:

Water is free. Therefore it is the easiest and readiest adulterant of alcoholic liquors. It is a question whether the water does not render it more injurious to man, in that the water acts as a carrier for the alcohol, causing it to act with more rapidity.

NORTH CAROLINA.

Director H. B. Battle, of the North Carolina Experiment Station, says: "We have no such laws specially relating to the subject of adulteration of food, drugs, and liquors."

OHIO.

Dairy and Food Commissioner Edward Bethel made a valuable and extended report to the governor of Ohio, February 7, 1891, from which the following extracts are taken. Ten thousand copies of the report were printed and distributed to manufacturers and dealers of food and drug supplies:

If this circular did not propose or promise to do more than the legislature had provided the means of doing, complainants will have to look for the grounds of their grievances in the inadequate provision made by that body in its appropriation bills. The mere enactment of laws, without the means of enforcing their execution, is of little or no effect.

So far as it has been within the legal power and authority of my assistants and myself to reach and enforce the food laws, the known violators have been prosecuted.

In speaking of lard, he says:

Consumers should look well to the sort of stuff they are purchasing in packers' lard. They had better buy and use no lard but such as they know was made in the country near home, or in rendering establishments known to be clean.

Of 437 samples of lard purchased and analyzed by direction of the State board of health of New Jersey in the year 1889, 274 were found composed of hog fat, and all others, 163 in number, were found adulterated with beef fat, cotton-seed oil, and beef stearine.

Violation of food laws are misdemeanors and are punishable as such. Like all other misdemeanors they are matters subject to be brought by any citizen to the attention and action of the grand jury.

WINES.

The law to regulate the manufacture and sale of compounded wines, and to prohibit the manufacture or sale of adulterated wines within the State of Ohio, makes the manufacture or sale of adulterated wines a misdemeanor, punishable by a fine of not less than $200 nor more than $1,000, or by imprisonment in the county jail for a term of not less than thirty days nor more than six months, or by both such fine and imprisonment, in the discretion of the court, and with liability to a penalty of $1 for each gallon thereof sold, offered for sale, or manufactured, together with forfeiture and destruction of the article. My attention has been especially called to the alleged adulteration of wines in the northwestern part of the State, and I have been requested to institute prosecutions against the alleged offenders. This complaint extends to the whole wine-producing district of that section. The legal remedy for such wide-spread evil in adulterated wine is provided by the law within each county. The law expressly says: "All penalties imposed by this act may be recovered, with costs of action, by any person in his own name, before any justice of the peace in the county where the offense was committed, where the amount does not exceed the jurisdiction of such justice; and such penalties may be recovered in the like manner in any court of record in the State. It shall be the duty of the prosecuting attorneys of the respective counties of this State, and they are hereby required, to prosecute or commence actions in the name of the State of Ohio for the recovery of the penalties allowed herein, upon receiving information thereof; and in all actions brought by such prosecuting attorneys, one-half of the penalty recovered shall belong to and be paid over to the person or persons giving the information upon which the action is brought." It is plain from this quotation that the wine law does not make the dairy and food commissioner the informer or prosecuting witness in such cases, but that any citizen or prosecuting attorney may prosecute alleged offenders.

VINEGAR.

Pure cider vinegar, or fermented apple juice, is the only article allowed by law to be manufactured, sold, or offered for sale as vinegar in this State. All cider vinegar made by other than domestic makers is required to be branded "cider vinegar," on each cask, barrel, or keg, with the name and residence of the manufacturer, and the date of its manufacture. I have inspected a number of the articles on sale as vinegar by sundry retail dealers in the city of Columbus, and found, by the chemist's analysis, that many samples sold as "vinegar" were spurious or adulterated. The dealers, I was convinced, were innocent of any intentional fraud in the matter, being unaware of the real character of the substance they were dealing in as vinegar. In each of such instances the article was either returned to the wholesale dealer, or destroyed, at the loss of the party having it in stock. I believe there is now comparatively little adulterated vinegar being kept on sale in Columbus."

MAPLE SIRUP.

This popular local product and delicious sweet is an object of adulteration and imitation to a remarkable extent. This result is largely the fault of purchasers themselves. I know of parties having made an excellent article of maple sirup, free from any adulteration, who visited dealers in Columbus and other cities, offering to sell their goods at 75 cents a gallon—a very reasonable price; but the dealers declined to buy from them, saying they could buy "maple sirup" for 55 cents a gallon, and that upon the latter, though not so pure and good, they could make more profit than they could on the genuine product. Thus, the true maple sirup and sugar makers, in such case, would have to submit to a loss, of over 26 per cent, at which rate the total loss on the whole amount of maple sirup made in the State would amount to about $120,000.

H. H. Hyman, assistant commissioner, in his report furnishes the following:

With pleasure I state that I have had very few prosecutions to make, as, with proper instructions on the part of the commission, most dealers are making an earnest effort to place only pure goods on sale.

The greatest difficulty to contend with is in articles of food and drugs manufactured outside of Ohio.

I have avoided, as much as possible, cause for being charged with persecution in the discharge of my duties, as I realize how easy it is for small dealers to be imposed upon.

The number of prosecutions is not as large as it might have been had I been desirous of prosecuting every technical violation of the law that has come to my notice; desiring only to prosecute where violations were willful, and required in the interest and well-being of the community, or to uphold the dignity of the law.

Final issue in cases is often delayed on grounds sufficient to the court, and based upon facts beyond the control of the commission.

I have discovered that in many cases prejudice against the commission, or sympathy for the offender, prevails against overwhelming evidence of guilt, and verdicts of acquittal are sometimes given accordingly.

The same gentleman suggests confiscation of all adulterated goods improperly branded as a means of making tradesmen more careful.

Also, an amendment to the act to prevent fraud in canned goods; that all articles intended for food or ingredients of food put up in tin shall have the month and year of canning stamped in the tin, and that any goods exposed or offered for sale without being so stamped should be subject to destruction by the commissioner or his assistants, provided the same could be constitutionally done.

Speaking of the enforcement of the laws in his district, Mr. Hyman itemizes as follows:

MILK.

During the past six months I have had inspected samples and generally found them of standard quality. Whenever creamery men remove any part of the cream from the milk they handle, they are very careful to have the milk up to the requirements of the statute when delivered to the customer. In most cases the adulteration is made after the milk reaches the street vender.

I am satisfied that more attention by dairymen should be given to the care of milk before it reaches the consumer, with a view to keeping everything clean and neat. The place where the milk is kept should have plenty of pure air, and be removed far enough from the stable and barnyard not to retain any of the odors.

Too much care can not be taken in keeping clean the utensils connected with the dairy. The cans in which the milk is shipped or carried should be thoroughly cleansed and scalded each time they are emptied, before refilling.

CHEESE.

The cheese interests of this district are in fair shape. There is apparently an honest and earnest effort on the part of most manufacturers to make clean, honest goods. Most of the "filled" cheese in the market is shipped in from other States, and wherever found I have notified the dealer, who has desisted from placing any more of it on sale, but he is the one who had to suffer the loss, as in most cases it had been paid for when delivered.

VINEGAR.

The vinegar law in this district is very generally complied with. I find grocers are very particular in purchasing to see that the product is all right; also, that in the quality of the vinegar offered for sale there is a marked improvement. Hardly any but fruit vinegar has been sold in this market.

MAPLE SIRUP.

The law governing maple sirup has been lived up to almost without a single exception in this district. In fact, I have not received a single complaint in regard to any violation of the same.

CANDY.

I can safely say that the statute governing the adulteration of candy has not been violated by the manufacturers in this district.

This is due in a great measure to the action of reputable manufacturers entirely discarding the use of anything in the way of adulterants, the rules of the Candy Manufacturers' Association, of which they are members, inflicting heavy fines and penalties on any member making anything but straight goods.

COFFEE AND SPICES.

The greatest fraud and deception now practiced in the market is in coffees and spices. They are placed on the market by unscrupulous manufacturers in connection with gift enterprises. I have now in the hands of Prof. Rosewater, State chemist for this district, several samples of this miserable stuff, and have already learned enough from him to enable me to commence and successfully prosecute the parties putting these goods on sale, which duty I shall perform when I receive his official report.

In conclusion, the larger number of tradesmen and dairymen in this district are honorable in their dealings, with no apparent intention to deceive their customers or violate the laws. There are a few, however, who, for profit's sake, would adulterate everything they sold, were it not for fear of the law and its execution.

It is a singular fact that there are to be found men who earnestly demanded the enactment of the oleomargarine and pure-food laws, and who are now screaming themselves hoarse for the rigid enforcement of same, who would not hesitate to adulterate their own products by every means possible.

Mr. P. McKeown, assistant commissioner, Cincinnati, says:

The vinegar manufacturers having thoroughly realized the salutary effects designed by the passage of the "pure vinegar law," are according a most commendable compliance to its requirements, and on this score no complaint is to be found.

In view of the fact that the interests of Cincinnati, relative to the quality of milk prepared for delivery to consumers, is looked after by the health department of the city, I deemed it unnecessary to give this matter that attention which I otherwise should. However, the vigorous and determined warfare inaugurated last spring by the health department, under the supervision of its excellent and efficient head, Dr. Prendergast, looking to the correction of the abuses and impositions practiced by unscrupulous dairymen in the character of the milk they sold for family use, can not be too highly indorsed. It is gratifying to note, as a result of this crusade against filthy and wretchedly managed dairies, that a decided and material improvement is now apparent in the character of the milk that supplies this market.

I am now engaged in trying to enforce "the pure food law," which went into effect September 1. To this end I have visited the leading grocery and drug firms here, and placed them in possession of a copy of the law, urging upon them the consequences of its violation. Further than this I have done nothing. It is a pity that this law, aiming as it does, to accomplish such laudable and meritorious ends, and to correct the long existing evils and deleterious effects of adulterated foods, can not be enforced, owing in large measure to the limited means at our disposal. You doubtless are aware that the last general assembly which passed the law, made no pecuniary provision for its enforcement.

*   *   *   *   *   *   *

The competition of manufacturers in outside States is another factor which should not be lost sight of, and one which much hampers the law's efficiency. For, with no restrictions placed upon the goods prepared by them, it is very evident that the home manufacturer has to cope for success under peculiar and unjustifiable disadvantages. Fearless and energetic federal legislation, coupled with a reasonable appropriation by the State, is, in my opinion, required to make the law a success. The enactment of such a law by Congress would go very far to obviate the difficulties which now beset this commission in securing a rigid enforcement of the pure-food law, and it is to be hoped that the National House of Representatives, in their wise judgment, may quickly see fit to frame so desirable and valuable a measure of legislation.

The State chemist for Ohio reports 105 analyses; among these the most interesting were the following:

Examinations for poisons in cheese (tyrotoxicon) failed to discover any of the poison.   •

The conclusions derived from the analysis are:

(1) That the Prussian-blue reaction is caused by the presence of an organic base, probably an amine.

(2) That the carbolic-acid reaction is due to butyric acid.

(3) That when both bodies are present in the same liquid both are extracted with ether from an altraline solution, probably in the form of a butyrate of the organic base.

(4) That both bodies are liable to occur in any old specimen of cheese, milk, or cream.

(5) That the presence of these two bodies causes artificial diazobenzole to give the orange-red reaction with carbolic acid, after being extracted from whey with ether which it does not give before.

CANNED GOODS.

An exhaustive investigation was made of the condition of foods packed in tin cans, including fruits, vegetables, fish, and condensed milk. The investigation was suggested by a case of poisoning reported from Mansfield, in which canned pumpkin was alleged to have been the cause. With the exception of the condensed milk every article examined was contaminated with salts of tin. In most cases the amount of tin present was so large that there can be no doubt of danger to health from the consumption of the food, especially if several kinds are consumed at the same meal. The goods were bought in open market as offered for sale, and no pains were taken to procure old samples. Since the completion of the work several other similar cases of poisoning have been reported.

The analyses are given in full and consist of the following:

ARTICLES CANNED.

Pumpkins, three samples; blackberries, salmon, pineapple, each two samples, and one each of squash, tomatoes, "petite pois," "champignons de choix," blueberries, sweet corn, Bartlett pears, peaches, red cherries, baked sweet potatoes, peas, string beans, and condensed milk. The samples, according to brand, came from Ohio, Michigan, New York, Bordeaux, France, Paris, New Brunswick, Oregon, California, Maryland, Virginia, Tennessee, and Wyoming, showing a pretty extended scope of territory.

The amount of tin found ran from 3.0 to 4.20 grains to the pound. Eleven samples contained less than 1 grain to the pound. Five samples contained between 1 and 2 grains. Five samples showed between 2 and 3 grains and the remaining two samples contained 3.11 and 4.20 grains.

COFFEE.

Five samples of ground coffee were examined—all adulterated. As curiosities they are given in full:

No. 600. Ash, 4.16; chicory and barley, 33⅓; peas, 33⅓; coffee 33⅓ per cent.

No. 609. Ash, 4.43; coffee, 25; chicory, 6; rye 69 per cent.

No. 610. Ash, 4.33; coffee, 25; chicory, 10; peas, 25; rye, 40 per cent.

No. 611. Ash, 6.70; coffee, 90; chicory and cedar wood, about 10.

No. 612. Ash, 4.20; coffee, 5; chicory, 5; peas, 8; rye with another substance not determined, 82 per cent.

LARD BLEACHERS AND SAUSAGE PRESERVATIVES.

Serial No. 606. Sample of lard bleacher received of Edward Bethel, November 30, 1890. Sent by B. A. Stevens, Toledo, Ohio. Labeled, the best lard bleacher and purifier, Wolf, Sayer & Heller, Chicago, Ill.

Tin can of 132 grams, about one-fourth pound, 25 cents per can for 30 gallons lard. This sample was found to be granulated caustic soda; price 11 cents per pound.

Serial No. 607. Sample of lard bleacher received of Edward Bethel, November 30, 1890. Sent by B. A. Stevens, Toledo, Ohio; labeled, "Snow White," S. Oppenheimer, Chicago, Ill. Tin can, 172 grams, about one-third pound, for 45 gallons lard.

    Boracic acid 10.86
    Borax 47.12
    Salt 41.13

Serial No. 608. Sample of "Preservative," received of Edward Bethel, November 20, 1890. Sent by B. A. Stevens, Toledo, Ohio, Wolf, Sayer & Heller, Chicago, Ill. Marked, B. Savaline, 1 pound, 16 cents; pink-colored salt.

    Boracic acid 16.26
    Salt 83.74
    Color...cochineal.

THE ACTION OF FOOD PRESERVATIVES ON SALIVARY DIGESTION.

On account of the prevalent use of borax, boracic acid, salicylic acid, and other antiseptics for the preservation of foods and drinks, the following investigation made in the laboratory of the writer by Mr. C. P. Fox will be of general interest. The analytical data are omitted for want of space. The method and conclusions alone will be given. The work covered the effect of salicylic acid, borax, sulphite of lime, and saccharine upon the salivary digestion of starch. No attention was given here to any deleterious therapeutic action of the drug in question.

The following method was adopted and strictly adhered to; the same conditions being observed in all cases.

One gram of the starch mixture was weighed off, transferred to a flask (250 cc. capacity), 10 cc. water added, and the mixture boiled for five minutes; 5 cc. of water added and the contents cooled to 40° C; 5 cc. of freshly secreted saliva is added and the flask shaken until the contents are thoroughly mixed, then placed in the oven and kept at the temperature of 40° C. for the required time.

On removing from the oven the action of the saliva was stopped by boiling. The contents of the flask were washed into a graduated cylinder, the solution rendered alkaline with sodium hydrate, and made up to 100 cc. The amount of grape sugar in this solution was determined with Fehling's solution.

Although the action of the saliva begins in the mouth, and the greater part of its work is done there, yet there is no reason why the process could not be carried on in the stomach.

For this reason the action was studied by leaving the starch and saliva in contact for different lengths of time; the periods being one, five, fifteen, thirty, and sixty minutes. While the hour test may be unnecessary, yet it is better to give the preservative every possible chance that its friends claim for it.

CONCLUSIONS.

The conclusions to be drawn from the results of these experiments are :

(1) That the use of salicylic acid, borax, sulphite of lime, and saccharine in the proportion of 1 part to $\frac{1}{2000}$ of food is not detrimental to the process of salivary digestion.

(2) That the use of the above preservatives in proportion of 1 part to 1,050 parts of

food shows no hindrance of the function, unless in case of borax, where there is a slight indication.

(3) That the use of the preservatives, salicylic acid and borax, in proportion of 1 part to 840 parts of food, shows a decided check of the action in the one-minute, five-minute and fifteen-minute tests, but disappears in the thirty and sixty minute trials.

(4) That where they are present in proportion of 1 part to 420 parts of food, the one-minute test shows that no sugar was formed where salicylic acid and saccharin were used, and only a trace where borax was present.

Five-minute test.—No sugar formed in the test with salicylic acid saccharin; an increase of sugar in the borax test.

Fifteen-minute test.—No change from five-minute test.

Thirty-minute test.—No sugar in the salicylic acid and saccharin trials; the difference between starch and the borax test has disappeared.

Sixty-minute trial.—No sugar in the salicylic acid and saccharin tests. The borax remains about the same as in the thirty-minute trial.

(5) When the preservatives are present in the proportion of 1 part to 210 parts of food, the entire action of the saliva is, without exception, suspended for five minutes. At fifteen minutes borax hinders the action. At thirty minutes borax still retards the action. At sixty minutes the digestive action is still checked slightly by borax. At the end of this period not a trace of sugar could be found in the trials with salicylic acid and saccharine. By inspection of these results, it will be seen that salicylic acid is the most dangerous of all the preservatives experimented with. Saccharin comes next and is nearly as strong. Borax is third, and sulphite of lime last. It will be seen that the safety limit for salicylic acid and saccharin is 1 to 1,050 parts of food. Borax may be used in proportion of 1 part to 840 parts. Sulphite of lime, 1 to 500 or 600 parts.

OREGON.

W. W. Baker, commissioner, writes:

I have been but thirty days in office. While I am satisfied that Oregon is a dumping ground, I have not had time to determine the extent of adulteration save in dairy products that have been imported here from other States. It is estimated that in the last six months some six carloads of oleomargarine have been imported into Portland.

PENNSYLVANIA.

H. D. Tate, esq., private secretary to the governor, writes as follows:

I am directed by Governor Pattison to state that upon receipt of the circular letter requesting information with regard to the adulteration of food, etc., each department under the State government was requested to furnish all the desired information in their possession. Inclosed herewith you will find reports made by them, and it is believed that those reports cover the case fully as far as Pennsylvania is concerned.

Dr. Benjamin Lee, secretary State board of health, in letter to Mr. Tate says:

I have been in communication with the food analyst of the State board of agriculture on the subject. Unfortunately the appropriation to our board is so meager that we have never been able to institute the observation and experiments that we would like in reference to this very important matter.

Thomas Edge, secretary State board of agriculture, writes Governor Pattison and says:

Dr. Leffman and Prof. C. B. Cochran, as microscopist and hygienists of our board, have made several examinations into the adulteration of food products and of milk, but not having any funds for such a purpose under our control nothing of any great value has been accomplished. In our annual report for 1890, pp. 89-94, you will find a somewhat extended report on the milk supply of Philadelphia, by Prof. Cochran.

Dr. Alonzo Robbins, president of the pharmaceutical examining board, Pennsylvania, writes Mr. Tate:

I herewith inclose copies of the report of the committee on adulterations of the Pennsylvania pharmaceutical association for the years 1889 and 1890, and also inclose a copy of a paper by Frank A. Hennessy on a new spice adulterant. This, I think, comprises all the investigations recently made in this State. Section 9 of the pharmacy act prohibits and provides a penalty for the adulteration of drugs and medicines, but the persons making the investigations recorded in the inclosed papers have been unwilling to go into court to testify. Recently, however, samples have been purchased and placed in the hands of an expert chemist for analysis; if his report warrants prosecutions will be promptly instituted. I regret that from so abundant a field I have so little to report.

Dr. H. B. Donnell, State College, Pa., reports sample of cream of tartar branded "Pure Cream of Tartar, Philadelphia," to have contained calcium phosphate with some calcium sulphate. He adds that the adulterants are probably not injurious.

Hon. H. Wharton Amerling, president of the American Society for the Prevention of Adulteration of Food, writes:

In accordance with your kindly request for information as to food adulteration would state that we have the honor to submit the results of some analyses of different articles of food made by chemist of our society in the year preceding May 1, 1891. The results show merely the average per cent of adulteration of the several articles of food named, as follows: Cream of tartar, 40 per cent; low grades of sugar, 18 per cent; olive oil, 54 per cent; castor oil, 20 per cent; ground pepper, in bulk, 60 per cent; ground cinnamon, 54 per cent; ground ginger, 40 per cent; ground nutmegs, 50 per cent; ground mace, 52 per cent; sirups, 30 per cent; milk, 40 per cent; beer, 40 per cent.

L. G. Groff, Lebanon, Pa., says:

The most injurious adulterant I now have in mind is that which has become wellnigh universal, of putting all the dust and dirt of all kinds removed from wheat into the bran and other feed products. This is a matter worth some attention.

Messrs. Powers & Weightman, Philadelphia manufacturing chemists, say:

There is no difficulty in procuring food, drugs, and liquors of the best quality in any city or town in the United States, provided there is a willingness to pay for them a just and proper price. If, on the other hand, consumers demand cheap goods, there are some, undoubtedly, who will adjust the goods to the price.

While there can be no doubt as to adulteration being carried on in all countries to a greater or less degree, we feel satisfied that the extent in this country has been greatly magnified and the trade grossly misrepresented.

If Messrs. Powers & Weightman are correct in their views of the matter, does it not show the absolute necessity for a law that will compel all who "adjust their goods to the prices" to publish the fact to their customers? The writer quite agrees with Mr. F. B. Thurber, of

New York, on this subject that the reputable houses desire a just and equitable law and would aid greatly in enforcing its provisions.

RHODE ISLAND.

Dr. Charles H. Fisher, secretary State board of health, writes as follows:

In reply to inquiries by circular of 19th instant in regard to adulterations of food, drugs, or liquors, allow me to say that very little investigation has been made in this State of the first two classes, because the legislature has not seen fit to make an appropriation therefor. This board made use of what little funds it could spare in 1890 from its appropriation of $3,000, and in some previous years the inspector of milk of the city of Providence has made in limited numbers analyses of milk when brought to him for that purpose. Liquors have been analyzed only when they have been seized under supposed violation of law. The results of such investigations as this board has been able to make show that, taking all parts of the State, 57.14 per cent of milk examined was below the legal standard of 12 per cent solids and 2½ per cent of fats. Some samples contained adventitious substances. Of a considerably large number of samples of milk analyzed by the recently appointed milk inspector of Providence City, I think he stated to me that 78 per cent was below the legal standard. Of the samples of molasses analyzed under the direction of the board and purchased in different sections of the State as best molasses, 1 sample only in every 8, or 12 per cent, was found to be true molasses.

Of vinegar, 55.17 per cent contained less than the legal standard of 2 per cent of vinegar solids or 4½ per cent of absolute acetic acid. Twenty-seven per cent of samples was other than cider vinegar. No attempt was made, in any case of purchase of any and all samples, of obtaining other than the best goods. I had an anti-adulteration bill before the legislature a year or more ago, but it was never reported back from the committee to whom it was referred, although several public hearings were given with general approval; opposed only by paid legal counsel and one large dealer in milk, a member of the committee. I have been unable thus far this session to get a hearing upon the merits of the bill. It is based on the laws of Massachusetts, New York, and New Jersey. I would like a more extensive investigation of articles of food if means could be obtained. I would undertake to furnish samples of various articles for analysis by your Department if such an arrangement could be made.

The law referred to by Dr. Fisher, he states in a subsequent letter, was not passed by the legislature.

Dr. Fisher, in another letter, further says:

From circumstances within my knowledge I believe that frauds are perpetrated in the necessary articles of food in this State to the extent of $1 per annum in the consumption of every individual of the population of 354,000 at date.

TEXAS.

Commissioner of Agriculture L. L. Foster writes from Austin:

I beg to state that there are no laws in this State upon this subject. *It is the prevailing opinion of the people that adulteration of food, drugs, and liquors is carried on to a considerable extent,* but this is not based on any reliable data.

The italics are supplied, and the opinion expressed by Commissioner Foster is backed up by resolutions of the State Grange of Texas and of letters received by the writer from Worthy Past Master A. J. Rose, of the Texas State Grange, and other prominent gentlemen in that State.

VERMONT.

Governor C. S. Page, of Vermont, was prompt and courteous in his reply to request for information. At the request of Governor Page Prof. W. W. Cook, director of the State agricultural station, furnished the following information:

In reply to your favor I would say that there is no person or department in this State whose duty it is to look into the question of the adulteration of food, liquors, etc. The nearest approach to it is in the question of oleomargarine, suspected samples of which may be sent to the experiment station for analysis. So far, of the few samples that have been sent to us, we have failed to find any thing but pure butter. In our station report for 1889, p. 37, there is an analysis given of adulterated cream tartar, which happened to come to the laboratory.

Secretary J. H. Hamilton, Richford, of the State board of health, furnished the following:

This board has not been asked to investigate the adulteration of food, drugs, or liquors, and no appropriation has been made by the State for this purpose. The statute prescribes a penalty for such adulterations, but provides no means for inspection (chapter 6, R. S.). A bill relating to this matter was killed by the legislature of 1890.

VIRGINIA.

Prof. Richard H. Gaines, Richmond, Va., reports as adulterated: "Butter, lard, pulverized sugar, baking powder, vinegar, lager beer, and whisky." The State Grange and the Farmers' Assembly have both repeatedly urged Congress to pass some stringent laws upon the subject of adulteration.

WEST VIRGINIA.

Mr. James W. Ewing, secretary to the governor, says: "This department will be unable to furnish any information on the subject of adulteration of food, drugs, and liquors."

The West Virginia State Grange passed strong resolutions urging the adoption of a pure food bill.

Nearly every article of food, drink, and drug used by man, and from recent reports, beasts should be added, is more or less adulterated. It has been stated that during the English examination every article in use was found in some way to be adulterated except common salt, which was too cheap to admit of the expense, and the old-fashioned loaf sugar. Whether this be true or not, it is now a pretty well established fact that every article in use has its " grades," " imitations," etc., and that nothing that enters largely into daily consumption is too cheap to be cheapened.

In the annexed list are arranged in alphabetical form the various articles adulterated and the adulterants used, so as to give some slight idea of the extent and character of sophistication in a shape that can be readily comprehended.

COMMON ADULTERANTS OF FOODS AND BEVERAGES.

As far as possible herein is given a classified list of common adulterants, together with comments and extracts relating to some of the most important ones as presented by various authorities. While many of these articles are perfectly harmless, the fraud consists in selling them under false and misleading brands, whereby the purchaser is sold one article when asking and paying for a different one. These adulterants are divided into two classes," Poisonous",and " Fraudulent" adulterants. While all poisonous adulterants are not only criminal but fraudulent as well, most of the fraudulent adulterants are not harmful.

One character of fraud now generally adopted in States where laws are enforced is for the manufacturer in branding his goods to use large letters to describe them and very small ones to define the fact, required by law, that they are compounded. For example:

PURE GROUND PEPPER COMPOUNDED

46

ALUM.

While not an acid salt gives the same practical result, carbonic acid being liberated by its use. It is often used in so-called cream of tartar powders. In such cases it is an adulterant.

ALCOHOLIC LIQUORS.

Fusel oil, tannin, logwood, water, coloring matter, burnt sugar.

Kirsch (German cherry brandy) is imitated by a mixture made from apricot and cherry seed, dried peach leaves, myrrh, and good-flavored alcohol.

Gin is the product of the juniper berry, often imitated with a whisky made from rye and barley, or potatoes and barley; also, adulterated with alum salts, spirits turpentine, and water and sugar.

Absinthe is adulterated or imitated by liquors undistilled—some distilled—with trois-six from beets, etc. Old and damaged material is used and others after distillation have added aromatic resins, such as benzoin, guaiacum, etc.

BUTTER.

Oleomargarine, cotton oil, olive oil, beef suet, and water. The proper proportion of water is 5 to 10 per cent, but, according to Hassell, Hilmer, Johanson, and others, it can be loaded with from 20 to 50 per cent.

Rancid butter and lard churned together in sweet milk, with alkalies, is another form of adulteration.

BAKING POWDERS.

Alum for cream of tartar, overdoses of starch and flour.

BLACK PEPPER.

Buckwheat flour and ground hulls, cracker crumbs, Indian meal, wheat flour, charcoal, sand, bran, linseed meal, cocoanut shells, mustard husks, sawdust, olive stones, cayenne, P. D., red clay, and ship bread (see Spices).

Gen. B. F. Butler claims that the pepper used to cure the hides sent from South America to this country is washed, dried, and sold as pure pepper. One can imagine how they would like salt from spoiled fish or decomposed meat; this class of pepper is no better.

Of thirteen samples analyzed by the Connecticut authorities, nine were adulterated.

BREAD.

Alum, sulphate of copper, ammonia, flours other than wheat, inferior grades of flour.

BEER.

Burnt sugar, licorice, treacle, quassia, coriander and caraway seed, cayenne pepper, soda, salicylic acid, and salt (increase thirst). Artificial carbonic gas, grains other than barley malt, glycerine, to increase its viscosity. Glucose* water is often added by retailers.

Tobacco or seed of *Cocculus indicus* are added as intoxicants.

In color and flavor burnt sugar, licorice, treacle, and other mixtures are added to disguise the taste of adulterants.

The very extended report of the Department of Agriculture in Bulletin No. 13, part 3, would seem to preclude the necessity of referring to beer, but as its consumption is almost as general as bread, it may not be out of place to refer to its composition, and to the unhealthy elements that investigation has found therein.

The age of good beer should be from twelve weeks to six months, according to different authorities. It is often sold in from two to three weeks after being made, and in such a state is not healthy. One report says:

Beer should stand from four to six months, so as to produce the needed carbonification to prevent the beer turning acid. Good beer, well made, allowed to stand the necessary time, has in itself sufficient carbonic acid gas to eject all fermentable matter without resorting to artificial or injurious fermentation. The beers that are sophisticated simply accuse themselves.

Webster defines malt as "Barley or *other grain* steeped in water until it germinates, then dried in a kiln, thus evolving the saccharine principle."

Hassal says:

The extract of malt contains a variety of other substances, organic and mineral, beside sugar, so that the beverage produced from brewing malt extracts and the mixture of this with sugar and various other substances is very different in its actual composition and in its diabetic properties and effects.

Hassal again says:

Malt beverages should consist solely of the product of malt and hops, the former of which has been subjected to fermentation, and all varieties of these beverages should be due to these and these alone. The color should be due solely to the degree of heat to which the malt has been subjected in the kiln and the ripeness and color of the hops employed, and adulteration is defined as follows: Any other substances than the constituents of malt and their derivatives, hops, and water, in such proportion as in the case of stout, strong, and pale ale, to reduce the absolute alcohol to less than 4.5 per cent, and in porter and beer to under 3.5 per cent. Although the law allows the addition of both sugar and salt, we regard these additions as adulteration.

Atcherly, in reference to what ought to be the composition of beer, says:

Beer is the fermented infusion of malted barley flavored with hops, which, by law (English), are the only substances permitted to be used in its manufacture. How far this law is carried out is a matter which only analysis can determine.

---

*Glucose, when properly made, is healthful, but if manufactured improperly is a dangerous article (see Glucose).

A gentleman who evidently takes a somewhat liberal view defines normal lager to be a fermented beverage not less than six months old, made from any starchy grain, and rendered bitter to suit the consumer's palate.

There seems to be, therefore, an agreement in defining malt beverages as being composed solely of malt and hops, but a difference in regard to the kind of grain from which malt is to be derived.

On page 416, New York State Board of Health Report for 1886, we find the following:

Dr. Bartley, of Brooklyn, speaks of the custom of brewers sending out to the market beers only fourteen days old, containing more or less yeast, and clarified by artificial means instead of in the natural way. He further shows that while bicarbonate of soda taken into the stomach in small quantities is quite harmless, yet in the frequent potations of habitual beer drinkers, who imbibe, say, thirty glasses per diem, an amount ranging from 180 to 200 grains of bicarbonate of soda may be introduced into the system with necessarily deleterious effect.

*   *   *   *   *   *   *

Another danger to be guarded against is at the retailers, where, it is alleged, adulteration is carried on, either with the object of increasing the quantity, its intoxicating power, its pungency, or to revive old beer and give it an artificial color, resulting, of course, in a deteriorated article.

*   *   *   *   *   *   *

No matter how good the beer may be when brewed, it is always liable to harmful manipulation in the hands of a conscienceless retailer. Water is added to increase the quantity with the result of lowering the proportion of its constituents and lessening its flavor. Tobacco or the seeds of *Cocculus indicus* are added for intoxicating effect; color and flavor are given by means of burnt sugar, licorice, treacle, quassia, coriander and caraway seeds. To increase the thirst of the consumer, salt and cayenne pepper are put in, and various mixtures are concocted to get rid of stale ale. For these the brewers are certainly not responsible.

COTTON SEED OIL.

This article has within the past few years created more discussion than any other adulterant, owing to the agitation arising from the Congressional investigation regarding the "Conger lard bill." The discussion has been so general that chemists in nearly all the States have investigated the article with more than the usual care. So far as I have seen, the opinion expressed by these gentlemen is to the effect that the oil from cotton seed is a healthful commodity, and but few persons have advanced any contrary opinion. The oil, however, is used to adulterate the food supply probably more than any other one substance, and is sold under the name of lard and olive oil more extensively than in any other form. It enters largely into the fraudulent manufacture of butter and cheese, its rich color making it a very valuable article in the hand of the unprincipled manufacturer who desires a cheap substitute for cream.

CHEESE, LARD, AND COTTON OIL.

The adulterants are oleomargarine, skimmed milk, and coloring matter, salts of mercury in the curd, and cotton seed oil.

Probably no one article is more extremely adulterated than this, and the extent to which the adulteration has been carried has excited considerable remark in foreign markets and materially interfered with the export of the article. The principal adulteration in this article, like most of the others, is harmless, being the extraction of the cream and addition of coloring matter, olio, and cotton oils.

The following is from the Ohio report, 1890:

A process has been invented and patented, and which has been in operation a number of years, by which about 14 per cent of lard is used with skimmed milk in making cheese. In this process about half of the fat removed in the skimming of the milk is replaced with lard, I do not believe there is any cheese of this sort made in Ohio. In this State the main cause of the poor and low grade cheese is the use of full skimmed milk.

What is called "filled cheese" is manufactured as follows, according to the New York Produce Exchange Bulletin:

"The process consists in taking all the cream out of the milk by the separator, and then taking the skim milk up and charging the vat just before it is set with deodorized lard, cotton seed oil, or other fat. The oil is taken up in the curd, and mechanically held there, the cheese curd simply being used as a capsule in which to carry it. There is no assimilation or chemical affinity between the curd and its contents."

CHROME YELLOW.

This dangerous article is, it is thought, used very carelessly by bakers and confectioners to add beauty of color to their goods to give the appearence of using eggs much more generally than is done. On this subject I quote from several distinguished authorities in Philadelphia.

The following is taken from the Third Annual Report State Board of Health of Pennsylvania:

Dr. Leffman, of Philadelphia, found 8 grains of lead chromate in a pound of a sample of Soup "noodles" placed there to color it in imitation of eggs. The baker from whom these noodles were purchased, one Krumm, of Philadelphia, stated he had habitually used this dye for thirteen years. Other samples were also found to contain lead.

Seventy-eight cases of lead poisoning were reported in Philadelphia by Dr. D. D. Stewart, chief of the medical classes in the Jefferson Medical College, from eating chrome yellow pound buns. Sixty-four cases were indisputably the result of the use of chrome yellow by two bakers, Schmid and Palmer; in the family of one, six deaths occured, and he was himself seriously ill from the use of "his own medicine."

The tea buns tested by Dr. Leffman yielded approximately 2 grains of lead chromate to each.

At the inquest on the Palmer and Dieble cases, by a member of a wholesale drug and paint supply house, before referred to, who, curiously enough, is a lecturer on food adulterations, as well as pharmacy, in the Medical University of Pennsylvania, that, to his knowledge 80 per cent of the bakers and confectioners in Philadelphia were very recently regularly using chrome yellow, and that it had been in constant use by them as an artificial color for many years. It was shown that all the chrome yellow so used came from this house. Coroner Ashbridge and Deputy Coroner Powers, both of whom took a very active part in the investigation that followed the report of the Palmer and Diebel cases to the district attorney, visited sixty-odd bakers, of which all but one were found to be using this dye, and it was ascertained that all were supplied directly or indirectly from this house.

It was shown at the inquest that chrome yellow had been kept on sale by this firm as bakers' and confectioners' yellow, in packages of one-quarter, one-half, and 1 pound, the latter being most frequently asked for, and that no warning had been given to those the clerks recognized as bakers as to the danger attending its use as a food dye. It was further shown that this firm employed a salesman who regularly visited bakers to solicit orders for chrome yellow, and that most of it disposed of in this way was marked "free from arsenic," which the coroner inferred was an attempt to mislead purchasers, and cause them to believe the color nonpoisonous. It appeared that baker Schmid attempted to purchase from this house a harmless dye, styled "extract of eggs," such as he had employed in his trade in Switzerland, and that he was furnished chrome yellow, in 1 and 2 pound lots, which he subsequently introduced into his cake dough regardless of quantity, and that, being entirely unaware of its poisonous properties, his wife and himself had eaten of the dyed cakes and had been made ill thereby. The thoroughness of the poisoning in nearly all of the reports of Schmid's victims indicated the recklessness with which he used the dye, but the fact that his wife and himself exhibited undoubted symptoms of plumbism points to his ignorance, that it is a poison.

Commercial chrome yellow is a rather variable chemical compound. It rarely, if ever, consists of pure lead chromate, but contains, as sold to bakers by the drug house before mentioned, usually from 65 to 93 per cent of this salt, and its chief diluent is calcium carbonate (whiting), though lead, calcium, and barium sulphate may also be used. When prepared for painters' use, lead carbonate is often added to render the mass more opaque and of a less decided yellow.

Because of the supposed insolubility of lead chromate and the number of cases I had indubitably traced to its use as a cake dye, Dr. Leffmann recently undertook some experiments to ascertain the possible presence of lead carbonate as an adulterant, fancying, naturally, the poisoning might have been due to the latter more soluble salt. He tested various samples of chrome yellow in the market and some procured from several bakers, including the sample obtained from Palmer, but was unable to find lead carbonate in any of them. He, however, ascertained that lead chromate, contrary to the generally received opinion, is freely soluble in very dilute solutions of the ordinary household acids, such as citric and acetic, in very dilute hydrochloric acid, and in very dilute solutions of hydrochloric acid and pepsin. A brief consideration of this important fact will explain the ease with which poisoning took place, and should not cause surprise at the statement that there is scarcely a doubt that many thousands of cases of poisoning have occurred in our city through lead-laden cakes during the past twenty years, many of which, it is feared, have been unrecognized by physicians and treated for other ailments. I have recently, in my service in the out-patient medical department of the Jefferson Medical College Hospital, seen not a few cases of plumbism, with obscure symptoms, none of which are ordinarily regarded as suggestive of poisoning by lead, yet the metal was found in the urine of a number of these, and, placing them on an antilead treatment, they have recovered. There is likewise a large group with more pronounced and characteristic symptoms that I have in most instances been unable to trace to other sources than dyed cakes. I have, however, refrained from placing any of these cases on record, not having had the opportunity of making an exhaustive search for other channels of poisoning, which, though, I believe I should not have found.

COFFEE.

Green coloring matter, polishing, burnishing, water, and lactoserine (the Swedish coffee bean), an almost exact imitation of the real bean, even to the crook in the seam.

Mr. Barrett tells of a case where green coffee was darkened by artificial means to supply the demand for a rich dark color. People are doubtless often fooled in buying various articles of food by the color. Appearance has little to do with any article in these days of paint, dye, polish, and powder.

Toasted coffee is often steamed to increase the weight.

Ground coffee.—Chickory, beans, peas, corn, rye, acorns, chefus nuts, almond or nut shells, burnt sugar, lower grade coffees, pea hulls.

Imitation coffee.—The Swedish "lactoserine" has gotten a strong hold through the country.

The following letter and accompanying articles from the Philadelphia Times need no explanation or comment. There is also published herewith an article from the American Analyst:

STATE BOARD OF HEALTH.

LEWISBURG, PA., *May* 4, 1891.

DEAR SIR: Some days ago I received circular from your Department asking for any knowledge I might possess on the subject of food adulteration. Since I wrote you my attention has been called to two bad adulterations.

(1) An imitation coffee, concerning which I send you recent clippings from the Philadelphia Times.

(2) The use of oat hulls to adulterate ground horse feed. An imitation "chop" is made using the hulls to produce the appearance of oats in the feed.

This, and the use of smut in feed, can, I think, be stopped.

Kindly acknowledge the receipt of this.

G. G. GOFF.

Hon. SECRETARY OF AGRICULTURE,
Washington, D. C.

A COFFEE SWINDLE.

The market flooded with perfect counterfeits, both green and roasted—Big shipments from the Brooklyn agent of a German firm—Varieties among local dealers—Hard, molded gritty pellets, heavy in weight and cheap in price, that are identical with the genuine coffee in appearance, but have no taste, manufactured for the purpose of mixing with the legitimate article—An imitation of green coffee beans that caused sickness.

Counterfeit coffee is the latest addition to adulterants. It is a manufactured bean, identical in appearance with genuine green or roasted coffee, and dealers in this city have recently been flooded with it. It is almost impossible to detect the fraud with the eye. It is apparently a hard-baked composition, molded by machinery in the same manner as druggists' pills.

It is very hard and gritty and not as easily broken as the genuine. Having little or no taste or odor, its sole mission is to increase the bulk and weight of the regulation article, and this it does admirably, its weight being more than double that of the legitimate bean.

This is the bogus coffee bean now most widely used. It is of German manufacture, and is supplied by a Brooklyn agent. Other varieties, similar in appearance and differing but slightly in composition and taste, are manufactured in this city and in New Jersey.

THE IMPORTED COUNTERFEIT.

Quantities of the imported coffee substitute have been sent to Philadelphia dealers since the first of the year by the Brooklyn agent, whose name is M. Kliemand, and whose office is at 327 Degraw street. Mr. Kliemand, or a representative, made several trips to this city, and received orders for considerable amounts of his stuff. To those who didn't order it he sent generous samples, and few local dealers have not met with it. Its sales are reported by the agents of local wholesale coffee dealers and roasters as enormous. As it is supplied at only 11 cents a pound, it leaves a big margin of profit to dealers who mix it with the genuine.

Dealers who have not consented to use the counterfeit have been at a loss as to what defense to make against its encroachments on their trade, since it is not sold to wholesalers as coffee, but as "coffee substitute," dealers being left to their own discretion in the matter of mixing and reselling as the genuine article.   One dealer who feared that it would be a hopeless task to invoke the aid of the law decided to draw public attention to the swindle by giving an exhibition of the samples.

THE PUBLIC WARNED.

The following notice is posted in the window of Harkness & Dering, dealers in teas and coffees, at 244 Chestnut street:

> **BEWARE**
> **OF**
> **COUNTERFEIT COFFEE.**
> A manufactured bean, made to resemble genuine roasted coffee and generally sold to consumers, mixed with the genuine.

The window is filled with samples of the "coffee substitute," which another sign announces are not for sale, but to be given away.   Naturally enough there hasn't been much request for them even on this basis, and the dealer has noticed that two or three persons who had the hardihood to take a little home to try have not returned for a further supply.

LETTER FROM A SUBSTITUTE DEALER.

Just what is claimed for the counterfeit coffee is shown by the following letter received by the firm:

M. KLIEMAND, COMMISSIONER AND REPRESENTATIVE,
327 Degraw street, Brooklyn, N. Y., January 14, 1890.

Messrs. HARKNESS & DERING, *Philadelphia, Pa.:*

GENTLEMEN: I beg to mail you a sample of a coffee substitute called "Kunst Kaffee," manufactured by Messrs. Erhorn & Dierchs, Hamburg, who appointed me general agent for the United States.

Advantages: It is animating but not exciting, and very nutritious and wholesome, softening the taste of the inferior coffees; quality unimpaired for twelve months and longer.

Roast: Light, middle, and dark.   (Sample is dark.)

Price: Eleven cents per pound, New York net, per Pennsylvania Railroad.

Packing: In bags of 75 kz. (161 pounds).

I inclose the official analysis from Dr. Ules, sworn trade chemist, and hope to receive your kind order.

Yours, very truly,

M. KLIEMAND.

The inclosed analysis to which Kliemand referred, gave a list of harmless ingredients, including water, carbon, etc.   This, with samples of the "coffee substitute," Mr. Harkness sent to Prof. Buckhaut, of State College, in Center County, with a request that he also should make an analysis.   Prof. Buckhaut has not yet reported.

IMMENSE SALE OF THE BEAN.

Mr. Harkness said yesterday: "The sale of the counterfeit beans in this city is tremendous.   I shouldn't be surprised to see a lot of manufactories starting up in this city, for there is so big a demand for the stuff that there is a quick fortune in making and selling it.   I have heard that similar counterfeits are made in Trenton, and other places in New Jersey, although there were some prosecutions there some time ago. Some parties must have been making the stuff in this city, too, as there are different varieties on the market.

"The counterfeit beans mix easily with the genuine, and the price, 11 cents a pound, leaves a big profit when the higher classes of coffees are so adulterated. Just what proportion is generally used in mixing I don't know—one-half would probably be too much. The bogus bean outweighs the genuine more than two to one."

THE GREEN BEAN COUNTERFEITED.

The worst counterfeit of the lot is a bean made to resemble the green coffee. A clerk in the drug store of H. P. John, 242 Chestnut street, had a number of the beans in his possession which he had discovered in an uptown grocery. The beans were apparently a hard-molded paste of starch or flour, in which some coloring material had been used.

Coffee Dealer Harkness, who has also seen specimens of the green counterfeit, said he had heard that one of the ingredients was Paris green, and that a family had been made very sick from its use. Where it was made was a mystery, but he was inclined to believe that it was procured not far from home, although it might be imported like the burnt samples.—Philadelphia Times, April 30, 1891.

COUNTERFEIT COFFEE.

The imitation green and roasted beans that are sold—How the stuff is made—Flour and water as the principal ingredients—Machinery that turns out great quantities in a short time—The local imitations in the market.

Coffee dealers yesterday had little else to talk about than the Times' exposé of the counterfeit coffee swindle. The market, they said, was flooded with the various grades of beans made to resemble in appearance the genuine articles, both roasted and green. Although most of the counterfeits have been shipped to the city within the past few weeks by the Brooklyn agent of the Hamburg "coffee substitute" manufacturing concern, a good deal of the stuff on the market is of local manufacture.

The imitation coffee bean now found in this market is harmless enough, being made for the most part of flour and water. The beans are manufactured by machinery, which has a capacity for turning out immense quantities in a very short time.

LOCAL IMITATION COFFEE.

Most of the counterfeit coffee of local manufacture now on the market is said by dealers to have been made by the Dowling Manufacturing Company, which had an office on Fifteenth street, above Arch. This firm manufactured coffee beans of flour and water, green and roasted, and sold them in packages labeled "Java coffee" in large letters, with the addition in very small type of the word "compound." The firm ceased doing business a short time ago and the office is now occupied by a real estate dealer. Immense quantities of the "Java coffee compound" were distributed throughout the city and New Jersey and are still to be found in the market. The selling price was 7 to 8 cents a pound. An attempt was made to form a stock company, and it was claimed that about $150,000 of capital had been secured.

North Dowling, the head of the company, is now associated with J. E. Burns & Co., spice dealers on Front street, above Chestnut, in the manufacture of "process coffee." This is also an imitation of the genuine coffee bean or berry, but it is not sold as the pure article and the business is legitimately conducted and a patent applied for. The "process coffee" is composed of 33 per cent of pure coffee mixed with rye and bears the indorsement of Dr. Genth, of this city. The mixture is turned into the bean shape by machinery made and patented for the work.

"BETTER THAN BAD COFFEE."

Mr. Burns said yesterday that he shipped the process coffee principally to the West and Southwest. He sold great quantities of it and considered it superior to the poorer grades of coffee sold generally as "siftings." The Dowling Manufacturing Company gave up its business because it didn't pay to make an imitation absolutely free from coffee. There was, too, considerable trouble over the sale of the counterfeit in New Jersey, where the law against adulteration is very strict.

The Chestnut street firm that advertised "Counterfeit coffee given away in samples" did a rushing business yesterday. All day people crowded the store in order to get samples to take home, many of them explaining that they were anxious to compare the bogus coffee with that they had been buying and drinking as the unadulterated article.

Jobbers are anxious to check the sale of the counterfeits because they are so widely used by dealers to mix with the genuine that less of the real article is sold than would otherwise be the case, but the manufacturers, as they do not label their production as pure coffee, can not be proceeded against.

HOW IT IS MADE.

"I read the exposure of the coffee swindle in this morning's Times with a great deal of interest," said a traveling salesman yesterday. "It recalled to mind a recent trip through the Southern States when I met a salesman in the coffee line. He let me into the secrets of the 'line' and showed me samples of his goods. The roasted whole beans that he was selling were similar to those described in the Times, and he told me of what they consisted. The exact formula I have forgotten, but I remember that flour paste, hardened by hydraulic pressure, was the basic component. The machine which makes these bogus beans is the invention of a shrewd Boston Yankee and is patented. It turns them out by the million. There is another patented machine used by the coffee adulterants, which is fed with a white bean about the size of a coffee berry. The machine splits and grooves the beans and they fall into a tub of cold water, where they are allowed to soak a few minutes. After this they are dumped into a stain, one of the ingredients of which is Paris green. Finally they are dried and run through a 'brush' machine which turns them out so closely imitating genuine green coffee berries that only an expert could detect the difference.

GROUND COFFEE COUNTERFEITED.

"The *ne plus ultra* of fraud in the 'coffee line' was a sample of 'ground' that he showed me. To the smell, touch, look, and taste it was wonderfully like the genuine article, and I told him that the adulteration was, in my opinion, a better article than most of the genuine that was sold. When he told me what it was made of I marveled greatly at man's ingenious rascality.

"Another machine, also the invention of the Boston coffee maker, a powerful grinding mill, was used in making this. The husks and shells of cocoanuts, which can be had at any of the large confectionery establishments at the cost of carting them away, were reduced to granules, and, without being doctored, looked very much and felt very much like genuine coffee. When soaked for several hours in a solution made by dissolving coffee essence in water the deception was perfect. After being dried at a slow heat no one could tell the difference between a sample of this and a sample of genuine Mocha or Java."—Philadelphia Times, May 1, 1891.

ARTIFICIAL COFFEE.—A SWEDISH SWINDLE, WITH HEADQUARTERS IN PHILADELPHIA.

"Lactoserin." What is it? It is an imitation of coffee—an excellent imitation, too—and it comes from Sweden. It looks like coffee and smells like coffee, but it isn't coffee, and consumers will, in the future, do well to look to what they are buying, as otherwise they may be made the victim of a remunerative Swedish "joke"—remunerative to the gentlemanly perpetrator in Sweden. The difference between genuine coffee and its Swedish imitation is very pronounced when the test is applied—the test of taste. The imitation looks like the genuine article, but does not taste like it. As soon as it is cracked by the teeth it resolves itself into small particles in the mouth. With a view to finding out something about the imitation, a reporter for the Blade called on Mr. Woolson, of the Woolson Spice Company, last evening, and asked him regarding it. "We have received several communications and samples of the 'coffee,'" said he, "but have paid no attention to them. The 'imitation' is, of course, a fraud, i. e., so far as it being equal to genuine coffee is concerned, and it may for a little time interfere in some degree with the legitimate coffee trade. One of our men last week visited a regular customer, and asked, as usual, for an order. The dealer told him he had bought coffee cheaper elsewhere and had made more money on it than he could on ours. Our agent wanted to see the coffee. After examining the package produced, and finding the contents to be a mixture, he purchased it, and here it is." The inventor of the "new coffee," William Rehnstrom, of Stockholm, Sweden, some days ago wrote a letter, it is learned, to the Dowling Manufacturing Company, of Philadelphia, in which he says he is glad his invention is getting on so well in the United States, and in which he declares it to be a merchandise just as good as it is valuable. He adds that by adding lactoserin to coffee "we have values in millions. The production of coffee is limited—of lactoserin unlimited, or the less coffee add the more lactoserin." The Dowling Manufacturing Company have a corner on the new merchandise, and are flooding the country with sample packages, and with each package goes a letter announcing that their long negotiations with the representatives of Mr. William Rehnstrom, of Stockholm, Sweden, have been successfully concluded, and that henceforth the exclusive use in the United States rests with them for "lactoserin" for and in combination with coffee. Here Mr. Woolson emptied the contents of the package on the table and leveled the pile. He then placed his hand on it and raised it quickly. "You see," said he, with a smile of triumph, "that the genuine coffee of the mixture will stick to the palm, the imitation won't. They can not put the gloss on the bogus article that beautifies the genuine." "Is the gloss put on coffee during the process of roasting it or afterwards?" "Afterwards; but to go on about 'lactoserin,' it may be said that it is liable to become a dangerous article in the coffee trade unless steps are taken to regulate it. I do not think it can be suppressed at once, as its inventor, William Rehnstrom, of Stockholm, Sweden, has patents on it in this country. The berry of the imitation, you see, is much heavier than the genuine, but it lacks the gloss, and the crease is not like that of nature's production. The imitation will be manufactured at 10 cents per pound. A half pound of coffee at 25 cents and half of 'lactoserin' at 10 would make a pound of mixture worth 17½ cents. It would sell readily at 25 cents, as the people know nothing of the new article, and have been paying 27 cents a pound, and the profit to the seller would be 9¼ cents. This is quite an item when it is taken into consideration that there is very little, if anything, made on coffee by the retail dealer. The genuine article costs him 25¾, and he grinds and sells it for 27. The temptation to make something will probably prove so strong that a good deal of 'lactoserin' will be sold. In ground coffee it can not easily be detected, as it has the color and odor of the genuine." "What do you think 'lactoserin" is made of Mr. Woolson?" "Probably musty flour, though I do not know. If it is made of flour it is not dangerous, but it can not be determined what its ingredients are. It may be a kind of clay."—Toledo Blade.

CIDER.

This very wholesome and refreshing drink does not escape the adulterator's art.

Prof. H. A. Weber, chemist of the Ohio State University, reported on these samples to Hon. F. A. Derthick, dairy and food commissioner for that State.

He states that all of the samples were branded pure cider. He found No. 388 sweet, showing no signs of fermentation, but containing a large amount of salicylic acid.

No. 389 was undergoing fermentation; it, too, contained "a large amount of salicylic acid."

No. 390. Marked, "S. R. & J. C. Mott's unfermented apple juice. 'Sweet cider.' Bouckville, Madison County, N. Y."

The following was copied from S. R. & J. C. Mott's card, which accompanied the sample: "Unfermented juice can not be kept for a long time without the use of powerful drugs, which not only ruin the flavor, but render it very injurious to the stomach. Our products are free from any such materials, and sweet juice can not be indefinitely guaranteed against fermentation."

This sample, when examined, was undergoing fermentation. It contained a large quantity of salicylic acid.

Cider is also adulterated with acids and other chemicals, and dried apples are used to give taste and color to the compound. This is especially the case when the fruit crop is scarce and high, but it is a well-established fact that the supply of cider never runs dry.

CREAM OF TARTAR.

Sulphate of lime, acid phosphate of lime, alum, corn starch, flour.

For weighting any white material, such as terra alba, plaster, flour, starch, etc,

Alum or tartaric acid gives it aerating qualities.

Pure cream of tartar should be guaranteed 98 per cent of tartrate (Connecticut report).

The following in regard to this article is taken from the 1890 New York State Report, page 466:

One hundred and fifteen samples collected from retail grocery stores in the city of Albany exclusively were examined, previous investigation having shown that a pure article is almost invariably sold by druggists. The results of the examination of these samples will be surprising to those who are not informed upon this subject, for only 30 of the samples, or 26 per cent of the total number, consisted of real and unadulterated cream of tartar. With the exception of 6 samples rated as fair, in which the amount of adulterants was comparatively small, the remaining 85 samples were either largely adulterated or entirely fictitious. Of this number, 19, rated as inferior, were adulterated, either with starch, acid phosphate of lime, or sulphate of lime, in varying quantities, not less than 80 per cent of the adulterant or make-weight being present in some instances. Fifty-eight of the samples were entirely fictitious, of which number 10 were chiefly acid phosphate of lime (containing considerable sulphate), 23 were chiefly acid phosphate of lime and starch, 11 were chiefly tartaric acid and sulphate of lime, and 14 consisted of tartaric acid, sulphate of lime, and starch; 2 samples consisted of poor baking powder sold by mistake for cream of tartar. The sale of such miserable imitations for real cream of tartar is evidently without excuse, and as the fraudulent substitute is frequently sold at the price of the genuine, with perhaps less than a quarter and seldom more than half of its strength, it is evident that the purchaser is both deceived and defrauded. These substitutes are to be condemned, also, as being, in all probability, less wholesome than the article they replace.

Of 12 samples analyzed by the Connecticut authorities, 8 were adulterated.

COPPER.

A dangerous poison when used by inexperienced or careless people. in Connecticut Report, p. 307, is found :

Even if the copper is in a poisonous form, of course the quantity present is not sufficient to produce immediate symptoms of poisoning, but the continued use of food containing small quantities of such a poison is quite probably injurious to health, especially as some people are affected by extremely slight doses. Sulphate of copper ought not certainly to find a place in an establishment where foods are being prepared. Although small quantities are intentionally used, the consumer, knowing from experience, how liable cooks are to oversalt their dishes, can not but think of what would be the consequence if, through some blunder, a poisonous dose had been added.

Blyth, the English analyst, says on this point :

Since coppered peas must either (1) have a toxic action if the copper is in a soluble form, or (2) if the copper is insoluble the pea must be deprived of some of its nutritive properties, the analyst need have no hesitation in certifying that pease made green with copper are adulterated under the sale of food and drug act.

CANNED GOODS.

Sulphate of copper is used to give a green color.   Meat damaged in the process of canning.

An examination by the Connecticut authorities showed in nine samples of French peas, one sample string beans, and one of mixed vegetables, that all contained copper.

CAYENNE PEPPER.

Red lead, ground rice, flour, salt, cracker dust, Indian meal, ship biscuit, " P. D.," and other like articles.

COCOA AND CHOCOLATE.

Oxide of iron and other coloring matter, starch, flour, sugar, animal fats, and caromel.

CONFECTIONERY.

The principal articles used are glucose, terra alba, arsenic, sulphate of copper, prussic acid, tartaric acid, fusil oil, analyne dyes, chrome yellow.

Several alleged cases of poisoning by confectionery in Massachusetts resulted upon examination in failure to find the alleged poison. The cause of illness is believed to have resulted more from the quantity consumed than from the quality.

CLOVES.

Arrowroot.

CINNAMON.

Spent bark.

FLOUR.

Not generally adulterated, but few cases reported.   Damaged pease, ground rice, corn meal.   It is sold musty and often contains smut.   Alum is sometimes put in some brands to give whiteness.

GREENING.

. This species of deception is dangerous and consists of using carelessly or wilfully copper salts copper coins, and vessels, to give a green color to preserves or pickles.

GINGER.

Turmeric, cayenne pepper, mustard, inferior and refuse ginger.

GLUCOSE.*

This article is used to adulterate very extensively the following articles: Sugar, cane and maple sirups, molasses, honey, jellies, jams, confectionery, beer, vinegar, liquors, wines.   Bakers use it for cakes, cooks for sauces; it is also used in tobacco.

Dr. Battershall, of New York, in his Food Adulteration and its Detection, says, on page 138:

The question of the sanitary effects of the use of artificial glucose as an adulterant of sugar and sirups, and as a substitute for malted grain in the manufacture of beer, has given rise to extensive controversy.   In this regard one fact seems to have been demonstrated.   Glucose, as it is now found in the market, is free from any appreciable amount of deleterious contamination.   The discovery of its artificial production has given birth to a very important branch of industry, and, according to all available reports, the commercial product at present met with is for many purposes an economical and harmless substitute for cane sugar, the chief objection to its application being the fact that it possesses considerably less sweetening power.

The Massachusetts board of health, as quoted from the New York American Analyst, February 15, 1886, has some very sensible comments on this glucose question, calculated to dispose of popular fallacies regarding its supposed dangerous qualities.   When properly and carefully manufactured it regards it as a wholesome food, deficient, however, in sweetening power; but a dangerous article to be taken into the system when carelessly prepared.   The question, then, turns upon its mode of preparation.   Glucose is usually made from the starch of corn by boiling it with dilute sulphuric acid, a process first discovered by Prof.

---

* When there is an excess of oil vitriol and lime it is dangerous.

Kircoff, a Russian chemist, in 1811, and largely practiced in Austria and Germany since that time; but only within a comparatively recent period introduced into this country. The process is thus described by the Massachusetts board of health:

The starch is first obtained in a pure condition from the corn, then mixed with water, and the mixture is heated to boiling. Sulphuric acid is added to the extent of about 2 per cent., and it is then boiled about three hours. The starch is by this time converted to sugar and dextrine, both of which are in solution. The free acid is then got rid of by the addition of chalk or marble dust, which, with the acid forms calcic sulphate, which settles to the bottom and leaves a clear, supernatant fluid, which yields glucose and dextrine. Should all of the acid not be removed or should the calcic sulphate be in any amount retained, it is evident that the product would not be entirely harmless, since disturbances of the digestion might follow its use. Moreover, the contaminations which are ordinarily present in commercial sulphuric acid will of course be present with the acid, and Johnston claims that such beer is deficient in the aromatic principle found in the skin of the grain.—[New York State Report, p. 415.

The following is taken from New York State report for 1890, pp. 79–82.

The National Academy of Sciences at the request of the Commissioner of Internal Revenue, made a report on the "composition, nature and properties," of glucose, from which I will extract as follows:

The starch sugar of commerce consists chiefly of dextrose, with varying quantities of another kind of sugar called maltose, and often more or less of dextrine or starch gum. Dextrose was first recognized as a peculiar variety of sugar, differing from cane sugar, by Lowitz, in 1792. It is generally known in chemical works as dextrose or dextro-glucose, but is also called glucose, glycose, grape sugar, starch sugar, potato sugar, etc. It is produced from starch by the action of dilute acids. In France and Germany potato starch constitute, the only available material for the manufacture of this sugar, but in the United States the starch of Indian corn or maize is invariably employed. The process consists, first, in extracting the starch from the corn in a state of sufficient purity, then transforming this into sugar by treatment with dilute acid, and subsequently neutralizing the acid, purifying and then concentrating the product.

The variety in which the conversion is the least complete is called "glucose," and remains liquid. That in which it is more complete, and which becomes solid, is called grape "sugar." Starch sugar appears in commerce in a variety of grades, under the following names:

The liquid varieties.

Glucose.	Corn sirup.
Mixing glucose.	Jelly glucose.
Mixing sirup.	Confectioners' crystal glucose.

The solid varieties.

Solid grape sugar.	Powdered grape sugar.
Clipped grape sugar.	Confectioners' sugar.
Granulated grape sugar.	Brewers' grape sugar.

This industry sprang into existence during the continental blockade under Napoleon I, after which it disappeared for some years. It has gradually revived, and is now an established industry both in continental Europe and in the United States. The irregularity of demand for the product depends largely upon the comparative price of corn, and of molasses and cane sugar. At the time of the last census the capacity of the factories in the United States was estimated at 43,000 bushels of corn per day.

Payen, in 1855, estimated the French production from potato starch at 5,500 tons per year; and Wagner, in 1874, estimated that of the German Empire at 19,800 tons of sirup and 27,500 tons of sugar per year.

The committee reported the following conclusions:

(1) That the manufacture of sugar from starch is a long-established industry, scientifically valuable and commercially important.

(2) That the processes which it employs at the present time are unobjectionable in their character, and leave the products uncontaminated.

(3) That the starch sugar thus made and sent into commerce is of exceptional purity and uniformity of composition, and contains no injurious substances.

(4) Though having at best only about three-fifths the sweetening power of cane sugar, yet starch sugar is in no way inferior to cane sugar in healthfulness, there being no evidence before the committee that maize-starch sugar, either in its normal condition or fermented, has any deleterious effect upon the system, even when taken in large quantities.

HORSE-RADISH.

Turnips.

HONEY.

Glucose, sugar sirups, molasses, and raw sugar.

Of five samples examined in Connecticut all were adulterated.

Bees are often fed sugar and glucose sugar by raisers, so as to increase the quantity of honey. Whether this is an adulteration the reader can determine for himself.

It has been stated that paraffine combs have been supplied the bees, so as to lessen their labors and increase the supply.

It has been learned from a gentleman that some samples were sold in Baltimore some years ago of comb honey, all of which was artificial. No trace has been secured or a sample obtained.

JAMS AND JELLIES.

Glucose, gelatin; coloring matter principally dyes, preservatives; gelatin apple jelly, artificial essences.

ISINGLASS.

Gelatin.

ICE CREAM.

Aniline and other coloring; for flavoring, essence of bitter almond.

LARD.

Cotton oil, beef and sheep stearin, caustic lime, and alum water (often as high as 20 to 35 per cent), and alkalies. For full report of lard and its adulterants see Dr. Wiley's report, Bulletin 13, Part IV, U. S. Department of Agriculture, and reports of investigation by the Fiftieth and Fifty-first Congresses. No one article has probably been more conspicuously adulterated.

MUSTARD.

Ground yellow cakes, flour, cayenne, chrome* yellow, Martin's yellow,* gypsum,† turmeric,† mustard cake colored with turmeric; diluted with starch, wheat and rice flour; weighted with terra alba.†

Of nineteen samples examined in Connecticut seventeen were adulterated.

MACARONI.

Saffron, turmeric,† and Martin's yellow.*

MOLASSES.

Glucose, sirups, tin salts.*

In Connecticut, of twenty-two samples examined nine contained glucose and salts of tin. An examination shortly afterwards showed all to be pure (fifteen samples). But in 1888 and 1889, of forty-two examinations made nineteen were fraudulent.

MEATS.

Diseased meats of all kinds are liable to transmit disease to the person eating, but so far as national legislation can well regulate this matter it is done by the meat inspection law passed by the Fifty-first Congress.

MILK.

The question of meat inspection has been acted on by Congress since my last report, both foreign and interstate, which, taken in connection with the oleomargarine law, pretty well covers the entire question, except as to

MILK AND CHEESE.

The various local laws regarding milk have created great improvement in the quality of the milk sold, as proven by inspection, and that it has done good is shown by the decreased death rate of infants in several of the larger cities where the inspection has been most thoroughly attended to.

The adulteration of milk, however, is a question that needs special and careful attention, as it is not only one of the most important articles of diet, but is undoubtedly the most susceptible of being contaminated by absorption of impurities from its surroundings, as well as being easily injured by the food given the cow, its purity depending largely upon what she eats and the water she drinks. The health of the animal is also another important question, as it is a well recognized fact that tuberculosis in the cow engenders it in the human system that uses the milk. As milk is largely an article of interstate trade and one upon which so much depends, it comes clearly within the province of the

---

Government to regulate the conditions of shipment and provide for its careful inspection both of the commodity and the animal from which it is taken.

The use of milk may be estimated by the following figures, which show the supply for 13 cities; population, 4,746,150 : Amount of milk used, 480,000,000 quarts; wholesale price, $19,260,000; retail price, $32,000,000.

Milk that contains less than 12 per cent of solids and more than 88 per cent of water is not good or wholesome.

The standard for milk by New York regulation is fixed at—

Fat	2.5
Solids not fat	9.0
Total solids	11.5
Water	88.5

The great importance of milk as an article of food ; its rapid deterioration upon exposure to the air, especially at high temperatures; its liability to convey the material of infection, make it imperative that its production and its sale should be conducted under the most careful supervision.—[Mass. Report, 1889, p. 91.

Prof. S. P. Sharpless, of Boston, says:

The milk law has probably been better and more fully enforced in this city than any other in the United States, not as a spasmodic effort, as in some other cities, but as a regular, constant business.

The Massachusetts report of 1874, page 476, shows the following adulterants : Water, flour, salt, sheeps' brains, gum arabic, annetto, caramel.

Dr. Chancellor, of Maryland, on page 32 of his report for 1888, says :

When we remember that 50,000 disease germs will thrive in the circumference of a pin head, we may form some idea of the great danger to health that arises from milk pollution.

The Massachusetts board inspected in 1889 1,955 samples, of which 1,108 were above the standard and 847 below. The percentage was 43.32 of an inferior quality. Twenty-five samples were skimmed and 34 colored.

The same report states that the milk of 601 animals was examined and the average total solids was 13.26. The average in 1888 was lower than in 1884–'85, and is explained by two reasons, neither of which the producer or dealer is responsible for, viz : An increase of rainfall in the months of September and October, when the samples were collected, was greater than for ten years previous. The report does not claim this to be a settled question, however. The other reason assigned is the introduction of Holstein cows, " whose milk is usually found to be below the legal standard of pure milk."

The following is taken from the report of Dr. C. W. Chancellor, secretary of the State board of health of Maryland :

But the worst effect of adulterated milk is to be found among young children, who feed so largely on milk, for not more than one mother in six is able to nourish her infant from her breast for one year. In 1868 the deaths from cholera infantum in Boston,

Mass., amounted to 437, while in an equal population outside of the city the deaths from the same cause during the same time were only 100. It was found that not more than 5 per cent of the milk sold in Suffolk was unadulterated. In New York, after the milk inspectors began their work, the infant mortality was 3,673 less in 1883 than in 1882, when there was no inspection. In Boston the milk inspection begun in 1883, and in that year there was an apparent lessening of deaths among children under five years of age from cholera infantum. In Baltimore, during the year 1885, there were upwards of 3,000 deaths of children under five years of age, and of this number it is fair to assume that one-sixth, or 500, were directly attributable to an inferior milk supply, and doubtless 500 of these could have been saved by an improved quality of milk. We can not replace milk with any other diet, and therefore the failure of the milk supply would in some respects be more disastrous than the failure of the wheat supply.

Prof. Babcock, who was the official analyst of Boston, a few years ago obtained samples of milk from some of the most respectable milkmen and grocers in the city, which were all sold as pure milk, and at the highest prices, and his examination of these samples goes to confirm the fact, which some milkmen themselves do not hesitate to admit, that in conducting the milk trade of our large cities adulteration is the rule. Nor is the evil unmixed. Much of the water of adulteration is derived from country wells and springs, added by persons in agricultural districts where typhoid fever may be rife. Recent investigations, conducted in the most thorough and searching manner by experts, have established the fact that epidemics of typhoid fever and of other infective diseases, such as scarlet fever, may be produced by infected milk, and this being the case, we can not but view with distrust and alarm this importation of country well water mingled with the milk we drink—[Maryland Report, 1886, p. 31.

In the report of the Massachusetts board for 1876 Dr. Bowditch states that typhoid fever may be produced by using milk polluted with water, and in the report for 1877, p. 122, the same doctrine is illustrated by Prof. William Riply Nichols in his article on the pollution of streams, etc., in which, among other things, he treats of watered milk.

In the report of the same board for 1878, p. 325, it is stated that scarlet fever germs are also carried in milk, and may be thus propagated. When we remember that 50,000 disease germs will thrive in the circumferance of a pin head, we may form some idea of the great danger to health that arises from milk pollution.

EFFECT OF MILK ON INFANT LIFE.

The following is taken from the report of Dr. Townsend, health officer of the District of Columbia:

Although the white population is estimated as being twice that of the colored, yet it will be seen that the deaths of the colored infants exceed the white by 200. This material difference in the death rate may be charged, to a great extent, to the location of the colored people in alleys and unhealthy parts of the city, and in their unsanitary surroundings; while there is no doubt but that a very large proportion of these children die in consequence of being fed improper and unhealthy food, especially cheap and badly-prepared condensed milk, and cow's milk which has been allowed to stand to the point of acidity after having been kept in vessels badly or unskillfully cleaned. It is a well-known fact that infant mortality in the country is much less than that in the cities. This difference can not be wholly attributed to the unsanitary conditions of the city. Much of it can be laid to the unnatural custom of urban mothers in depriving their offspring of the food nature has prepared. It is now a well-established fact that no artificial food has as yet been manufactured which will convey the same amount of nutriment to the child, without causing functional derangement, as mother's milk.

Mr. Charles O. Flagg, president of the Rhode Island State Agricultural School, sends the following from the Providence Evening Bulletin of March 20:

ADULTERATION OF MILK.

The following communication was received by the city council:

From the inspector of milk to the honorable the Mayor and Board of Aldermen:

I most respectfully beg to draw your attention to the requirements of my office.

In entering upon my duties I find that adulteration is practiced very extensively and openly; the examination by the State board of health proved 72 per cent of purchased samples to be adulterated, and my own experience thus far fully corroborates this condition of the milk sold in Providence. I estimate that there are fully 75,000 quarts of milk sold daily in this city. At 6 cents per quart this represents a value of $4,500 per day, or $1,500,000 per annum.

On the 14th instant I spent the time from 2 a. m. to 7:30 a. m. inspecting milk among the peddlers, and have analyzed twenty of the samples taken, finding eighteen adulterated. The forms of adulteration are skimming, adding water, coloring, and in some cases substances to conceal watering, also preservatives to keep the milk from souring. The last additions are acknowledged by physicians to be injurious to the health, especially when taken daily by children and invalids.

I am of the opinion that not less than 10 per cent of the fluid sold as milk is adulteration; matter foreign to pure milk; this represents $450 per day, or $165,000 per annum, for added water and the like, which the people of Providence are paying to-day.

It at first seems that active work for a short time followed by prosecution might stop this fraud, but the experience of Boston shows that only constant vigilance will insure the offering for sale of milk of standard quality.

During the past week I visited the inspector of milk of Boston and examined the system so successfully in operation there.

The city has furnished a laboratory in one of its buildings. The working force consists of: Inspector, salary, $3,000; assistant chemist, salary, $1,800; clerk, salary, $1,500; three collectors, at $3 per day each.

During the year 1889 the entire expenses of the office were $9,478.20.

The income from license fees was $604, from fines $7,480; total, $8,084, making the net cost of the office to the city $1,394.20.

To fully cope with the present condition of milk adulteration in our city will require systematic and thorough inspection; so complete that every dealer in milk, whether peddler or storekeeper, will feel that he is likely to have his stock inspected at any moment and on any day including Sundays.

No reliable tests of milk, except in case of considerable adulteration by water and skimming, can be made on the premises where the milk is sold or the wagon from which it is delivered. Such tests can only be properly made in a laboratory provided with suitable facilities for chemical analysis. This involves the collection of samples and their removal to the laboratory for examination. Therefore to carry out the intentions of the law and to provide pure milk for the citizens of Providence will require a much larger appropriation, and I respectfully request that a committee be appointed to examine into the matter.

Yours respectfully,

GEORGE E. PERKINS,
Inspector.

Alderman Harris introduced the following resolution :

Resolved, That Aldermen ——, together with such as the common council may add, be, and they are hereby, appointed a joint special committee to examine into the matter of the adulteration of milk, as reported by the inspector of milk in his communication, this day presented to the board of aldermen, with authority to report to either branch of the city council.

The resolution passed and Mayor Smith appointed from the board Aldermen Harris, West, and Dyer as the committee on examination.

MILK PRESERVATIVES.

The Connecticut report says :

The use of preserving chemicals is highly objectionable for two reasons :

(1) Because the continued use of boraic acid, borax, and salicylic acid, the principal substances used for this purpose, is considered by physiologists of the highest authority injurious to health.

(2) When such preservatives are used there is a strong temptation to neglect in the dairy that cleanliness which otherwise is so essential for the proper preservation of milk.

Although large quantities of milk preservatives are sold in various parts of the country no evidence can here be presented regarding their use in Connecticut since the work of collecting and testing milk was carried on the latter part of autumn, when preservatives are not so much needed and are probably not used. During the summer, especially, when ice is scarce, there is an incentive to the use of preservatives, since, where they are used, ice can be dispensed with. In a circular recently sent out by the manufacturers of a well-known milk preservative the following statement appears : "We know that many unscrupulous persons have recommended such chemicals as salicylic acid, borax, boracic acid, and benzoic acid as proper articles to preserve milk, but a little investigation will show these, by reason of their action on the human system and the health of people, to be unfit for use, and, in fact, quite injurious." Since the preparation which this philanthropic company offers for sale consists, according to analyses by reliable chemists, largely of boracic acid, the public, in the light of this quotation, can decide as to the advisability of its use.

MILK FROM DISEASED COWS.

The use for human food of milk from diseased cows is not only a disgusting but a dangerous practice. It is well known that many serious or even fatal cases of illness among children may be traced to the sickness of the cows on whose milk they were fed.

We have a law forbidding the sale of milk from cows "affected with tuberculosis or other blood disease;" but until we have an official inspection of milk farms, this law will be of little value in protecting the public against milk of such a dangerous character.

NOODLES (FOR SOUP).

Chrome yellow * to color.

OLIVE OIL.

Cotton seed, peanut, cocoa, and other vegetable oils.

---

* Poisonous.

The following from the American Analyst is of such an interesting character, in connection with oil adulterations and the question generally, that I reproduce it:

OLIVE OIL FRAUDS.—THE IMPORTED ARTICLE MADE OF PEANUTS AND SEEDS.

In a recent issue of the San Francisco Argonaut a letter was published from a gentleman of that city, who, after graduating from the University of California, went to Europe for several years to study all that relates to the culture of the vine and the olive tree, and the making and treatment of wine and oil, and has been in France and Italy for several years. In view of the growth of those industries in California, the following extract may interest some of our readers:

"MONTPELLIER, FRANCE, *April*, 1891.

"One hears so much of the adulteration of almost all articles of daily consumption, that a few words about what I saw in this line may be of interest. While at Marseilles I visited the magnificent docks and saw thousands of tons of peanuts and other grains from which oil is made. Great iron steamers were unloading heavy cargoes of these grains. Most of it came from Africa or Asia, where slave labor makes their production very cheap. The next day I visited some of the large oil mills in the outskirts of Marseilles. Here I saw these peanuts, cotton seeds, colza, sesame, etc., ground up and pressed. It was an interesting sight I assure you, but apart from the fine machinery in use, the names on the barrels of oil were of great wonder to me. Afterward at Nice, the most important oil center in the world, I found that among all the numberless oil merchants not more than *three* ever sell really pure olive oil. Leaving the warehouses and docks, I rode through the beautiful olive-covered country and was astonished to see so many acres of magnificent olive trees being cleared and planted in grass. Questioning the men, I found that the price of genuine olive oil had been so reduced by competition with grain oils under the name of olive oil that the poor producers could not pay expenses and were forced to uproot these grand old trees and plant something that could not be pirated by unscrupulous merchants. In other industries the law compels everyone to sail under his own colors. When the oleomargarine threatened to ruin all the buttermakers of France, the law compelled the merchants to 'call a spade a spade.' Recently, plastered wine became omnipresent. The Government put an end to plastering, not by forbidding it, but simply by compelling merchants to indicate the nature of the product they offered for sale. Needless to say, no one would buy plastered wine if they knew it as such. The reason that cotton seed, peanut, etc., oils are allowed to be sold as 'pure olive oil' is twofold. First, because the oil merchants are united against attempts to interfere with their trade; second, because, up to very recently, it was almost impossible to detect mixtures of cotton-seed oil, etc., with the pure product of the olive. Recently, however, the much-talked-of difficulty in detecting falsifications has been swept away by the discovery of a simple and cheap detective that gives infallible results. The Italians claim that it was Prof. E. Bechi, of the royal station of Florence, who first discovered it. The French say that it is due to the labors of Mr. R. Brulé, director of the government station Agronomique de Nice. I do not wish to enter into the controversy. Suffice it to say the two methods differ but little, and great credit is due both gentlemen, for their discoveries were made, I believe, independently.

I had occasion to pass several days in the government laboratory at Nice each time I passed through that city, and I made experiments with pure oil and mixtures. I was able to detect unmistakably 5 per cent of cotton-seed oil in olive oil and less than 3 per cent of oleomargarine in butter—for it works even more perfectly with butter than with oil. Some day, when you have an hour to spare, you can do all the tests yourself. You need but a solution of nitrate of silver, twenty-five for one thousand in alcohol of wine at 95° a few test tubes 6 inches long, and a basin of water kept at boiling point over an alcohol lamp or stove of some sort,

Put in one test tube pure olive oil in another pure cotton-seed oil, and then make any mixture you choose. In each case use 12 cubic centimeters of the oil you wish to test and 5 cubic centimeters of the reactive. Put the tubes in the bath of boiling water and watch the results. You can do six or eight dozen at a time by numbering your test tubes. The whole operation lasts but thirty minutes at most. Pure olive oil, well made, remains clear and of a greenish tint. Cotton-seed oil turns black, and mixtures vary in color. Poorly made oil of the second pressure clouds up at first, but soon regains a greenish color. This test is *infallible*, and once seen never can lead to mistakes. When this discovery was first made known, the oil falsifiers took prompt steps to muzzle the press and buy off all who attempted to make it known generally. They were at first successful; but thanks to the outside press and the patient and determined efforts of a few people, the cat got out of the bag, and a great commotion ensued. Buyers of oil now demand Brule's analysis, sworn to before the consul, before they will accept shipments. I know of one man who is making a great deal of money by offering, as an inducement, Brule's analysis *free*, thereby proving the old saying that honesty is the best policy. If this crusade against falsifications continues to be as successful as it has been thus far, I have no doubt that the culture of the olive will regain its former importance, and the poor peasants will be once more happy, as they were before cotton seed and peanuts gained the mastery.

The grower of olives in California should be careful to fight the adulterators before they gain too much power. Steps should be taken to establish laboratories where consumers could have analyses made without trouble or expense. The slight cost of such stations would be paid for a hundred-fold by the increase in price of the pure article. Why should not Congress extend the oleomargarine law to oils, and compel various oils to sail under their own flags."

OLEOMARGARINE.

Refuse pork (liable to produce trichinæ), bone fats, candle and soap grease, horse fat.

PICKLES.

Poor vinegar, poor spices, and copper greening.

PEAS.

Of nine samples of French pease examined in Connecticut for copper all contained it, while two American samples examined contained none.

PIMENTO.

Ship bread.

PRESERVES.

Glucose, gelatin,* preservatives, and coloring matter, apples, pumpkins, molasses, etc.

SAGO.

Potato starch.

RUM.

Cayenne pepper, artificial essences, water.

---

* Injurious.

SUGARS.

Granulated sugar is not easily adulterated. Loaf, pulverized, and brown are found adulterated with grape sugar, flour, starch, terra alba,* clay,* sand,† bean dust, salts of tin,‡ lead ‡ and gypsum,* and rice flour.

Sugar is often injured by being purified with putrid blood.

SPICES.

Every character of spices is adulterated with a great variety of things. Among them are starch, flour, shells, ground beans and pease, turmeric, buckwheat flour and hulls, chromate of lead,‡ sulphate of lime* (plaster), yellow lake.‡

In this connection is given a paper from the American Journal of Pharmacy, June, 1890, read by Frank A. Hennessy, Ph. G., before the pharmaceutical meeting May 20.

A NEW SPICE ADULTERANT.

[Contribution from the chemical laboratory of the Philadelphia College of Pharmacy—No. 72. Read at the pharmaceutical meeting, May 20, by Frank A. Hennessy, Ph. G.]

Some time ago the attention of the writer was called to some samples of "artificial ground spices" which bore a close resemblance to the pure articles. It was learned that the production of these goods was the result of numerous experiments, and subsequent investigation succeeded in bringing to light a branch of manufacturing industry of no small magnitude, which has for its sole object the production of articles known to the trade as "spice mixtures." The manufacture of these articles is conducted in a large steam bakery in Philadelphia. Samples of the materials used have been secured from time to time, and these are presented with this paper.

The substance which forms the base for all these mixtures, and which is designated in the sample as "meal," was found on inquiry among several millers to be a very low grade of wheat.

It is not known to them by any special name, but might be called "blow-room stuff." It is a little better than feed, to which it is sometimes added to improve the quality, but is a lower grade than middlings. Samples from lots which had been delivered to the bakery at different times were identical.

The meal is made into a dough with water, rolled out and cut in the same manner as soda crackers, and baked in an oven.

These crackers or "biscuits," as they are termed, are then allowed to dry thoroughly when they are ready for grinding.

The different shades are obtained by the use of coloring matters which are mixed with the meal when it is being made into dough.

The "white" biscuit is made from the plain meal without coloring. The "yellow" is made with the aid of turmeric, a little of which goes a great way in imparting a rich yellow hue, such as is peculiar to mustard.

A sample of the coloring matter used in the "brown" biscuits is also presented. An analysis shows this to be a mixture of about equal parts of Spanish brown and turmeric.

Charcoal is used in the "black" biscuits.

Some biscuits having a red color, such as might have been used to adulterate cayenne pepper, were seen, but it was impossible to secure samples at the time.

---

* Injurious.   † Not often.   ‡ Poisonous.

Large quantities of these spice biscuits have been delivered to a spice house in Philadelphia, and it is not known that any have been shipped out of the city. As they are all sent to the spice dealers in the whole condition, probably on account of the lack of facilities for grinding, the samples of powders which are presented were ground by the writer in a small drug mill, and may only roughly resemble the powders prepared by the spice millers.

However, they will serve to show how closely the ground spices may be imitated. The sample labeled "pepper mixture" is made up of the "black," "white," and "brown" powders—the one labeled "clove mixture" of the "brown" and "black."

"Cracker dust" is said by many investigators to be used as a spice adulterant, and a sample of this material from the same bakery is presented, although it has never been used in the manufacture of these biscuits. It consists altogether of stale bread, which accumulates in large quantities, and which is thoroughly dried and ground.

An analysis of the spice biscuits gave the following results, the "black" and "white" powders and the original meal being taken:

	White.	Black.	Meal.
Moisture	7.52	8.27	....
Soluble ash (HCl)	3	4.98	2.95
Insoluble ash (HCl)	Trace	4.45	....
Total ash	3	9.43	2.95
Glucose	14.51	14.51	14.51
Cane sugar	6.03	3.02	11.02
Residue after treatment with cold H_2O and dried at 100° C	75.8	83.2	65.8
Charcoal and matter insoluble in boiling H_2O	....	54.1	....
Ash of same	....	15.57	....

The ash consisted of Na, K, Cu, Mg, chiefly as phosphates, with some sulphates, the insoluble portion of the "black" being fine sand.

It is evident that without the most careful examination the presence of these mixtures in ground spices might often escape notice.

The starch granules are usually so much altered in the process of baking as to render their identifications almost impossible.

As pure ground pepper, for instance, yields:

Moisture... 8–10
Ash 2–5
Starch 34–43
Total reducing sugar equivalent.......................... 42–55

It is obvious that in case of admixture with this material the determination of any or all of these constituents would be of no value, and it is probable that the only reliable results would be obtained from estimating the amount of piperin and resin, which is quite constant.

Some points of similarity to other spices might be mentioned to show how admirably these mixtures are adapted to their purpose; but the object of this paper is simply to call attention to what is believed to be the latest development of inventive genius in this direction.

SIRUPS.

Glucose, salts of tin,* dextrine.

TEA.

Exhausted leaves, once used dried, facing with Prussian blue,* plumbago gum; weighting* nitric acid, sand, soapstone, china clay, and gypsum.

---

* Poisonous.

Of eighteen samples examined in Connecticut, all were found to contain Prussian blue, which was identified under the microscope.

Tea is generally faced or painted with clayey matter, Prussian blue, plumbago; also a yellow dye, probably turmeric.

Extractive matter in genuine unadulterated tea should generally reach 30 per cent. The Connecticut authorities found in pure tea from 31 to 39 per cent.

VEAL.

Should not be eaten when under a month old. The practice of killing and selling younger calves is reprehensible; there is little nutriment in the meat, it is not easily digested, and should be condemned.

VINEGAR.

Oil vitriol,* hydrochloric, and pyroligneous acid, and rarely burnt sugar, water, wine and meal vinegars sold for cider.

Of 206 samples analyzed for acids by the Connecticut officials 82, or 39 per cent, fell below the legal requirement.

Of 163 analyzed by the same authorities for solids 74, or 46 per cent, fell below the standard.

WINES.

If all that is claimed about this article be true, but little pure wine can be found. Many wines are heavily fortified with alcohol, coloring matter is extensively used, inferior wines are mixed, acids are added, and it is asserted in many cases all kinds of refuse matter is used that will ferment. Analine colors, crude brandy, water.

CHEMICAL COMPOSITION OF WINE.

It contains a large proportion of water, a little undecomposed glucose, traces of soluble azotized matter or ferment, alcohol in variable proportions (from $7\frac{1}{2}$ to 24 per cent), peptine and mucilage, some tannin, free malic and tartaric acids; a coloring matter, yellow in white wine and red in dark wines, acetic and œnanthic acids, an aromatic principle or *bouquet*, and *œnanthic ether*, an essential oil of vinous odor; and finally, all the vegetable and mineral salts contained in the latest McKenne's translature of Duplais, alcoholic liquors, p. 99.

Champagnes contain an appreciable quantity of carbonic acid gas in addition to the above.

WHITE PEPPER.

Starches, flour. Of four samples analyzed in Connecticut, two were adulterated.

----

* Poisonous.

ADULTERANTS OF DRUGS.

Drugs are often tinctured with an excess of alcohol, so that the strength of the mixture becomes a matter of great uncertainty. Dr. Chancellor, secretary Maryland State board of health says:

As regards the purity of medicine, we all know that this varies; and this variance is, unfortunately, not always due to natural cause. Sometimes it is, but only too often do we find it to be the work of persons who have a sole regard for the "filthy lucre" with which they hope to fill their purses, and who are utterly indifferent to the evil consequences which their wicked deeds may bring upon suffering mankind. Yet there is no law in our State to correct this growing evil, no law to punish the wretch mean enough to rob from his unsuspecting, suffering fellowman what is often the last anchor of hope. There exists a rivalry in the commerce in medicine as there is in the commerce as in all other merchantable articles, and if one only seeks he can purchase them at almost any price. There is no class of articles so important to the people as medicine, and at the same time no class of articles of which the people are so poor a judge, and in which fraud can be so easily and so deeply hidden, and in which this fraud is so difficult of exposure.

On page 502 of the New York report, Prof. Willis G. Tucker, State analyst says:

The work done during the past four years has received the hearty commendation of both manufacturers and leading dealers throughout the State, and is believed to have had an important influence in improving the quality of the drugs dispensed and in inciting dealers to greater carefulness in their preparation and sale.

SALICYLIC ACID.

This article is extremely dangerous as an adulterant, being used so indiscriminately and so profusely. A man who drinks a glass of beer may not feel the effects of the drug, but as many people drink twenty to thirty glasses, it can readily be seen that an undue quantity of this preservative may be absorbed in the system, especially if vegetables are eaten that have it used to preserve them, to which may be added a moderate amount to preserve the meat eaten, and when we remember that it will keep preserves and pickles, and jellies, and keep fruits, one can readily see how easy it is to dose oneself upon this wonderful preservative of everything but the human system.

Prof. H. A. Weber, of the Ohio University, Columbus, in a report to State dairy and food commission, makes the following somewhat extended statement, but the subject-matter is of such importance that it is given in full:

In connection with this discovery of the use of salicylic acid in such a common and liberally-consumed article as sweet cider, it may be well to mention that in recent years recipes, claimed to be patented and guaranteed to be perfectly harmless, have been sold by the thousands to private families all over the country for preserving fruits, vegetables, etc. In one of these recipes the following quantities of salicylic acid are prescribed :`

For small fruits, as currants, strawberries, raspberries, etc., 18 grains salicylic acid to 1 quart of water.

For hard fruit, as peaches, pears, watermelons, etc., 35 grains salicylic acid to 1 quart of water.

For vegetables, as beans, pease, green corn, asparagus, etc., 52 grains of salicylic acid to 1 quart of water.

For pickles, 24 grains of salicylic acid to 1 quart of vinegar.

For sweet pickles, the same.

For preserves, jams, and apple butter, 14 grains dry salicylic acid to 1 gallon of fruit and 1 quart of sugar, after cooking to a thick preserve.

That salicylic acid is employed in enormous quantities as a food preservative may be inferred from the fact that a single druggist of this city sold during the past season 500 ounces of the drug, all of which, he thinks, was used for this purpose.

When a drug is used thus extensively, and in such a variety of articles of daily food, it is due the public to be informed of its nature and effects, and for this purpose the following is respectfully submitted :

Preparation.—Salicylic acid occurs in nature in the oil of wintergreen as an ether, methyl salicylate. From this substance it was formerly prepared. It is now made artificially from phenol (carbolic acid). When pure it forms white, needle-shaped crystals, without odor, and of a sweetish taste.

Properties.—Salicylic acid is a powerful antiseptic, *i. e.*, it retards the action of organized ferments like the yeast plant and putrefactive bacteria. Thus it hinders or prevents fermentation, the souring of milk and other liquids, the putrefaction of meat, etc. It is this property which has brought it into such a common use as a preservative of food. But the action of salicylic acid upon unorganized ferments is even more powerful. Thus it prevents the formation of prussic acid by amygdalin in emulsions of almond seeds. It completely arrests the conversion of starch into grape sugar by diastase and pancreatic extracts as first shown by H. Leffman and W. Beam (Analyst, volume 13, p. 103), and corroborated by experiments in the physiological laboratory of our own townsman, Dr. A. M. Bleile. The minute quantity of one part of the acid in one-thousand parts of the mixture is sufficient to produce this effect. As this action is diametrically opposed to the process of digestion, the use of salicylic acid in daily articles of food should be condemned for this reason alone.

Physiological effects.—The dose of salicylic acid as a medicine is from 10 to 40 grains. For children the dose is much smaller. Although the maximum dose would rarely, if ever, be reached in the consumption of food preserved with the drug, yet the minimum dose if continued for a long time might produce equal disorders, and this dose can readily be exceeded, especially if a variety of foods and drinks thus preserved are consumed at the same meal. This danger is increased by the fact that several days may intervene before the drug is completely eliminated from the system after it is taken, although it speedily enters into the circulation.

From the physiological actions of the drug as reported in the National Dispensatory, the following may be cited :

"Plants watered with a solution of salicylic acid speedily die. One grain of sodium salicylate introduced under the skin of a frog renders the animal languid and then occasions complete motor paralysis and arrest of the heart. Guinea pigs, after a dose of 60 to 70 grains, grow rapidly weak, lie down and drag their limbs, which move spasmodically; then respiration grows shallower until it ceases.

"Experiments on dogs: (1) moderate doses occasion nausea, salivation, vomiting, and diarrhea; (2) the senses of sight and hearing appear somewhat dull; (3) the respiration is quickened, the temperature increased, except in fever, when it is reduced; (4) the central nervous system is affected only by large doses, which abolish sensibility and vitality, and spasms precede death; (5) after death, the stomach, intestines, liver, and kidneys are congested; the brain and spinal cord also.appear congested.

"Effects on man: In full medicinal doses salicylic acid usually caused buzzing, humming, and rushing sounds in the ears, with more or less deafness. Headache is not unusual and may be attended with dullness and an uncertain gait. Blindness for ten hours is reported. When fever exists delirium is readily induced by the medicine, especially in nervous patients, and it is apt to be accompanied with phantasms and violence, as in delirium tremens. Difficulty of breathing and palpitation of the heart are ordinary effects of the medicine. Hence it should be a rule never to prescribe the medicine in case of heart or lung troubles. In cases of disease, enormous doses have been given without any apparent serious effects. On the other hand, cases of death are reported by doses not exceeding 150 grains per day, and one case after four doses of only 15 grains had been taken."

Fortunately the toxical effects of the drug are counteracted by the nutrients of the food taken. Otherwise the results of its general and indiscriminate use would be baneful indeed. But this statement does not justify its employment as a food preservative. The property of the drug pointed out above is not changed by the presence of nutrients, and its physiological actions are of such a nature that it should be administered only under the direction and care of a competent physician, and not be taken indiscriminately by everyone in all conditions of health and disease.

Salicylic acid can, therefore, find no legitimate place in our daily food. Its use by private families should be discontinued, and its occurrence in commercial food products should be condemned by all who are interested in public welfare.

PENNSYLVANIA AND NEW YORK REPORTS.

The reports herein contained, taken from the Pennsylvania and New York reports, are very extended and probably confined to too circumscribed a territory, but as undoubtedly more attention is given to the adulteration of drugs in these two States than any other, the reports quoted are not only the most reliable that can be obtained, but they certainly are the fairest to the manufacturer, and dealers, as they having had the fullest knowledge of the law on the subject and the intention of the authorities to inspect them, if they continued to sell adulterated goods it was done with a full knowledge of the consequences.

MISCELLANEOUS REPORTS.

REPORT OF COMMITTEE ON ADULTERATIONS AND DETERIORATIONS OF PENNSYLVANIA PHARMACEUTICAL ASSOCIATION, 1889.

[Extracts Pennsylvania Pharmaceutical Association.]

The work carried on by the committee this year has been greatly advanced by a few members furnishing samples. The number, however, that responded to the appeal for samples was a very small proportion of the total membership—they can easily be counted—as follows: Messrs. J. H. Stein, B. A. Kelly, L. Emanuel, C. A. Randolph, J. F. Patton, G. W. Kennedy, W. H. McGarrah, S. S. Jones, and M. N. Kline.

A number of students in the chemical laboratory of the Philadelphia College of Pharmacy also contributed their time and made a number of analyses. Mr. William

Handler examined six samples of simple sirup purchased of retail druggists in Philadelphia, with the following results:

Sample.	Cane sugar.	Glucose.	Remarks.
	Per cent.	Per cent.	
A....................	60.00	1.28	
B....................	65.30	0.38	Contained traces of ultramarine.
C....................	66.30	0.38	
D....................	40.00	5.87	Had fermented.
E....................	64.13	1.98	Yellow in color. Called white rock candy sirup.
F....................	68.16	0.39	

Mr. Charles A. Schwacke assayed eight samples of household ammonia. All were in 1-pint bottles except sample 5, which measured 12 ounces The results were as here tabulated:

Sample.	Ammonia, NH_3	Price.	Source.	Remarks.
	Per cent.	Cents.		
1..............	3.72	20	Retail drug store	
2..............	4.52	20	Retail grocery store	Contained borax.
3..............	5.25	9	Dry goods store	
4..............	5.35	15	......do	Do.
5..............	6.75	8	......do	
6..............	7.49	25	Retail drug store	
7..............	8.58	15	Dry goods store	
8..............	10.00	15	Wholesale drug store............	

It will be seen from this that price does not always indicate quality.

Mr. Harry S. Wood determined the strength of commercial glacial acetic acid and found two qualities in the market under that name, one containing about 80 per cent and the other 99 to 100 per cent of the absolute acid. In this case the price is a consideration, the absolute acid can always be gotten, generally with the exact percentage strength on the label, if the pharmacist is willing to pay the price. The absolute acid is easily recognized by its power to dissolve an equal volume of fresh oil of lemon.

Mr. Charles E. McCloskey found powdered belladonna root from different wholesale druggists of Philadelphia to yield from 0.2 to 0.4 per cent, and the leaves 0.04 to 0.24 per cent of alkaloid.

Mr. A. G. Hostetter, noticing the statement frequently made that potassium tartrate is often impure or adulterated, found all the samples from the manufacturers in this State to be very good, containing only traces of calcium salts, sulphuric, hydrochloric, and carbonic acids.

Mr. G. M. Grosse found reduced iron to be of poor quality, one sample only answering to the requirements of the Pharmacopœia. They ranged from 18.43 to 83.40 per cent, the highest being of German and the lowest of French manufacture. Those of American make, being obtained from the stock bottles of retail pharmacists, had no doubt deteriorated by long exposure to the oxidizing action of the air.

Mr. O. Y. Owings determined the sodium carbonate and bicarbonate of commerce to be of very good quality, there being little or no difference between the English and American brands. Mr. H. J. M. Schroeter (Am. Journal of Pharmacy, December, 1888), has also shown that the commercial bicarbonate responds to the requirements of the Pharmacopœia for a pure salt.

Mr. Joseph Lowenberg examined five samples of morphine sulphate. All were found to be pure, but an English sample contained only 6.94 per cent of water of crystallization, instead of 11.87 per cent, as allowed by the Pharmacopœia. A sample of morphine acetate was not easily dissolved in water, and yielded 1.81 per cent of residue on igniting.

Mr. S. A. Wagaman assayed five samples of one-fourth grain granules of morphine sulphate. Finding that a small quantity of morphine was lost in the assay, he used as a check a calculation based on the amount of sulphuric acid found to be present. In this way he obtained higher results than by the morphine assay, but still below what should have been in the samples. A single granule should contain one-fourth or twenty-five one hundredths of a grain; he found 20, 22, 18, 21, and 17 one hundredths of a grain, respectively, in the five samples. One hundred granules should contain 25 grains of morphine sulphate, but one sample only weighed 32 grains with the coating, two others weighed 36 grains each, thus showing that quality was probably sacrificed for elegance. These assays, which were repeated as well as compared with one made on a weighed quantity of the salt mixed with gum and sugar, indicate that pharmacists should exercise great caution in buying morphine granules. Competition in them is very sharp, and wherever the price is kept so near the cost it is well to look out for deterioration.

Mr. Clarence S. Eldridge investigated the quality of twenty-five samples of lime water, purchased of retail pharmacists in Philadelphia and its vicinity. The results indicate gross carelessness in the manner of making and keeping this important preparation. Eight of the samples contained 0.15 per cent of calcium hydrate, and were, therefore, equal to the Pharmacopœia requirements; eight more were nearly up to the standard, and the remaining nine rapidly descended on the scale of strength to two, which failed to show any alkaline reaction by litmus paper.

Notices have appeared in different journals during the past year of adulterated copaiba. Through Mr. Kline, who has given the subject considerable attention, four samples were obtained, together with valuable information concerning them. One of the samples responded to all known tests of purity; two by the United States Pharmacopœia test showed gurjin balsam, one of these also contained turpentine; the fourth sample was of a character that indicated adulteration, without one being able to determine exactly the nature of the admixture. The subject of adulterated copaiba is one that is sadly in need of further investigation, with the special object of giving simple and more reliable tests for the genuine article.

A sample of yellow wax was found to contain 50 per cent of paraffin, thus showing that this old trick has not been forgotten.

A bottle of essence of peppermint, put up in Lancaster for country trade, was found deficient in oil and alcohol, the deficiency being made up with water.

Epsom salts, from Pittsburg, was shown to be pure, but much effloresced.

Quinine is now selling at such a low price that during the last few years we have heard nothing of its adulteration; but great care should still be exercised in purchasing. One suspicious sample has been received. It was found to contain the cheaper alkaloids in greater amount than permitted by our national standard.

Most of the sugar of milk received in Philadelphia is of German brand, and all appears to be from the same source. In physical properties it does not compare favorably with the powdered crystals, as the taste is quite earthy, but chemical tests failed to reveal any adulteration. The ash, however, was in excess of that required by the advocates of homœopathy, who think it should not exceed 0.02 per cent. The crystals, as received in this country, yield about 0.06 per cent of residue on ignition.

The adulteration of certain kinds of cream of tartar has nearly come to the point of being a recognized business. No one acquainted with the first principles of preparing goods for the grocery trade will question this. A sample from Altoona, labeled "Pure Cream of Tartar," consisted largely of calcium phosphate. It scarcely charred when heated, thus indicating the absence of any organic substance like tartaric acid; it, however, did show a faint acid reaction, due no doubt to the presence of small quantities of acid phosphate. Two samples from Pittsburg did not char on heating, were faintly acid to litmus, and consisted of calcium sulphate and phosphate.

One of the most glaring examples of willful substitution was given me by the clerk in a retail pharmacy in Philadelphia, where I was purchasing laudanum for the purpose of assay. The sample in question was called blue ointment, but I was informed that it consisted of lard colored with Prussian blue. A subsequent examination of it failed to detect the presence of a trace of mercury, and to fully confirm the information received in regard to it, Mr. Walter B. Crawford assayed seven samples of laudanum with the following results:

No.	Morphine.	Bought from —
	Per cent.	
1	1.23	Retail drug store in Chambersburg.
2	1.30	Retail drug store in Fayetteville.
3	0.42	Grocery store, bottled in Baltimore.
4	0.61	Grocery store, bottled in New York.
5	0.18	Grocery store, bottled in Baltimore.
6	0.70	Grocery store, bottled in Harrisburg.
7	0.52	Grocery store, bottled in Baltimore.

Mr. A. H. Benerman assayed fourteen samples of the same preparation. No. 1 to 3, inclusive, were obtained of retail pharmacists in Philadelphia. No 4 to 8, inclusive, from manufacturers and bottlers. No 9 to 14, from patent medicine dealers and others who sold the bottled article. He also estimated the percentage of alcohol by volume.

No.	Morphine.	Alcohol.	No.	Morphine.	Alcohol.
	Per cent.	Per cent.		Per cent.	Per cent.
1	1.18	60.97	8	0.57	45.71
2	1.15	53.91	9	0.41	28.68
3	0.92	49.71	10	0.77	47.02
4	0.36	17.08	11	0.00	21.59
5	0.17	60.47	12	1.00	57.88
6	0.36	44.55	13	0.84	47.78
7	0.51	53.81	14	0.17	11.52

In addition to the above, your chairman received fifty-six samples from different parts of the State, which were assayed as tabulated.

Officinal laudanum should contain from 1.2 to 1.6 per cent morphine.

No.	Morphine.	Whence procured.
	Per cent.	
1	0.97	Retail drug store in Philadelphia.
2	0.82	Do.
3	0.88	Retail drug store in Delaware County.
4	0.03	Retail drug store in Chester.
5	1.22	Retail drug store in Philadelphia.
6	1.10	Do.
7	0.86	Sent from Pittsburg, origin unknown.
8	0.38	Do.
9	0.21	Sent from Scranton, origin unknown.
10	0.65	Do.
11	0.93	Do.
12	0.00	Sent from Pottsville, strong odor of licorice.
13	0.69	Sent from Carbondale.
14	0.07	Sent from Carbondale. Strong odor of licorice.
15	0.63	Retail drug store in Dillsburg.
16	0.51	Retail drug store in Delta.
17	0.02	Country store, bottled in Chester.
18	0.37	Country store, bought in bulk.
19	0.56	Retail drug store in Wilkesbarre.
20	0.26	Country store near Wilkesbarre, bottled in New York.
21	0.97	Bottled in New York.
22	0.72	Retail drug store in Wilkesbarre.
23	0.52	Do.
24	0.52	Do.
25	0.46	Retail drug store in Scranton.

No.	Mor-phine.	Whence procured.
	Per cent.	
26	0.00	Country store near Wilkesbarre.
27	0.57	Retail drug store in Wilkesbarre.
28	0.00	Grocery store in Wilkesbarre, bottled in Philadelphia.
29	0.84	Retail drug store in Wilkesbarre.
30	0.00	Wholesale grocery store in Wilkesbarre.
31	1.00	Retail drug store in Wilkesbarre.
32	0.00	Retail drug store in Philadelphia.
33	0.62	Country store in Delaware county, bottled in Philadelphia.
34	0.45	Drug store in Reading, bottled for country trade.
35	0.58	Wholesale drug store in Philadelphia, bottled for country trade.
36	0.26	Do.
37	0.65	Do.
38	0.40	Do.
39	0.49	Wholesale drug store in Reedsville, bottled for country trade.
40	0.61	Wholesale drug store in Pittsburg.
41	0.96	Do.
42	0.38	From Pittsburg, bottled and labeled " Pure Laudanum."
43	0.27	Bottled in New York.
44	0.16	Bottled in Philadelphia.
45	0.29	Bottled in Lancaster.
46	0.61	Retail drug store in Denver, Pa.
47	0.52	Retail drug store in Liverpool.
48	0.66	Retail drug store in Millersburg.
49	0.50	Do.
50	0.87	Retail drug store in Lititz.
51	0.36	Retail drug store in Myerstown.
52	0.50	Retail drug store in Womelsdorf.
53	0.33	Bottled in Philadelphia, for country trade.
54	0.51	Do.
55	0.31	Do.
56	1.40	Wholesale drug store in Philadelphia.

The results may be briefly summed up as follows: There were in all seventy-seven samples assayed. Four were of full officinal strength, nine more were near enough to come within the limits of reasonable error, and five failed to yield a weighable amount of morphine. One of these five, No. 32, was according to information received, made from the following formula :

Opium, 1 ounce.

Alcohol, 1¼ pints.

Caramel to color.

Tr. gentian to give bitter taste.

Water, a sufficient quantity to make 1 gallon.

It will probably be granted that an assay would fail to indicate a weighable quantity of morphine, as the opium was no doubt poor in quality to begin with. It may further be stated that this sample originated in the same store as the artificial blue ointment and that the proprietor is a graduate in pharmacy as well as a graduate of a medical college in good standing.

Is the association now ready to take any further action than that of listening to, adopting, and printing these reports ? For the healthy growth of every association, society, or individual, it is necessary to have some great object in view, some important principle at stake. Is it too much, then, to suggest that this is the opportunity of the Pennsylvania Pharmaceutical Association ? Let it be our object to rid the profession of this curse. It has been suggested that homeopathy owes its success to our failure to have drugs fully up to the standard ; so many disappointments occur from the use of impure drugs that people naturally drift into experiments. Great as are the theoretical errors of homeopathy, one branch of it is conducted, as a rule, with the most scrupulous care, and that is the pharmaceutical branch.

We must all admit that it is of importance not only to the public, but also to the pharmaceutical profession, to have every remedy kept up to the very highest standard. When a pharmacist sells an inferior preparation, he not only injures the buyer, but the physician and his brother pharmacist as well. It was pointed out a year ago that it was impossible to buy reliable male fern in the market, and that condition has not changed. What would be the verdict of both physician and patient when the drug as it now offered was tried? Take the case of the lime water mentioned in this report, that had not strength enough to turn litmus paper, and consider if the sale of such a preparation does not injure both the pharmaceutical and medical professions.

It is admitted that we should have obtained samples that would have responded to the requirements of our standard, but does the public know where to go in order to do this? Can the physician be sure that his patient will not stray into one of those places that dispense colored lard for blue ointment?

There is a class to which the attention of the association is especially directed, namely, those who manufacture and bottle for the country trade. The country tradesman is utterly ignorant of everything about the remedies he sells, except the money value.

Certainly it is not with him that we must first deal, but with the one who supplies him with inferior or worthless goods. One of these manufacturers recently purchased laudanum of full strength and then complained because he could not mix an indefinite amount of water with it and still have a clear mixture for bottling.

The same enterprising individual revealed the method of manufacturing an "extract of ginger" with diluted alcohol and at the same time retaining the property of becoming cloudy on addition of water by the judicious use of guaiac. Any deficiency in pungent property was made good with capsicum.

It is hoped, by the relation of these few facts, that the association will realize it is not the ignorant country merchant who is responsible, but the more educated manufacturer, who can only be met by superior education and the strong arm of law and justice.

HENRY TRIMBLE, *Chairman.*

C. D. LIPPINCOTT.

P. W. LASCHEID.

REPORT OF COMMITTEE ON ADULTERATIONS AND DETERIORATIONS, OF PENNSYLVANIA PHARMACEUTICAL ASSOCIATION, 1890.

[Extract from Pennsylvania Pharmaceutical Association—reprint.]

One of the most important disclosures during the year has been that of Frank A. Hennessy (American Journal of Pharmacy, 1890, p. 276), who has described the systematic production, on a large scale, of crackers which are specially designed for the adulteration of ground spices.

The commercial name of these crackers is "spice biscuit." They are made by taking a low grade of "meal" from wheat, together with bakery sweepings, moistening with water, and baking the resulting dough, after it has been rolled and cut into proper sizes, until a very hard brown biscuit results. By the addition of coloring matter, three or four different varieties are made, turmeric, Spanish brown, and charcoal, and mixtures of these are used to give the different colors, which vary from a light brown to black. After the thorough baking, the biscuits are ground into powders of various degrees of fineness, and then by a proper mixing the different ground spices are imitated and flavored by the addition of volatile oil or a small quantity of the genuine spice. This industry is carried on by a large steam bakery company in Philadelphia, and they have delivered large quantities of these biscuits to a spice house in the same city. These facts have been communicated by a person having access to the building, who, in addition to what he saw, received much information from the workmen.

While the use of "cracker dust" has frequently been noticed as an adulterant of spices, this particular form appears to be new. The high temperature to which the biscuits are submitted and the careful adjustment of the amount of ash are such as to render their chemical detection a matter of considerable difficulty,

Several investigations, as well as the preceding, have been carried out by students in the chemical laboratory of the Philadelphia College of Pharmacy, under the direction of your chairman. Of these William D. Barnard examined commercial ground cloves. Of ten samples three were adulterated to the extent of 50 per cent (as shown by the deficiency in volatile oil), two were pure, and the remaining five were inferior. Frank A. Hennessy found in a standard sample of lupulin 6.05 per cent of ash and 66.64 per cent of ether extract. One other sample was similar to this, while eight others contained ash varying from 16.02 to 32.68 per cent, with a corresponding diminution of the oleoresin. The ash was made up largely of sand, which in one sample amounted to 26.49 per cent of the drug.

Abraham L. Besore determined eight samples of lycopodium to be free from adulteration, although the amount of ash was found to be from 1.4 to 2.2 per cent, instead of 4 per cent as usually given in the books. This low ash has also been found by A. Langer (Archiv der Pharm., March and April, 1889, and Proc. American Pharm. Asso., 1889, p. 430).

David J. Reese had difficulty in procuring genuine saffron in the market; one contained as much as 49.3 per cent of ash and several others were an artificially colored material which bore no resemblance to the true article.

George D. Feidt found, on examining nine samples of powdered rhubarb, that two of them showed the presence of excessive amounts of ash; the others were of good quality.

Jerome P. Churchill analyzed eight samples of potassium nitrate and found two of them to be pure. The others contained from 26 to 46 per cent of sodium nitrate and small quantities of potassium chloride, which in no case exceeded 3 per cent. These results throw some light on the fact that this salt is sold at very variable prices.

Franklin I. Adams purchased twelve samples of lead water from as many retail druggists of Philadelphia and found the preparation to differ in physical properties as well as in actual strength. Six of them were deficient, one to the extent of 66 per cent, while the other six were too strong, three of them indicating that Goulard's extract had been dispensed, although "lead water" was on the labels. Gross carelessness is certainly the rule with this preparation, a condition sometimes noticed with other cheap preparations, and such a practice can not be too strongly condemned.

Two members of the association have contributed samples during the year. Mr. Joseph L. Lemberger sent a sample of saffron which contained dried fiber and a large percentage of inorganic matter.

Mr. William L. Turner sent the result of picking 100 grains of anise, which amounted to 20 grains of small fragments of stones, evidently especially prepared for the purpose. The anise was free from dust and other adulterations.

Such an instance shows the importance of examining the whole as well as the powdered drugs.

Your committee take this opportunity to call the attention of the association to the national adulteration bill recently pending before Congress at Washington. We think we express the sentiment of this association when we say that any law which would properly regulate the adulteration of drugs and medicines would be welcome. This bill was calculated to work a great injustice on the whole drug trade, and if passed would undoubtedly have failed to accomplish the purpose for which it was created.

HENRY TRIMBLE,
A. GLAMSER,
W. M. L. WELLS,
Committee.

Examinations by Dr. Tucker, of the New York State Board, in 1890, show the following results:

Alcohol, 16, of which 14 were good, 1 was fair, and 1 compound spirits of ether of inferior quality—the dealer having attached a wrong label to the bottle.

Benzoic acid, 6 samples examined; all good.

Subnitrate of bismuth, 5 samples; all good.

Oxalate of cerium, 4 examinations; 1 good, 2 fair, and 1 inferior, containing traces of metallic impurities.

Chloral, 10 examinations; 6 good, 3 fair, and 1 inferior, containing traces of hydrochloric acid and other impurities.

Chloroform, 21 examinations. The United States Pharmacopœia requires specific gravity 1.485–1.490, 15° C. (59° F). Of the samples examined, 15 were good, 5 fair, and 1 inferior. The grade of this article is reported as greatly improved.

Stronger ether (United States Pharmacopœia specific gravity, 0.725, at 15° C. and about 6 per cent of alcohol), 68 samples examined; 40 good, 4 fair, 22 inferior; 1 consisted of compound spirits of ether, and 1 of sweet spirits of niter, "most carelessly sold for the article called for."

Diluted hydrobromic acid (United States Pharmacopœia, 10 per cent absolute acid), 38 samples examined; good quality, 25; fair, 1; inferior, 6, and of excessive strength, 6.

Diluted hydrochloric acid (United States Pharmacopœia, 10 per cent absolute acid), 10 samples examined; 4 good, 4 fair, and 2 inferior, running 4.40 and 6.60.

Ipecac, 5 examined; 4 good and 1 fair.

Diluted nitric acid (United States Pharmacopœia, 10 per cent of absolute acid), 4 tests; 1 good, 3 of excessive strength, running from 13.40 to 16.70.

Tartrate of pottassium and sodium, 3 tests made; all good.

Iodide of potassium, 8 examinations made: 3 good and the remainder fair.

Santonin, few samples; all good.

Seidlitz powders, 7 examinations; 4 of good weight and quality, 2 rated fair, one being 17 and the other 20 per cent short in weight of blue paper, and 1 inferior, the blue paper weighing 26 per cent short.

Diluted sulphuric acid (United States Pharmacopœia, 10 per cent of officinal sulphuric acid, and have a specific gravity of about 1.067), 53 samples examined; 38 good, 5 fair, 1 inferior (7 per cent); 9 possessed excessive strength, running from 14.10 to 24.80 per cent.

PROFESSOR CALDWELL'S REPORT.

Prof. G. C. Caldwell, public analyst, New York, in report of 1890, states he made 275 examinations of alkaloidal preparations, 7 of canned vegetables, and 5 of kerosene. Samples bought on open market.

The American canned peas and beans were all found to be free from poisonous metals.

He summarizes the alkaloidal preparations as follows:

Good 177
Passable... 13
Considerably deficient.. 85

The last class contained about 30 per cent of the whole as against 34 per cent the previous year.

Sulphate of quinine, 15 samples; 7 contained large excess of foreign alkaloids, as indicated by Kerner's tests, 2 contained some, and 6 none.

Capsules of quinine sulphate: 41 analyses were made of these. Not one contained what was claimed for them, some being slightly higher than was claimed, but the majority falling below. Two samples were noticeably deficient. One claimed 500 grains and contained 50.8. The other claimed 200 and contained 51. Both contained " very much " excess of foreign alkaloids, and both came from Syracuse.

Quinine pills : 99 samples reported as examined. As in the case of the capsules, none were what was claimed for them.

Citrate of iron and quinine, 14 samples, 5 of which contained " much " foreign alkaloids, and 1 "some." The percentage of quinine found varied from 7.39 to 11.52.

Sulphate of morphia pills, 35 analyses; over 50 per cent were found to fall from, 10 to 33 per cent below the claim.

Hypodermic tablets of morphine sulphate, 12 samples examined, which varied in actual and claimed weights from 10 per cent to 30 per cent.

Tincture of opium (United States Pharmacopœia) should contain 1.2 grams morphia in 100 grams of tincture.

Fifteen samples examined, which ran from 0.6 to 0.89 per cent only.

Compound spirit of ether.—Forty-nine samples examined, of which 4 were of good quality, while there were of fair quality 4, and inferior 39. One sample consisted of alcohol and another of a mixture of alcohol and chloroform. Concerning this article I quote from my last annual report :

"Compound spirit of ether, or ' Hoffman's anodyne,' is frequently prescribed by physicians and often employed as a household remedy, and while an article of good quality can be procured from responsible manufacturers or prepared without difficulty by the intelligent and careful pharmacist, the fact is that a spurious article answering to none of the requirements of the Pharmacopœia is generally sold in its stead, because it is cheaper. Hoffman's anodyne is openly quoted at 50 cents a pound in a recent price list published in a leading pharmaceutical journal, which is about one quarter the price of the real article. This cheap, spurious, and worthless article, obtained as a secondary product in the manufacture of ether, consists chiefly of alcohol, ether, and water, with little or none of the ethereal oil upon which the virtue of the preparation largely depends. Dealers may urge that the sale of this spurious article as a household remedy to people who would complain of the price necessarily charged for a genuine article is excusable ; but without admitting this as a valid excuse for dispensing a fraudulent and worthless drug, it is evident that its sale in response to a physician's prescription or written order giving full title and specifying ' U. S. P.' is entirely inexcusable and unwarranted, and equally blameworthy, whether due to ignorance or cupidity. The habit of keeping two qualities of officinal drugs can not be too strongly condemned, but the results of the above explanation would seem to show that many dealers, so far as this preparation is concerned, keep only one, and that a spurious article. When officinal preparations are called for they should be furnished by the dealers or no sale made."

The specific gravity of this preparation is not stated in the Pharmacopœia, but it should be about 0.796. As made by the process laid down in the Pharmacopœia of 1870, in which ether, and not stronger ether, was employed and more of the ethereal oil was used, it had a specific gravity of 0.815 ; but the specific gravity alone is no criterion of quality.

DILUTED ACETIC ACID.—Forty samples examined, of which there were of good quality 9, fair 6, inferior 19, and of excessive strength, 6. The Pharmacopœia requires 6 per cent of absolute acetic acid. These samples varied from 1.90 to 32.80 per cent, and, rejecting the 6 samples of excessive strength, averaged 4.6 per cent. Some of these samples have been prepared without any regard to accuracy, and in some cases the practically undiluted acid has been sold. It is not to be expected that such preparations will be made with scientific precision, but gross carelessness in their manufacture is inexcusable. Diluted acetic acid is employed in the preparation of "spirit of mindererus," and if it is below or above the proper strength this solution will be either too weak or too strong, neither of which conditions is desirable.

SAFFRON.—Twenty-one samples examined, of which 2 were of good quality, 1 was of fair quality, and of the remaining number 17 consisted of "safflower" (*Carthamus tinctorius*) and one of "crocus martis," or red oxide of iron. Concerning the substitution of safflower for saffron, I quote from my last annual report: The saffron of the Pharmacopœia consists of the stigma of *Crocus sativus* and is often known in the trade as Spanish saffron or true saffron. No other kind of saffron is recognized in the Pharmacopœia, and when it is called for by its officinal name no other article should be substituted for it. Safflower is very cheap, and is often called for, verbally, as a domestic remedy, under the name of saffron, but when the demand is for the pharmacopœial drug it should not be dispensed. At all events, if offered in its stead, the substitution should be explained; but no such explanation was made in any of the above cases.

PRECIPITATED SULPHUR.—Thirty-one samples examined, of which but 6 were of good quality, 2 were of fair quality, 17 were of inferior qualitity, one of those being strongly acid and the others containing large quantities of sulphate of lime, while 6 consisted of washed sulphate ignorantly or carelessly sold for precipitated sulphur. Concerning this article I quote from my last annual report:

"The sale of common *lac sulphur* for the officinal precipitated sulphur is entirely inexcusable. It is loaded with sulphate of lime, and since precipitated sulphur of good quality is easily obtainable in the market at a slightly higher price, this substitution ought never to be made; but the above results show that the proper article was sold in less than half the cases. Pharmacists ought to be familiar with the various grades of the medicinal articles in which they deal, and a good result will be accomplished if, by calling attention to errors of this kind, an improvement in this respect can be brought about. The tests by which genuine precipitated sulphur can be distinguished from the impure commercial article are laid down in the Pharmacopœia, and are easily applied by the retailer. In this case, however, he hardly needs even to make a test, for the price he pays and name under which he buys sufficiently indicate the quality of the article supplied him."

QUININE.—Fifteen different pill masses were made from different samples of quinine sulphate that gave no reaction with Kerner's test; the residue of quinia obtained by precipitation with sodium hydrate from the solution of each of these pill masses, and extraction with ether, was dissolved in dilute sulphuric acid, the solution was nearly neutralized with ammonia, and allowed to crystallize. The sulphate thus obtained was collected on a filter, dried, and subjected to Kerner's test, precisely as described in my report for 1886 (Seventh Annual Report, New York State Board of Health, p. 438). In no case was any reaction obtained.

Ten samples of citrate of iron and quinine, prepared also from sulphate of quinine that gave originally no reaction with Kerner's test, were treated in a similar manner and with like results. It may be considered as satisfactorily established by the results of these 25 tests that if in the manufacture of pills of sulphate of quinine, or of citrate of iron and quinine, a quinia salt is used that will give no reaction for excess of foreign alkaloids with Kerner's test, the recrystallized sulphate prepared in the manner described above from the quinia weighed in my assays will not give the reaction; and that if it does give the reaction, the inference is a fair one that the salt used in the preparation of the sample would itself have shown evidence of excess of foreign alkaloids.

A large number of samples of capsules of sulphate of quinine have been examined in the course of the past year. Some of the results show what might be expected from the manner in which the capsules are sometimes filled, that the quantity of the salt contained in different capsules put up in the same pharmacy, in some cases varies so widely that the variation may be a matter of considerable importance, to say nothing of the oftentime serious deficiency or great excess in amount. Three different assays of one 2-grain sample gave 172, 192, and 202 grains of sulphate per hundred capsules; of another, a 3-grain sample, 269, 363, and 352 grains per hundred capsules; of another, 5-grain, 497, 465, and 423 grains per hundred capsules; of another, 5-grain, 348, 392, and 368 grains, instead of 500 claimed; of another, 5-grain, 61, 49, and 43 grains, instead of 500, and so on. That the fault was in the capsules and not in the analysis was shown by the fact that if a large number of them were dissolved up together and carefully weighed portions of this solution were analyzed, closely agreeing results were obtained.

Concerning citrate of iron and quinine, some druggists make it according to the Pharmacopœia of 1870, requiring that it shall contain but 10 per cent of quinia. A similar course appears to be followed in some cases in regard to tincture of opium, which the later Pharmacopœia requires to be of a higher strength than the older one demands. Further, some druggists use the gum opium, or sometimes what they call puddled opium, in making the tincture instead of the powdered opium, as required by the Pharmacopœia of 1880. To avoid any ambiguity in the requirement in section 3, article 1, of the act to prevent the adulteration of food or drugs, chapter 407, Laws of 1881, which might be used as a cover for incorrect practice, I would suggest that for the word "therein" the words "in the latest authorized edition thereof" be substituted.

The importance of continuing to devote a large part of the work to quinine preparations is, I think, justified by the statement made to my collector that some druggists sell as many as 200,000 2-grain pills annually, and that 50,000 is the estimate made of the average number sold by a druggist doing an ordinary business.

POISONS IN MANUFACTURED ARTICLES.

While doubtless outside of the legitimate province of this report, notice is taken of the following cases to show the extent to which the practice of imitation and deterioration is carried for the purpose of making money.

The dyes in stockings is a common process of poisoning. The lead used in hat bands has been found to create headache and in one case caused serious illness. Wall papers are often the source of poisoning cases, and the dyes in stockings have been known in several instances to cause death. The most recent case of this character brought to my attention was the death in Philadelphia during the past year of a lady from "blood poisoning," caused by wearing a pair of Lisle gloves, the coloring matter from which got into the blood from a needle prick on her finger. Grange No. 38, Massachusetts, directed attention to this matter on June 29, 1878, and Worthy Master Ware, of the State Grange, issued a cautionary circular on the subject. This circular can be found on page 43 of the Maryland Health Report for 1888. It is an interesting article.

STATE AND OTHER LAWS RELATING TO FOODS AND BEVERAGES.

ILLINOIS LAWS.

AN ACT to prevent and punish the adulteration of articles of food, drink, and medicine, and the sale thereof when adulterated.

Be it enacted by the people of the State of Illinois represented in the general assembly, That no person shall mix, color, stain, or powder, or order or permit any other person in his or her employ to mix, color, stain, or powder any article of food with any ingredient or material so as to render the article injurious to health or depreciate the value thereof, with intent that the same may be sold; and no person shall sell or offer for sale any such article so mixed, colored, stained, or powdered.

Sec. 2. No person shall, except for the purpose of compounding in the necessary preparation of medicine, mix, color, stain, or powder, or order or permit any other person to mix, color, stain, or powder any drug or medicine with any ingredient or material so as to affect injuriously the quality or potency of such drug or medicine, with intent to sell the same, or shall sell or offer for sale any such drug or medicine so mixed, colored, stained, or powdered.

Sec. 3. No person shall mix, color, stain, or powder any article of food, drink, or medicine, or any article which enters into the composition of food, drink, or medicine, with any other ingredient or material, whether injurious to health or not, for the purpose of gain or profit, or sell or offer the same for sale, or order or permit any other person to sell or offer for sale, any article so mixed, colored, stained, or powdered, unless the same be so manufactured, used, or sold, or offered for sale, under its true and appropriate name, and notice that the same is mixed or impure is marked, printed, or stamped upon each package, roll, parcel, or vessel containing the same, so as to be and remain at all times readily visible, or unless the person purchasing the same is fully informed by the seller of the true name and ingredients (if other than such as are known by the common name thereof) of such article of food, drink, or medicine, at the time of making sale thereof, or offering to sell the same.

Sec. 4. No person shall mix oleomargarine, suine, butterine, beef fat, lard, or any other foreign substance with any butter or cheese intended for human food without distinctly marking, stamping, or labeling the article, or the package containing the same, with the true and appropriate name of such article, and the percentage in which such oleomargarine or suine enters into its composition; nor shall any person sell, or offer for sale, or order or permit to be sold or offered for sale, any such article of food into the composition of which oleomargarine or suine has entered, without at the same time informing the buyer of the fact and the proportions in which such oleomargarine, suine, or butterine, beef fat, lard, or any other foreign substance has entered into its composition: *Provided,* That nothing in this act shall be so construed as to prevent the use of harmless coloring matter in butter and cheese or other articles of food.

Sec. 5. Any person convicted of violating any provision of any of the foregoing sections of this act shall, for the first offense, be fined not less than twenty-five dollars ($25) nor more than two hundred dollars ($200); for the second offense he shall be fined not less than one hundred dollars ($100) nor more than two hundred dollars ($200), or confined in the county jail not less than one month nor more than six months, or both, at the discretion of the court, and for the third and all subsequent offenses he shall be fined not less than five hundred dollars ($500) nor more than two thousand dollars ($2,000), and imprisoned in the penitentiary not less than one year and not more than five years.

SEC. 6. No person shall be convicted under any of the foregoing sections of this act if he shows to the satisfaction of the court or jury that he did not know that he was violating any of the provisions of this act, and that he could not with reasonable diligence have obtained the knowledge.

SEC. 7. The State's attorneys of this State are charged with the enforcement of this act, and it is hereby made their duty to appear for the people and to attend to the prosecution of all complaints under this act in their respective counties in all courts.

SEC. 8. All acts and parts of acts inconsistent with the provisions of this act are hereby repealed.

Approved June 1, 1881.

PENALTY FOR ADULTERATION OF BUTTER AND CHEESE.

AN ACT to prevent the adulteration of butter and cheese, or the sale or disposal of the same, or the manufacture or sale of any article as a substitute for butter or cheese, or any article to be used as butter and cheese.

Be it enacted by the people of the State of Illinois represented in the general assembly, That whoever manufactures out of any oleaginous substances, or any compound of the same other than that produced from unadulterated milk, or cream from the same, any article assigned to take the place of butter or cheese produced from pure, unadulterated milk, or cream of the same, and shall sell, or offer for sale, the same as butter or cheese, or give to any person the same as an article of food, as butter or cheese, shall, on conviction thereof, be fined not less than twenty-five dollars ($25) nor more than two hundred dollars ($200).

SEC. 2. All acts or parts of acts inconsistent with this act are hereby repealed.

Approved June 1, 1881.

INDIANA.

In reply to a letter of inquiry addressed to Dr. C. W. Metcalf, secretary of the State Board of Health, he wrote as follows: "We have no dairy and food commissioners and no laws upon the subject."

IOWA.

[CHAPTER LII.]

AN ACT to prevent deception in the manufacture and sale of imitation butter and cheese.

Be it enacted by the general assembly of the State of Iowa, That for the purposes of this act every article, substance, or compound other than that produced from pure milk, or cream from the same, made in the semblance of butter, and designed to be used as a substitute for butter made from pure milk, or cream from the same, is hereby declared to be imitation butter; and that for the purposes of this act every article, substance, or compound other than that produced from pure milk, or cream from the same, made in the semblance of cheese, and designed to be used as a substitute for cheese made from pure milk, or cream from the same, is hereby declared to be imitation cheese: provided that the use of salt, rennet, and harmless coloring matter for coloring the product of pure milk or cream, shall not be construed to render such product an imitation.

SEC. 2. Each person who manufactures imitation butter or imitation cheese shall mark by branding, stamping, and stenciling upon the top and sides of each tub, firkin, box, or other package in which such articles shall be kept, and in which it shall be removed from the place where it is produced, in a clear and durable manner, in the English language, the name of the contents thereof as herein designated, in printed letters in plain Roman type, each of which shall not be less than one inch in length by one-half of an inch in width. Every person who by himself or another violates the provisions of this section, shall be deemed guilty of a misdemeanor, and upon conviction thereof shall be fined not to exceed two hundred and fifty dollars, or by imprisonment in the county jail not to exceed sixty days.

SEC. 3. No person by himself or another shall knowingly ship, consign, or forward by any common carrier whether public or private, any imitation butter or imitation cheese, unless the same be marked as provided by section two of this act; and no carrier shall knowingly receive for the purpose of forwarding or transporting any imitation butter or imitation cheese, unless it shall be marked as hereinbefore provided, consigned, and by the carrier receipted for by its name as designated by this act; provided that this act shall not apply to any goods in transit between foreign States and across the State of Iowa.

SEC. 4. No person shall knowingly have in his possession or under his control any imitation butter or imitation cheese unless the tub, firkin, box, or other package containing the same be clearly and durably marked, as provided by section two of this act; provided that this section shall not be deemed to apply to persons who have the same in their possession for the actual consumption of themselves or family.

SEC. 5. No person by himself or another shall knowingly sell or offer for sale imitation butter or imitation cheese under the name of or under the pretense that the same is pure butter or pure cheese; and no person by himself or another shall knowingly sell any imitation butter or imitation cheese, unless he shall have informed the purchaser distinctly at the time of the sale that the same is imitation butter or imitation cheese, as the case may be, and shall have delivered to the purchaser at the time of the sale a statement clearly printed in the English language, which shall refer to the articles sold, and which shall contain in prominent and plain Roman type the name of the article sold, as fixed by this act, and shall give the name and place of business of the maker.

SEC. 6. No keeper of a hotel, boarding house, restaurant, or other public place of entertainment shall knowingly place before any patron for use as food any imitation butter or imitation cheese, unless the same be accompanied by a placard containing the name in English of such article, as fixed by this act, printed in plain Roman type. Each violation of this section shall be deemed a misdemeanor.

SEC. 7. No action can be maintained on account of any sale or other contract made in violation of or with intent to violate this act by or through any person who was knowingly a party to such wrongful sale or other contract.

SEC. 8. Every person having possession or control of any imitation butter or imitation cheese which is not marked as required by the provisions of this act, shall be presumed to have known during the time of such possession or control the true character and name as fixed by this act of such imitation product.

SEC. 9. Whoever shall efface, erase, cancel, or remove any mark provided for by this act, with intent to mislead, deceive, or to violate any of the provisions of this act, shall be deemed guilty of a misdemeanor.

SEC. 10. Whoever shall violate any of the provisions of the third, fourth, and fifth sections of this act shall, for the first offense, be punished by a fine of not less than fifty dollars nor more than one hundred dollars, or by imprisonment not exceeding thirty days, and for each subsequent offense shall be punished by a fine of not less than two hundred and fifty dollars nor more than five hundred dollars, or by imprisonment in the county jail not less than thirty days nor more than six months, or by both such fine and imprisonment, in the discretion of the court.

SEC. 11. The governor shall, on or before the first day of April of each even-numbered year, appoint an officer, who shall be known as the Iowa State dairy commissioner, who shall have practical experience in the manufacture of dairy products, and who shall hold his office for the term of two years from the first day of May following his appointment, or until his successor is appointed and qualified. Said commissioner shall give an official bond conditioned for the faithful performance of the duties of his office in the sum of ten thousand dollars, with sureties to be approved by the governor. He may be removed from office by the governor, with the approval of the executive council, for neglect or violation of duty. Any vacancy shall be filled by the appointment of the governor, and with the advice and consent of the executive council.

SEC. 12. The State dairy commissioner shall receive a salary of fifteen hundred dollars per annum, payable monthly, and the expenses necessarily incurred in the proper discharge of the duties of his office: *Provided*, That a complete itemized statement of all expenses shall be kept by the commissioner, and by him filed with the auditor of State after having been duly verified by him before receiving the same. He shall be furnished a room in the agricultural department of the capitol at Des Moines, in which he shall keep his office and all correspondence, documents, records, and property of the State pertaining thereto, all of which shall be turned over to his successor in office. He may, if it is found to be necessary, employ a clerk, whose salary shall not exceed the sum of fifty dollars per month, said salaries and expenses to be paid from the appropriation provided for in section seventeen of this act. The commissioner provided for by this act shall hold no other official position under the laws of Iowa, or a professorship in any of the State institutions.

SEC. 13. It shall be the duty of the State dairy commissioner to secure, so far as possible, the enforcement of this act. He shall collect, arrange, and present in annual reports to the governor, on or before the first of November of each year, a detailed statement of all matters relating to the purposes of this act, which he shall deem of public importance, including the receipts and disbursements of this office. Such report shall be published with the report of the State Agricultural Society.

SEC. 14. The State dairy commissioner shall have power in all cases where he shall deem it important for the discharge of the duties of his office, to administer oaths, to issue subpœnas for witnesses, and to examine them under oath, and to enforce their attendance to the same extent and in the same manner as a justice of the peace may now do, and such witnesses shall be paid by the commissioner the same fees now allowed witnesses in justices' courts.

SEC. 15. Whoever shall have possession or control of any imitation butter or imitation cheese contrary to the provisions of this act shall be construed to have possession of property with intent to use it as a means of committing a public offense within the meaning of chapter 50 of title 25 of the code: *Provided*, That it shall be the duty of the officer who serves a search warrant issued for imitation butter or imitation cheese, to deliver to the State dairy commissioner, or to any person by such commissioner authorized in writing to receive the same, a perfect sample of each article seized by virtue of such warrant, for the purpose of having the same analyzed, and forthwith to return to the person from whom it was taken the remainder of each article seized as aforesaid. If any sample be found to be imitation butter or imitation cheese it shall be returned to and retained by the magistrate as and for the purpose contemplated by section 4648 of the code, but if any sample be found not to be imitation butter or imitation cheese, it shall be returned forthwith to the person from whom it was taken.

SEC. 16. It shall be the duty of the court in each action for the violation of this act to tax as cost in the cause the actual and necessary expense of analyzing the alleged imitation butter or imitation cheese, which shall be in controversy in such proceedings, provided that the amounts so taxed shall not exceed the sum of twenty-five dollars. It shall be the duty of the district or county attorney, upon the application of the dairy commissioner, to attend to the prosecution, in the name of the State, of any suit brought for the violation of any of the provisions of this act within his district; and in case of conviction he shall receive twenty-five per cent of the fines collected, which shall be in addition to any salary he may receive, to be taxed as costs in the case.

SEC. 17. That the unexpended portion of the appropriation provided for by section 17 of the 52d chapter of the twenty-first general assembly, is hereby appropriated for the next biennial period, or so much thereof as may be necessary for the proper carrying out of the purposes of the act; but not more than one-half of said unexpended balance shall be drawn from the State treasury prior to the 1st day of May, 1889. The amount hereby appropriated shall be expended only under the direction and with the approval of the executive council. And all salaries, fees, costs, and expenses of every kind incurred in the carrying out of this law shall be drawn from the sum so appropriated.

SEC. 18. Chapter 39 of the acts of the eighteenth general assembly of Iowa, and all acts and parts of acts in conflict with this act are hereby repealed.

SEC. 19. This act being deemed of immediate importance, shall take effect and be in force from and after its publication in the Iowa State Register and Iowa Homestead, newspapers published in Des Moines, Iowa.

Approved March 27, 1886.

Amendments approved March 28, 1888.

Law pertaining to milk, as enacted by the thirteenth general assembly, and found in the code of Iowa, chapter 156, section 4042.

ADULTERATED MILK, CHEESE, OR BUTTER.

SEC. 4042. If any person knowingly sell to another, or knowingly deliver or bring to another to be manufactured, to any cheese or butter manufactory in this State, any milk diluted with water, or in any way adulterated, or milk from which any cream has been taken, or milk commonly known as "skimmed milk," or shall keep back any part of the milk known as "strippings," with intent to defraud, or shall knowingly sell the milk, the product of a diseased animal or animals, or shall knowingly use any poisonous or deleterious material in the manufacture of cheese or butter, he shall, upon conviction thereof, be fined in any sum not less than twenty-five dollars nor more than one hundred dollars, or be liable in double the amount of damages to the person or persons, firm, association, or corporation upon whom such fraud shall be committed.

MAINE.

LARD LAW.

[State of Maine in the year of our Lord one thousand eight hundred and eighty-nine.]

AN ACT to prevent fraud in the sale of lard.

Be it enacted by the senate and house of representatives in legislature assembled, No manufacturer or other person shall sell, deliver, prepare, put up, expose, or offer for sale any lard, or any article intended for use as lard, which contains any ingredient but the pure fat of swine, in any tierce, bucket, pail, or other vessel or wrapper, or under any label bearing the words "pure," "refined," "family," or either of them, alone or in combination with other words, unless every vessel, wrapper, or label in or under which such article is sold or delivered or prepared, put up or exposed for sale, bears on the top or outer side thereof, in letters not less than one-half inch in length and plainly exposed to view, the words "compound lard."

SEC. 2. Any person who violates any provision hereof shall forfeit the sum of fifty dollars to the use of any person suing therefor, in an action of debt.

IN HOUSE OF REPRESENTATIVES, *March* 1, 1889.
This bill having had three several readings, passed to be enacted.

FRED. N. DOW, *Speaker.*

IN SENATE, *March* 2, 1889.
This bill having had two several readings, passed to be enacted.

HENRY LORD, *President.*

MARCH 2, 1889.

Approved.

EDWIN C. BURLEIGH, *Governor.*

ADULTERATION OF FOOD AND DRINKS.

A part of chapter 128 of the revised statutes of Maine, and amendments belonging thereto, relating to adulteration of food and drinks.]

SECTION 1 * * *   Whoever sells diseased, corrupted, or unwholesome provisions for food or drink, knowing it to be such, without informing the buyer, or fraudulently adulterates for the purpose of sale, any substance intended for food, or any wine, spirits, or other liquors intended for drink, so as to render them injurious to health, shall be punished by imprisonment for not more than five years, or by fine not exceeding one thousand dollars, etc.

SEC. 3 (as amended by public laws, 1885). Whoever, by himself or his agent, manufactures, sells, exposes for sale, or has in his possession with intent to sell any article, substance, or compound made in imitation of butter or cheese, or as a substitute for butter or cheese, and not made exclusively and wholly of cream or milk, or containing any fats, oils, or grease not produced from milk or cream, whether said article, substance, or compound be named oleomargarine, butterine, or otherwise named, forfeits for the first offense one hundred dollars and for the second and each subsequent offense two hundred dollars, to be recovered by individual with costs, etc.

SEC. 7. Whoever adulterates sugar or molasses, or knowingly, willfully, or maliciously sells or offers or exposes for sale sugar or molasses, adulterated with salts of tin, terra alba, glucose, dextrine, starch sugar, corn syrup, or other preparation from starch, shall be punished by a fine not exceeding five hundred dollars or by imprisonment for not more than one year.

SEC. 8. Whoever manufactures for sale or knowingly offers or exposes for sale, or knowingly causes to be branded or marked as cider vinegar any vinegar not the legitimate product of pure apple juice, known as apple cider, and not made exclusively therefrom, but into which any foreign substance, ingredient, drug, or acid has been introduced as appears by proper tests, shall for each offence be fined not less than fifty nor more than one hundred dollars.

[Chapter 244 of public laws of the State, 1889.]

No manufacturer or other person shall sell, deliver, prepare, put up, expose, or offer for sale any lard, or any article intended for use as lard, which contains any ingredient but the pure fat of swine, in any tierce, bucket, pail, or other vessel or wrapper, or under any label bearing the words "pure," "refined," "family," or either of them alone or in combination with other words, unless every vessel, wrapper, or label in or under which such article is sold or delivered or prepared, put up or exposed for sale, bears on the top or outer side thereof, in letters not less than one-half inch in length and plainly exposed to view the words "compound lard." Penalty, fifty dollars.

[Chapter 257 of the public laws of the State, 1889.]

No manufacturer or other person shall sell, prepare, deliver, put up, expose, or offer for sale any article, substance, or compound under or by the name of wheat, meal, graham meal, or graham flour made in imitation of pure wheat meal and not consisting exclusively and wholly of pure wheat meal, unless every box, bucket, barrel, or wrapper in or under which such article is sold, delivered, or exposed for sale bears on the top or outer side thereof, in letters not less than half inch in length, and plainly exposed to view the words "compound wheat." Penalty, fifty dollars.

MARYLAND.

[Chapter 604 of the acts of 1890.]

AN ACT to add additional sections to article forty-three of the code of public general laws, title "Health," to be numbered "sections forty-eight, forty-nine, fifty, fifty-one, fifty-two, fifty-three, fifty-four, fifty-five, fifty-six and fifty-seven," so as to provide for the prevention of the adulteration of articles of food and drink, and the sale thereof when adulterated or unwholesome.

Be it enacted by the general assembly of Maryland, That the following sections shall be added to article forty-three of the code of public general laws, to read as follows:

SEC. 48. That no person shall mix, color, stain, or otherwise sophisticate any article of food or drink with any other ingredient or material for the purpose of gain or profit, nor shall sell or offer for sale or order or permit any employé or other person to sell or offer for sale any article so mixed, colored, stained, or otherwise sophisticated, unless the same be so manufactured, used, or sold, or offered for sale under its true and appropriate name, and unless a notice that the same is mixed or impure is marked, printed, or stamped upon each package, roll, parcel, or vessel containing the same, so as to be and remain at all times readily visible, or unless the person purchasing the same is fully informed by the seller of the true name and ingredients (if other than such as are known by the common name thereof, of such article of food or drink at the time of making sale thereof or offering to sell the same.

SEC 49. That no person shall mix any glucose, grape sugar, or other article of adulteration with any syrup, honey, or sugar intended for human food, or any oleomargarine, suine, beef-fat, lard, or any other foreign substance with any butter, cheese intended for human food, nor mix or mingle any glucose, grape sugar, oleomargarine, or other adulterant, with any article of food or dietetics without distinctly marking, stamping or labeling the article or the package containing the same with the true and appropriate name of such adulterant, and the percentage in which it is used for the purpose of adulteration, or enters into the composition of the article so adulterated; nor shall any person sell, offer for sale, or permit to be sold or offered for sale any article of food or drink or dietetics into the composition of which any adulterant has entered without at the same time informing the buyer of the fact, and the proportion in which such adulterant has been used : *Provided,* That nothing in this section shall be construed to prevent the use of glucose or grape sugar in the manufacture of candy.

SEC. 50. That no person shall adulterate or sophisticate any wine, vinegar, spirituous, or malt liquors used or intended for drink or dietetic purposes by mixing the same in the manufacture or preparation thereof or otherwise, with any deleterious drug, substance, or liquid which is poisonous or injurious to health ; and no person shall use or offer for sale or import into this State for sale, any wine, vinegar, spirituous, or malt liquor intended to be used for drink or dietetic purposes knowing the same to be adulterated or in any way sophisticated.

SEC. 51. That if any person shall fraudulently adulterate for the purpose of sale, or shall sell or offer for sale any substance intended for the food of man, or any wine, vinegar, spirits, malt liquors, or other liquor intended for drink or dietetic purposes, knowing the same to be adulterated or in any way sophisticated, he shall be punished by imprisonment in the county jail not longer than one year, or by fine not exceeding five hundred dollars, and the article so adulterated shall be forfeited and destroyed or so disposed of as to prevent it from being exposed for sale or used for the food of man.

SEC. 52. That if any person shall sell or offer for sale any kind of diseased, corrupted, or unwholesome provisions such as poultry, game, flesh, or preparation of flesh, fruits, vegetables, bread, flour, meal, milk, or other things intended to be used for human food, he shall be punished by imprisonment in the county jail not more than one year, or be fined not exceeding five hundred dollars, or be both fined and imprisoned, in the discretion of the court having jurisdiction, and the unwholesome provisions offered or exposed for sale shall be forfeited and destroyed or so disposed of as to prevent their being used for food : *Provided*, That nothing in this section shall apply to the shippers or consigners of green fruits or vegetables that may be spoiled *in transitu.*

SEC. 53. That the State board of health shall be charged with the duty of rendering effective the provisions of this act, and shall take such steps and do such things as the board may deem necessary, to detect and publicly expose any adulteration or corruption of all articles sold or liquid intended or offered for sale as food or drink ; and shall, when deemed necessary, have the suspected article subjected to chemical or other scientific examination in order to establish more clearly the fact and degree of adulteration.

SEC. 54. That whenever the said board of health, or its proper officer, shall be satisfied that any article of food, condiment, or drink has been adulterated, or is otherwise unsound or unwholesome, the said board, or its proper officer, shall forbid the sale or disposal of such article for human food and order it to be destroyed or disposed of so as to prevent it from being exposed for sale or used for the food of man, and the person or persons to whom the same belongs, or did belong at the time of exposure for sale, or in whose possession or on whose premises the same was found, refusing or neglecting to destroy or otherwise dispose of such unsound or unwholesome article as directed, shall be liable to the penalty imposed under the provisions of the fifty-second section of this act.

SEC. 55. That the said board of health, or its proper officer, or any inspector or inspectors appointed by said board, are empowered at all reasonable times to inspect and examine any live animal, carcass meat, poultry, game, flesh, fish, fruits, vegetables, bread, milk, wine, spirits, malt, or other liquors or things exposed for sale, or deposited in any place for the purpose of sale, or of preparation for sale and intended for the food of man, the proof that the same was not exposed or deposited for any such purpose, or was not intended for the food of man, resting with the party charged; and if such animal, carcass, meat, poultry, game, flesh, fish, fruits, vegetables, bread, milk, or other things appear to the said board, or its proper officer, or inspector, to be diseased or unsound or unwholesome and unfit for the food of man, the said board, or its proper officer, shall issue an order preventing the sale of such article or articles for human food, and any person neglecting or refusing to obey such an order shall be deemed guilty of a misdemeanor, and shall be punished by fine in any sum not less than fifty dollars, and in default of the payment thereof, by imprisonment in the public jail not more than six months.

SEC. 56. That it is hereby made the duty of the prosecuting attorneys of this State to appear for the people and to attend to the prosecution of all complaints under this act in all the courts of their respective counties or the city of Baltimore, as the case may be.

SEC. 57. That the sum of twenty-five hundred dollars, or so much thereof as may be necessary, be annually appropriated for defraying the expenses of chemical and scientific examination of suspected articles of food or drink, for salary of inspectors and other necessary expenses, to be paid by the treasurer of the State on the warrant of the comptroller, at such times and in such sums as the board may direct.

SEC. 9. That this act shall take effect from the date of its passage.

Approved April 8, 1890.

MASSACHUSETTS.

GENERAL LAWS RELATING TO ADULTERATION.

FOOD AND DRUGS.

SECTION 1. No person shall, within this Commonwealth, manufacture for sale, offer for sale, or sell any drug or article of food which is adulterated within the meaning of this act.

2. The term "drug" as used in this act shall include all medicines for internal or external use, antiseptics, disinfectants, and cosmetics. The term "food" as used herein shall include all articles used for food or drink by man.

3. An article shall be deemed to be adulterated within the meaning of this act—

(a) *In the case of drugs.*—(1) If, when sold under or by a name recognized in the United States Pharmacopœia, it differs from the standard of strength, quality, or purity laid down therein, unless the order calls for an article inferior to such standard, or unless such difference is made known or so appears to the purchaser at the time of such sale; (2) if, when sold under or by a name not recognized in the United States Pharmacopœia, but which is found in some other pharmacopœia, or other standard work on *materia medica*, it differs materially from the standard of strength, quality, or purity laid down in such work; (3) if its strength or purity falls below the professed standard under which it is sold.

(b) *In the case of food.*—(1) If any substance or substances have been mixed with it so as to reduce, or lower, or injuriously affect its quality or strength; (2) if any inferior or cheaper substance or substances have been substituted wholly or in part for it; (3) if any valuable constituent has been wholly or in part abstracted from it; (4) if it is an imitation of or is sold under the name of another article; (5) if it consists wholly or in part of a diseased, decomposed, putrid, or rotten animal or vegetable substance, whether manufactured or not, or in the case of milk, if it is the product of a diseased animal; (6) if it is colored, coated, polished, or powdered, whereby damage is concealed, or if it is made to appear better or of greater value than it really is; (7) if it contains any added or poisonous ingredient, or any ingredient which may render it injurious to the health of a person consuming it.

4. The provisions of this act shall not apply to mixtures or compounds recognized as ordinary articles of food or drinks, provided that the same are not injurious to health and are distinctly labeled as mixtures or compounds. And no prosecutions shall at any time be maintained under the said act concerning any drug the standard of strength or purity whereof has been raised since the issue of the last edition of the United States Pharmacopœia, unless and until such change or standard has been published throughout the Commonwealth.

5. The State board of health, lunacy, and charity shall take cognizance of the interests of the public health relating to the sale of drugs and food and the adulteration of the same, and shall make all necessary investigations and inquiries in reference thereto, and for these purposes may appoint inspectors, analysts, and chemists, who shall be subject to its supervision and removal.

Within thirty days after the passage of this act the said board shall adopt such measures as it may deem necessary to facilitate the enforcement hereof, and shall prepare rules and regulations in regard to the proper methods of collecting and examining drugs and articles of food. Said board may expend annually an amount not exceeding ten thousand dollars for the purpose of carrying out the provisions of this act: *Provided, however,* That not less than three-fifths of the said amount shall be annually expended for the enforcement of the laws against the adulteration of milk and milk products.

6. Every person offering or exposing for sale, or delivering to a purchaser, any drug or article of food included in the provisions of this act shall furnish to any analyst or other officer or agent appointed hereunder, who shall apply to him for the purpose and shall tender him the value of the same, a sample sufficient for the purpose of the analysis of any such drug or article of food which is in his possession.

7. Whoever hinders, obstructs, or in any way interferes with any inspector, analyst, or other officer appointed hereunder, in the performance of his duty, and whoever violates any of the provisions of this act, shall be punished by a fine not exceeding fifty dollars for the first offense, and not exceeding one hundred dollars for each subsequent offense.

8. The State board of health, lunacy, and charity shall report annually to the legislature the number of prosecutions made under said chapter, and an itemized account of all money expended in carrying out the provisions thereof.

9. An inspector appointed under the provisions of said chapter two hundred and sixty-three of the acts of the year eighteen hundred and eighty-two shall have the same powers and authority conferred upon a city or town inspector by section two of chapter fifty-seven of the public statutes.

10. Nothing contained in chapter two hundred and sixty-three of the acts of the year eighteen hundred and eighty-two shall be in any way construed as repealing or amending anything contained in chapter fifty-seven of the public statutes.

11. Before commencing the analysis of any sample, the person making the same shall reserve a portion which shall be sealed ; and in case of a complaint against any person the reserved portion of the sample alleged to be adulterated shall upon application be delivered to the defendant or his attorney.

12. Whoever knowingly sells any kind of diseased, corrupted, or unwholesome provisions, whether for meat or drink, without making the same fully known to the buyer, shall be punished by imprisonment in the jail not exceeding six months, or by fine not exceeding two hundred dollars.

13. Whoever fraudulently adulterates, for the purpose of sale, bread or any other substance intended for food, with any substance injurious to health, or knowingly barters, gives away, sells, or has in possession with intent to sell, any substance intended for food, which has been adulterated with any substance injurious to health, shall be punished by imprisonment in the jail not exceeding one year, or by fine not exceeding three hundred dollars ; and the articles so adulterated shall be forfeited and destroyed under the direction of the court.

14. Whoever adulterates, for the purpose of sale, any liquors used or intended for drink, with Indian cockle, vitriol, grains of paradise, opium, alum, capsicum, copperas, laurel-water, logwood, Brazil wood, cochineal, sugar of lead, or any other substance which is poisonous or injurious to health, and whoever knowingly sells any such liquor so adulterated, shall be punished by imprisonment in the State prison not exceeding three years ; and the articles so adulterated shall be forfeited.

15. Whoever fraudulently adulterates, for the purpose of sale, any drug or medicine, or sells any fraudulently adulterated drug or medicine, knowing the same to be adulterated, shall be punished by imprisonment in the jail not exceeding one year or by fine not exceeding four hundred dollars ; and such adulterated drugs and medicines shall be forfeited and destroyed under the direction of the court.

16. Whoever sells arsenic, strychnine, corrosive sublimate, or prussic acid without the written prescription of a physician shall keep a record of the date of such sale, the name of the article, the amount thereof sold, and the name of the person or persons to whom delivered ; and for each neglect shall forfeit a sum not exceeding fifty dollars. Whoever purchases deadly poisons as aforesaid and gives a false or fictitious name to the vendor shall be punished by fine not exceeding fifty dollars.

CHAP. 171.—AN ACT concerning the adulteration of food and drugs.

Be it enacted, etc., as follows :

Section two of chapter two hundred and sixty-three of the acts of the year eighteen hundred and eighty-two is hereby amended so as to read as follows: The term "drug" as used in this act shall include all medicines for internal or external use, antiseptics, disinfectants, and cosmetics. The term "food" as used herein shall include confectionery, condiments, and all articles used for food or drink by man,

Approved April 29, 1886.

RULES AND REGULATIONS OF THE STATE BOARD OF HEALTH, LUNACY, AND CHARITY OF MASSACHUSETTS RELATIVE TO THE INSPECTION AND ANALYSIS OF FOOD AND DRUGS.

1. The State board of health, lunacy, and charity shall appoint analysts and inspectors, as provided in section 5 of chapter 263, acts of 1882.

2. It shall be the duty of the inspectors to procure samples of drugs and articles of food at such times and places as the health officer shall direct, in the manner provided in section 6 of chapter 263 of the acts of 1882, and in section 3 of chapter 289 of the acts of 1884, and in all acts amendatory of said provisions.

3. Under the direction of the health officer, one of the inspectors shall, for the identification of samples, affix a number to each sample of food or drugs obtained by him, beginning with number one, and taking every alternate or odd number thereafter, without limit; and the other inspector shall use and affix each alternate or even number, beginning with number two, and following such form of numbering, without limit, also, as far as may be directed. Under no circumstances shall an inspector convey any information to an analyst as to the source from which any sample was obtained.

4. The inspectors shall keep records of each sample, each record to include the following items:

(*a*) The inspector's number.

(*b*) The date of purchase or receipt of sample.

(*c*) The character of the sample.

(*d*) The name of the vender.

(*e*) The name of the city or town and street and number where the sample is obtained, and in the case of a licensed milk peddler, the number of his license.

(*f*) As far as possible the names of manufacturers, producers, or wholesalers, with marks, brands, or labels stamped or printed upon goods.

5. It shall be the duty of the analysts so appointed to determine, under the direction of the health officer, by proper examination and analysis, whether articles of food and drugs, manufactured for sale, offered for sale, or sold within this Commonwealth, are adulterated within the meaning of chapter 263 of the acts and resolves passed by the general court of Massachusetts in 1882, and all acts amendatory thereof, adulteration being defined as follows, viz:

In the case of drugs: (1) If sold under or by a name recognized in the United States Pharmacopœia, it differs from the standard of strength, quality, or purity laid down therein, unless the order calls for an article inferior to such standard, or unless such difference is made known or so appears to the purchaser at the time of such sale. (2) If, when sold under or by a name not recognized in the United States Pharmacopœia, but which is found in some other pharmacopœia or standard work on materia medica, it differs materially from the standard of strength, quality, or purity laid down in such work. (3) If its strength or purity falls below the professed standard under which it is sold.

In the case of food: (1) If any substance or substances have been mixed with it, so as to reduce or lower or injuriously affect its quality or strength. (2) If any inferior or cheaper substance or substances have been substituted, wholly or in part, for it. (3) If any valuable constituent has been wholly or in part abstracted from it. (4) If it is an imitation of or is sold under the name of another article. (5) If it consists wholly or in part of a diseased, decomposed, putrid, or rotten animal or vegetable substance, whether manufactured or not, or in the case of milk, if it is the produce of a diseased animal. (6) If it is colored, coated, polished, or powdered, whereby damage is concealed, or if it is made to appear of better or of greater value than it really is. (7) If it contains any added poisonous ingredient, or any ingredient which may render it injurious to the health of the person consuming it.

6. It shall also be the duty of the analysts to receive such specimens of food and drugs for analysis as may be delivered to them by the health officer, or by the in-

spectors, and to examine the same. To avoid, as far as possible, all suggestion or danger of specimens having been tampered with, each analyst shall keep each specimen in his possession in a suitable and secure place, labeled in such a manner as to prevent any person from having access to the same without the knowledge and presence of the analyst.

Analyses of perishable articles should be made promptly after they are received.

7. An analyst shall give no information, under any circumstances, regarding the result of any analysis to any person except to the health officer of the board, prior to any trial in court in reference to such analysis.

The analysts shall carefully avoid any error regarding the inspector's number attached to each sample, and shall report the results of their work in detail to the health officer.

In the case of all articles having a numerical standard provided by statute, the result of the analysis should show their relation to such standard.

8. Before beginning the analysis of any sample the analyst shall reserve a portion, which shall be sealed, and in the event of finding the portion analyzed to be adulterated, he shall preserve the sealed portion, so that in case of a complaint against any person the last-named portion may, on application, be delivered by the health officer to the defendant or to his attorney.

9. Each analyst shall present to the health officer on the Thursday before the first Saturday of each month a summary of the analyses made by him during the previous month.

Each analyst shall also present, on or before the first of January of each year, an annual report of the work done for the year ending on the 30th of September preceding.

10. The health officer shall have charge of the reports of analyses, and shall cause cases founded on such reports to be submitted to the courts for prosecution.

In each case of a retailer, and of every dealer not a manufacturer or producer, he may, if the party has not been previously complained of in court, issue a notice or warning of any violation of the law relative to the adulteration of food and drugs, and of the offender's liability to prosecution on a repetition of the sale.

11. Should the result obtained by any analyst be questioned in any given case, another analyst shall repeat the analysis, unless otherwise instructed by the board, provided a sufficient sum to meet the expense of the analysis be deposited with the health officer by any interested party feeling aggrieved, which sum will not be returned unless the second analysis fails to confirm the first in essential particulars.

12. Any appeal from the decision of an analyst shall be filed with the health officer, who shall report it and any matter in controversy to the board, giving his judgment thereon, and the board shall supervise and control the action of its officers in executing law.

13. Where standards of strength, quality, or purity are not fixed by the act, the analysts shall present to the health officer such standard as in their judgment should be fixed and the health officer shall report the same to the board for its action. The standard set by the British Society of Public Analysts will be followed as nearly as practicable, until otherwise ordered.

14. Whenever a drug or preparation not described in a national pharmacopœia or other standard work on materia medica shall be manufactured, offered for sale, or used in this State, the standard of such drug, and the standard and proportion of the ingredients of such preparation, and the range of variablility from such standard or standards shall be ascertained by the analysts, who shall report the same through the health officer to the board.

15. The analysts shall occupy such time in the performance of their respective duties as a reasonable compliance with the terms of the statute shall require, and shall be present one hour of each day at such time of the day and at such place as shall be designated by the committee on health of the board, to meet the convenience of interested parties and the public.

16. The compensation of the analysts of articles of food shall be at the rate of $1,500 per annum and that of the analysts of drugs shall be at the rate of $1,000.

That of the analyst of milk for the ten eastern counties of the Commonwealth shall be at the rate of $800 per annum and that of the analysts of the four western counties shall be at the rate of $500 per annum.

The compensation of each inspector shall be at the rate of $1,000 per annum.

MICHIGAN.

The laws of Michigan are as follows :

ADULTERATION OF FOODS, DRINKS, DRUGS, OR MEDICINES.

208. (7727.) SEC. 2. If any person shall fraudulently adulterate, for the purpose of sale, any substance intended for food, or any wine, spirits, malt liquor, or other liquor intended for drinking, he shall be punished by imprisonment in the county jail not more than one year or by fine not exceeding three hundred dollars, and the article so adulterated shall be forfeited and destroyed.—§ 9317.

209. (7723.) SEC. 3. If any person shall fraudulently adulterate, for the purpose of sale, any drug or medicine, in such manner as to render the same injurious to health, he shall be punished by imprisonment in the county jail not more than one year or by fine not exceeding four hundred dollars, and such adulterated drugs and medicines shall be forfeited and destroyed.—§ 9318.

ADULTERATION OF FOODS, DRINKS, AND MEDICINES, AND SALE THEREOF WHEN ADULTERATED.

Act No. 254, laws of 1881, entitled "An act to prevent and punish the adulteration of articles of food, drink, and medicine, and the sale thereof when adulterated."

210. SECTION 1. *The People of the State of Michigan enact,* That no person shall mix, color, stain, or powder, or order or permit any other person to mix, color, stain, or powder any article of food with any ingredient or material so as to render the article injurious to health, with the intent that the same may be sold ; and no person shall knowingly sell or offer for sale any such article so mixed, colored, stained, or powdered.—§ 9324.

211. SEC. 2. No person shall, except for the purpose of compounding in the necessary preparation of medicine, mix, color, stain, or powder, or order or permit any other person to mix, color, stain, or powder any drug or medicine with any ingredient or ingredients or materials so as to affect injuriously the quality or potency of such drug or medicine, with intent to sell the same, or shall sell or offer for sale any such drug or medicine so mixed, colored, stained, or powdered.—§ 9325.

212. SEC. 3. No person shall mix, color, stain, or powder any article of food, drink, or medicine, or any article which enters into the composition of food, drink, or medicine, with any other ingredient or material, whether injurious to health or not, for the purpose of gain or profit, or sell or offer the same for sale, or order or permit any other person to sell or offer for sale any article so mixed, colored, stained, and powdered, unless the same be so manufactured, used, or sold, or offered for sale under its true and appropriate name and notice that the same is mixed or impure is marked, printed, or stamped upon each package, roll, parcel, or vessel containing the same, so as to be and remain at all times readily visible, or unless the person purchasing the same is fully informed by the seller of the true name and ingredients (if other than such as are known by the common name thereof) of such article of food, drink, or medicine at the time of making sale thereof or offering to sell the same.—§ 9326.

213. SEC. 4. No person shall mix any glucose or grape sugar with syrup, honey, or sugar, intended for human food, or any oleomargarine, suine, beef fat, lard or any other foreign substance with any butter or cheese intended for human food, or shall

mix or mingle any glucose or grape sugar or oleomargarine with any article of food, without distinctly marking, stamping, or labeling the article or the package containing the same with the true and appropriate name of such article and the percentage in which glucose or grape sugar, oleomargarine, or suine enters into its composition; nor shall any person sell, or offer for sale, or order or permit to be sold, or offered for sale, any such food into the composition of which glucose, or grape sugar, or oleomargarine, or suine has entered, without at the same time informing the buyer of the fact, and the proportions in which such glucose or grape sugar, oleomargarine, or suine has entered into its composition.—§ 9327.

214. SEC. 5. Any person convicted of violating any provision of any of the foregoing sections of this act shall be fined not more than fifty dollars or imprisoned in the county jail not exceeding three months.—§ 9328.

215. SEC. 6. It is hereby made the duty of the prosecuting attorneys of this State to appear for the people and to attend to the prosecution of all complaints under this act in all the courts in their respective counties.—§ 9329.

216. SEC. 7. All acts and parts of acts inconsistent with the provisions of this act are hereby repealed.—§ 9330.

MINNESOTA.

MILK.

CHAPTER 247 GENERAL LAWS OF 1889. (S. F. NO. 243.)

AN ACT to amend chapter one hundred and forty (140), an act to prevent deception in the sale of dairy products, and to preserve the public health, being supplementary to and in aid of chapter one hundred and forty-nine (149) of the laws of one thousand eight hundred and eighty-five (1885), entitled "An act to prohibit and prevent the sale or manufacture of unhealthy or adulterated dairy products."   •

Be it enacted by the Legislature of the State of Minnesota, That chapter one hundred and forty (140) of the General Laws of Minnesota for the year one thousand eight hundred and eighty-seven (1887) be, and the same is hereby, amended so as to read as follows:

SEC. 1. No person or persons shall sell or exchange or expose for sale or exchange any unclean, unhealthy, adulterated, or unwholesome milk, or shall offer for sale any article of food made from the same or of cream from the same. This provision shall not apply to pure skim-milk cheese made from milk which is pure, healthy, wholesome, and unadulterated, except by skimming. Whoever violates the provisions of this section shall be deemed guilty of misdemeanor and shall be punished by a fine of not less than ten dollars ($10) nor more than one hundred dollars ($100) or by imprisonment of not less than one (1) month or more than three (3) months, or both such fine and imprisonment for the first offense and by three (3) months' imprisonment for each subsequent offense.

Section two (2) of said act is hereby amended so as to read as follows.

SEC. 2. No person shall keep cows for the production of milk for market, or for sale or exchange, or for manufacturing the same, or cream from the same, into articles of food, in a crowded or unhealthy condition, or feed the cows on food that is unhealthy or that produces impure, unhealthy, diseased, or unwholesome milk. No person shall manufacture from impure, unhealthy, diseased, or unwholesome milk, or of cream from the same, any article of food. Whoever violates the provisions of this section is guilty of a misdemeanor, and shall be punished by a fine of not less than ten dollar ($10) nor more than one hundred dollars ($100) or by imprisonment of not less than one (1) month or more than three (3) months, or by both such fine and imprisonment for the first offense and by three (3) months' imprisonment for each subsequent offense.

Section three (3) of this act is hereby amended to read as follows:

Sec. 3. No person or persons shall sell, supply, or bring to be manufactured, to any butter or cheese manufactory, any milk diluted with water, or any unclean, impure, unhealthy, adultered, or unwholesome milk, or milk from which any cream has been taken (except pure skim milk to skim cheese factories), or shall keep back any part of the milk commonly known as "strippings," or shall bring or supply milk to any butter or cheese manufactory that is sour (except pure skim milk to skim cheese fac tories). No butter or cheese manufactories, except those who buy all the milk they use, shall use for their own benefit or allow any of their employés or any other person to use, or the product thereof brought to said manufacturers, without the consent of the owners thereof. Every butter or cheese manufacturer, except those who buy all the milk they use, shall keep a correct account of all the milk daily received, and of the number of pounds and packages of butter, the number and aggregate weight of cheese made each day, the number of packages of cheese and butter disposed of; which shall be open to inspection to any person who delivers milk to such manufacturer. Whoever violates the provisions of this section shall be deemed guilty of a misdemeanor, and shall be punished for each offense by a fine of not less than ten ($10) dollars or more than one hundred ($100) dollars, or not less than one (1) month or more than three (3) months' imprisonment, or by both such fine and imprisonment.

Section four (4) of said act is amended so as to read as follows:

Sec. 4. No person shall manufacture out of any oleaginous substance or substances, or any compound of the same, or any other compound, other than that produced from unadulterated milk or of cream from the same, any article designed to take the place of butter or cheese, produced from pure, unadulterated milk or cream from the same, or shall sell or offer for sale the same as an article of food. This shall not apply to pure skim milk cheese made from pure skim milk. Whoever violates the provisions of this section shall be deemed guilty of a misdemeanor and be punished by a fine of not less than one hundred dollars ($100) or more than five hundred dollars ($500) or not less than six (6) months' or more than one (1) year's imprisonment, or by both such fine and imprisonment for the first offense, and by imprisonment for one (1) year for each subsequent offense.

Section five (5) of said act is hereby amended so as to read as follows:

Sec. 5. No person, by himself or his agents or servants, shall render or manufacture out of any animal fat, or animal or vegetable oils not produced from unadulterated milk or cream from the same, any article or product in imitation or semblance of or designed to take the place of natural butter or cheese produced from pure, unadulterated milk or cream of the same, nor shall he or they mix, compound with or add to milk, cream, or butter any acids or other deleterious substance or any animal fats or animal or vegetable oils not produced from milk or cream with designs or interest to render, make, or produce any article or substance for human food in imitation or semblance of natural butter or cheese, nor shall he sell, keep for sale, or offer for sale any article, substance, or compound made, manufactured, or produced in violation of the provisions of this section, whether such article, substance, or compound shall be made or produced in this State or in any other State or country. Whoever violates the provisions of this section shall be deemed guilty of a misdemeanor, and be punished by a fine of not less than one hundred dollars ($100) nor more than five hundred ($500) nor less than six (6) months' or more than one (1) year's imprisonment for the first offense, and by imprisonment for one (1) year for each subsequent offense.

Nothing in this section shall impair the provisions of section four (4) of this act.

Section six (6) of said act is hereby amended so as to read as follows:

Sec. 6. No person shall manufacture, mix, or compound with or add to natural milk, cream, or butter any animal fats or animal or vegetable oils, nor shall he make or manufacture any oleaginous substance not produced from milk or cream with intent to sell the same for butter or cheese made from unadulterated milk or cream, or have the same in his possession, or offer the same for sale with such intent, nor shall any article or substance or compound so made or produced be sold for butter or cheese, the product of the dairy. If any person shall coat, powder, or color with annatto or any coloring matter whatever, butterine or oleomargarine or any compounds of the same, or any products or manufacture made in whole or in part from animal fats, or animal or vegetable oils not produced from unadulterated milk or cream, whereby the said product, manufacture, or compound shall be made to resemble butter or cheese, the product of the dairy, or shall have the same in his possession, or sell or offer for sale, or have in his possession any of said products which shall be coated or colored in semblance of or to resemble butter or cheese, it shall be prima facie evidence of an intent to sell the same for butter or cheese, the product of the dairy. Whoever violates any of the provisions of this section shall be deemed guilty of misdemeanor and punished by a fine of not less than one hundred dollars ($100) nor more than one thousand dollars ($1,000).

This section shall not be construed to impair or affect the prohibition of sections four (4) and five (5) of this act.

Section seven (7) of said act is hereby amended so as to read as follows:

SEC. 7. No person shall offer, sell, or expose for sale butter or cheese branded or labeled with a false brand or label as to the quality of the article, or to the county or State in which the article is made.

The Minnesota State dairy and food commissioner is hereby authorized and directed to procure and issue to the cheese manufacturers of the State, upon proper application therefor, and under such regulations as to the custody and use thereof, as he may prescribe, a uniform stencil brand bearing a suitable device or motto and the words "Minnesota State Full Cream Cheese." Every brand issued shall be used upon the outside of the cheese and also upon the package containing the same, and shall be a different number for each separate manufactory, and the commissioner shall keep a book in which shall be registered the name, location, and number of each manufactory using the said brand, and the name or names of the persons at each manufactory authorized to use the same.

It shall be unlawful to use or permit such stencil brand to be used upon any other than full cream cheese or packages containing the same. Minnesota State full cream cheese, of which there be less than forty (40) per centum of fats to total solids, shall be deemed, for the purpose of this act, to be adulterated. Whoever violates the provisions of this section shall be deemed guilty of a misdemeanor, and for each and every cheese or package so falsely branded shall be punished by a fine of not less than twenty-five dollars ($25) or more than fifty dollars ($50), or imprisonment of not less than fifteen (15) days or more than thirty (30) days.

Section eight (8) of said act is hereby amended so as to read as follows:

SEC. 8. The governor shall appoint a commissioner who shall be known as the State dairy and food commissioner, who shall be a citizen of this State, and who shall hold his office for a term of two (2) years, or until his successor is appointed, and shall receive a salary of eighteen hundred ($1,800) dollars per annum and his necessary expenses incurred in the discharge of his duties under this act, and shall be charged, under the direction of the governor, with the enforcement of the various provisions thereof. Said commissioner may be removed from office at the pleasure of the governor and his successor appointed as above provided for. The said commissioner is hereby authorized and empowered to appoint a secretary whose salary shall be twelve hundred (1,200) dollars per year, and such assistant commissioners, and to employ such experts, chemists, agents, and such counsel as may be deemed by him necessary for the proper enforcement of this law, their compensation to be fixed by the commissioner. The sum of fifteen thousand dollars ($15,000) annually is hereby appropriated, to be paid for such purposes out of any moneys in the treasury not otherwise appropriated. All charges, accounts, and expenses authorized by this act shall be paid by the treasurer of the State upon the warrant of the State auditor. The entire expenses of said commissioner shall not exceed the sum appropriated for the purpose of this act. The said commissioner shall make biennial reports to the legislature not later than the fifteenth (15th) day of January, of his work and proceedings, and shall report in detail the number of assistant commissioners, experts, chemists, agents, and counsel he has employed, with their expenses and disbursements. The said commissioner shall have a room in the capitol, to be set apart for his use by the governor. This section shall not affect the tenure of office of the present commissioner, nor to be construed to impair or affect any of the provisions in section seven (7) of chapter one hundred and forty-nine (149) of the law of one thousand eight hundred and eighty-five (1885), except in the sum of money appropriated.

SEC. 9. The said commissioner and assistant commissioners, and such experts, chemists, agents, and counsel as they shall duly authorize for the purpose, shall have access, ingress, and egress to all places of business, factories, farms, buildings, carriages, cars, vessels, and cans used in the manufacture and sale of any dairy product or any imitations thereof. They also shall have power and authority to open any package, can, or vessel containing such articles which may be manufactured, sold, or exposed for sale, in violation of the provisions of this act, and may inspect the contents therein, and may take samples therefrom for analysis.

All clerks, bookkeepers, express agents, railroad officials, employés, or common carriers shall render to them all the assistance in their power, when so requested, in tracing, finding, or discovering the presence of any prohibited article named in this act.

Any refusal or neglect on the part of such clerks, bookkeepers, express agents, railroad officials, employés, or common carriers to render such friendly aid shall be deemed a misdemeanor, and be punished by a fine of not less than fifty dollars ($50) nor more than one hundred dollars ($100) for each and every offense.

SEC. 10. The commissioner shall provide blanks, which shall be furnished to all proprietors or managers of creameries, cheese factories, or milk dairies that ship milk to the cities, and all the venders or pedlers of milk in the cities, within the State, for the purpose of making a report of the amount of milk and dairy goods handled, and all owners or managers of such creameries and cheese factories shall, on the first (1st) day of November of each year, send to the dairy and food commissioner a full and accurate report of the amount of business done during the year, and all milk dairies, milk venders, or milk pedlers shall send to the State dairy and food commissioner quarterly reports of all the business done by each and every such person, firm, or company in handling dairy products during the last three (3) months past, as designated under the different headings of such printed blanks.

Any neglect or failure, or false statement on the part of any proprietor or manager of such creamery, cheese factory, dairy, or any milk vender or milk peddler shall be considered guilty of a misdemeanor, and be punished by a fine of not less than ten dollars ($10) nor more than one hundred dollars ($100).

Section eleven (11) of said act is hereby amended so as to read as follows:

SEC. 11. No person shall sell or offer for sale any cream taken from impure or diseased milk, or cream that contains less than twenty (20) per centum of fat. Whoever violates the provisions of this section shall be deemed guilty of a misdemeanor and shall be punished by a fine of not less than ten dollars ($10) nor more than one hundred dollars ($100).

Section twelve (12) of said act is hereby amended so as to read as follows:

SEC. 12. In all prosecutions under this act relating to the sale and manufacture of unclean, impure, unhealthy, adulterated, or unwholesome milk, if the milk be shown to contain more than eighty-seven (87) per centum of water fluids or less than thirteen (13) per centum milk solids, of which less than three and one-half ($3\frac{1}{2}$) per centum shall be fat, shall be declared adulterated, and milk drawn from cows within fifteen (15) days before and four (4) days after parturition, or from animals fed on distillery waste or brewers' malt, or any unhealthy food whatever, shall be deemed, for the purpose of this act, to be unclean, impure, unhealthy, and unwholesome milk. The penalties for any violation of this section are the same as those of section two (2) of this act. This section shall not prevent the feeding of ensilage from silos.

No person shall sell or expose for sale in any store or place of business or on any wagon or other vehicle used in transporting or selling milk from which cream has been removed, or milk commonly called "skimmed milk," without first marking the can or package containing said milk with the words "skimmed milk" in large, plain, black letters, each letter being at least one inch high and one-half inch wide. Said words to be on the top or side of said can or package, where they can be easily seen.

Whoever violates the provisions of this section shall be deemed guilty of a misdemeanor, and shall be punished by a fine of not less than twenty-five (25) nor more than one hundred (100) dollars for each and every offense.

SEC. 13. Every person who conveys milk in carriages, carts, or otherwise for the purpose of selling the same in any city or town of two thousand inhabitants or more in the State of Minnesota, shall annually, on the first day of May, or within thirty days thereafter, be licensed by the State dairy and food commissioner to sell milk within the limits of said city or town, and shall pay to the said State dairy and food commissioner the sum of one dollar ($1) each to the use of said dairy and food commission.

Licenses shall be issued only in the names of the owners of carriages, carts, or other vehicles, and shall, for the purpose of this act, be conclusive evidence of ownership. No license shall be sold, assigned, or transferred. Each license shall record the name, residence, place of business, number of carriages, carts, or other vehicles used, the name and residence of every driver, or other person engaged in selling said milk, and the number of the license. Each licensee shall, before engaging in the sale of milk, cause his name, the number of his license and his place of business to be legibly placed on each outer side of all carriages, carts, or other vehicles used by him in the conveyance and sale of milk, and he shall report to the State dairy and food commissioner any change of driver or other person employed by him which may occur during the term of his license. Whoever, without being first licensed under the provisions of this section, sells milk, or exposes it for sale from carriages, carts, or other vehicles, or has it in his custody or possession with intent to sell, and whoever violates any of the provisions of this section, shall, for the first offense, be punished by a fine of not less than ten dollars ($10) nor more than fifty dollars ($50). For a second offense by a fine of not less than fifty dollars ($50) nor more than one hundred dollars ($100), and for a subsequent offense by fine of fifty dollars and imprisonment in the county jail for not less than thirty (30) nor more than sixty (60) days.

SEC. 14. Every person, before selling milk, or offering it for sale in a store, booth, stand, or market place, in the respective towns or cities, as designated in this act shall procure a license from the State dairy and food commissioner or his authorized agents, and shall pay to said commissioner or his agents the sum of one dollar ($1). And whoever neglects to procure said license shall be deemed guilty of a misdemeanor and shall be punished for each offense by a fine not exceeding twenty-five dollars ($25).

SEC. 15. That all moneys received as license fees, or from the sale of any and all goods confiscated by the State dairy and food commissioner under said act shall be received and disbursed the same as money appropriated for the use of said dairy and food commission.

SEC. 16. The having in possession by any person or firm of any articles or substances prohibited by this act shall be considered *prima facie* evidence that the same is kept by such person or firm in violation of the provisions of this act, and the commissioner shall be authorized to seize upon and take possession of such articles or substances, and upon the order of any court which has jurisdiction under this act he shall sell the same for any purpose other than to be used for food, the proceeds to be placed to the credit of the State dairy and food commissioners' fund.

Section seventeen (17) of said act is hereby amended so as to read as follows:

SEC. 17. The district and municipal courts and all justices of the peace of this State shall have jurisdiction of all cases arising under this act, and their jurisdiction is hereby extended so as to enable them to enforce the penalties imposed by any or all of the sections hereof.

Section eighteen (18) of said act is hereby amended so as to read as follows:

SEC. 18. In all prosecutions under this act the cost thereof shall be paid in the manner now provided by law, and the rest paid to the credit of the State dairy and food commissioners' fund.

SEC. 19. All acts and parts of acts now in force and inconsistent with this act are hereby repealed.

SEC. 20. This act shall take effect and be in force from and after its passage.

Approved April 20, 1889.

IMITATION BUTTER.

CHAP. 11, GENERAL LAWS OF 1891. (S. F., NO. 467.)

AN ACT relating to the sale of imitation butter.

Be it enacted by the legislature of the State of Minnesota, Whoever, by himself or his agent, shall sell, expose for sale, or have in his possession with intent to sell, any article or compound made in imitation of butter or as a substitute for butter, and not wholly made from milk or cream, and that is of any other color than bright pink, shall be subject to the payment of a penalty of fifty (50) dollars, and for a second and each subsequent offense, a penalty of one hundred (100) dollars, to be recovered with costs in any court in this State of competent jurisdiction.

SEC. 2. Samples or specimens of any articles in imitation of butter, suspected of being of a spurious character, shall be analyzed or otherwise satisfactorily tested as to color and compounds; and a certificate of the analysis, sworn to by the analyzer, shall be admissible as evidence in all prosecutions under this act.

SEC. 3. The having in possession by any person or firm of any articles or substance prohibited by this act shall be considered *prima facie* evidence that the same is kept by such person or firm in violation of the provisions of this act, and the State dairy and food commissioner shall be authorized to seize upon and take possession of such article or substance, and upon the order of any court which has jurisdiction under this act he shall sell the same for any purpose other than to be used for food ; the proceeds derived from fines and the sale of imitation butter shall be paid into the State treasury to be placed to the credit of the State dairy and food commissioner's fund.

SEC. 4. For the purpose of this act the term butter shall be understood to mean the product usually known by that name, and which is manufactured exclusively from milk or cream or both.

SEC. 5. This act shall take effect and be in force from and after its passage.

Approved April 21, 1891.

CHAP. 141. (S. F., NO. 657½.)

AN ACT to prevent fraud in dairy products and to preserve health.

Be it enacted by the legislature of the State of Minnesota, Any person or firm who shall make or manufacture imitation butter, or butter made of part cream and part caseine and other ingredients under what is known as the "Quinness patent" or process, or any other similar process, whereby the caseine of milk and other ingredients are made to imitate and resemble genuine butter made from cream, shall stamp each package of the same on the top and sides with lampblack and oil, the words "patent butter" in letters at least one-fourth (¼) of an inch wide and one-half (½) of an inch long.

Whoever violates the provisions of this section is guilty of a misdemeanor, and shall be punished for each offense by a fine of not less than twenty-five ($25) dollars nor more than one hundred ($100) dollars.

SEC. 2. Whoever sells or offers for sale any imitation or patent butter, as described in section one (1) of this act, shall give to each purchaser of said goods a printed card stating correctly the different ingredients contained in the said compound.

Whoever violates the provisions of this section is guilty of a misdemeanor, and shall be punished for each offense by a fine of not less than twenty-five ($25) dollars nor more than one hundred ($100) dollars.

SEC. 3. This act shall take effect on and after its passage.

Approved March 7, 1887.

FOOD LAWS.

CHAP. 12, GENERAL LAWS OF 1891.   (H. F., No. 1237.)

AN ACT in relation to the manufacture and sale of lard and of lard compounds and substitutes, and of food prepared therefrom, to prevent fraud and to preserve the public health.

Be it enacted by the legislature of the State of Minnesota, No person shall within this State manufacture for sale, have in his possession with intent to sell, offer or expose for sale, or sell, as lard, any substance not the legitimate and exclusive product of the fat of the hog.

SEC. 2. Every person who manufactures for sale within this State, has in his possession with intent to sell, offers or exposes for sale, or sells, as lard, or as a substitute for lard, or an imitation of lard, any mixture or compound which is designed to take the place of lard and which is made from animal or vegetable oils or fats, or any mixture or compound consisting in part of lard in mixture or combination with animal or vegetable oils or fats, unless the same shall be branded or labeled as hereinafter required and directed, shall be guilty of a misdemeanor and shall upon conviction be subject to the penalties hereinafter provided in this act. ·

SEC. 3. Every person who manufactures for sale, has in his possession with intent to sell, offers or exposes for sale or sells, any substance made in the semblance of lard, or as an imitation of lard, or a substitute for lard, and which is designed to take the place of lard, and which consists of any mixture or compound of animal or vegetable oils or fats other than hog fat in the form of lard, shall cause the tierce, barrel, tub, pail, or package containing the same to be distinctly and legibly branded or labeled in letters not less than one (1) inch in length with the name of the person or firm making the same, together with the location of the manufactory, and the words "Lard Substitute," and immediately following the same, in letters not less than one-half ($\frac{1}{2}$) inch in length, with the names and approximate proportions of the several constituents which are contained in the mixture or compound.

SEC. 4. Every person who manufactures for sale, has in his possession with intent to sell, offers or exposes for sale, or sells any substance made in the semblance of lard, or as an imitation of lard, or as a substitute for lard, and which is designed to take the place of lard and which consists of any mixture or compound of lard with animal or vegetable oils or fats, shall cause the tierce, barrel, tub, pail, or package containing the same to be distinctly and legibly branded or labeled in letters not less than one (1) inch in length, with the name of the person or firm making the same, together with the location of the manufactory, and the words "Adulterated Lard," and immediately following the same, in letters not less than one-half ($\frac{1}{2}$) inch in length, with the names and approximate proportions of the several constituents which are contained in the mixture or compound.

SEC. 5. Every dealer or trader who, by himself or his agent, or as the servant or agent of another person, offers or exposes for sale or sells any form of lard substitute or adulterated lard as hereinbefore defined, shall securely affix or cause to be affixed to the package wherein the same is contained, offered for sale, or sold, a label, upon the outside and face of which is distinctly and legibly printed, in letters not less than one-half ($\frac{1}{2}$) inch in length, the words "Lard Substitute" or "Adulterated Lard," and immediatley following the same, in letters not smaller than long primer, the name and approximate proportions of the several constituents which are contained in the mixture or compound, and shall furnish to the purchaser at the time of sale a card, upon which is distinctly and legibly printed the name of the article as hereinbefore defined, and a list of the several components of the mixture.

SEC. 6. Every person who manufactures for sale, or who offers or exposes for sale or sells, or who serves to guests as keeper of hotel, restaurant, dining-room, or in any other capacity, articles of food which have been prepared, either wholly or in part, with lard substitutes, or adulterated lard as hereinbefore defined, shall at the time of sale furnish to the purchaser a card upon which is distinctly and legibly printed the words, "This food is prepared with lard substitute (or adulterated lard)," or in case no bill of fare is provided, there shall be kept constantly posted upon each of the sides of the dining-room, in a conspicuous position, cards upon the face of which is distinctly and legibly printed in the English language, and in letters of sufficient size to be visible from all parts of the room the words: "Lard substitute (or adulterated lard) is used in the preparation of the food served here."

SEC. 7. The having in possession of any lard substitute or adulterated lard, as hereinbefore defined, which is not branded or labeled as hereinbefore required and directed upon the part of any dealer or trader, keeper of hotel, restaurant, bakery, or person engaged in the public sale of such articles or of food prepared therefrom, shall for the purpose of this act be deemed *prima facie* evidence of intent to sell the same or to use the same in an illegal manner.

SEC. 8. The district and municipal courts and justices of the peace of this State shall have jurisdiction of all cases arising under this act, and their jurisdiction is hereby extended so as to enable them to enforce the penalties imposed by this act.

SEC. 9. It shall be the duty of the State dairy and food commissioner and his assistants, experts, chemists, and agents by him appointed to enforce the provisions of this act. The said commissioner is hereby authorized and empowered to employ such experts and chemists as may be deemed by him necessary for the proper enforcement of the law, their compensation to be fixed by the commissioner. All charges, accounts, and expenses authorized by this act shall be paid by the State treasurer upon a warrant drawn by the State auditor.

SEC. 10. The said commissioner and assistant commissioners, experts, chemists, and others by him appointed, shall have access, ingress, and egress to all places of business, factories, and buildings where the same is manufactured or kept for sale; they shall also have power and authority to open any package, car, or vessel containing such articles which may be manufactured, sold, or exposed for sale in violation of the provisions of this act, and may inspect the contents therein and take samples therefrom for analysis. All clerks, bookkeepers, express agents, railroad officials, employés, or common carriers, shall render them all the assistance in their power, when so requested, in tracing, finding, or discovering the presence of any prohibited article named in this act. Any refusal or neglect on the part of such clerk, bookkeeper, express agent, railroad officials, employés, or common carriers to render such friendly aid shall be deemed a misdemeanor and be punished by a fine of not less than twenty-five (25) dollars or more than fifty (50) dollars for each and every offense.

SEC. 11. In all prosecutions under this act the costs thereof shall be paid in the manner now provided by law, and such fine shall be paid into the State treasury, and placed to the credit of the State dairy and food commissioner's fund.

SEC. 12. Any person violating any of the provisions of this act shall be deemed to be guilty of a misdemeanor, and upon conviction shall be punished by a fine of not less than twenty-five (25) dollars or more than one hundred (100) dollars and costs for each offense, or by imprisonment in the county jail for not less than thirty (30) days or more than ninety (90) days.

SEC. 13. All acts and parts of acts inconsistent with this act are hereby repealed.

SEC. 14. This act shall take effect and be in force from and after its passage.

Approved April 20, A. D. 1891.

AN ACT to amend chapter seven (7) of the General Laws of one thousand eight hundred and eighty-nine (1889), an act entitled "An act in relation to the manufacture and sale of baking powders, sugars and syrups, vinegars, lard, spirituous and malt liquors, to prevent fraud, and to preserve the public health."   Approved April 24, A. D. 1889.

Be it enacted by the legislature of the State of Minnesota, Every person who manufactures for sale within this State, or offers or exposes for sale, or sells any baking powder, or any mixture or compound intended for use as a baking powder, under any name or title whatsoever, which shall contain, as may appear by the proper tests, any alum, in any form or shape, unless the same be labeled, as hereinafter required and directed, shall be deemed guilty of a misdemeanor, and upon conviction, shall, for each offense, be punished by a fine not less than twenty-five ($25), or more than one hundred dollars ($100) and;costs, or by imprisonment in the county jail not exceeding thirty days.

Sec. 2. Every person making or manufacturing baking powder, or any mixture or compound intended for use as a baking powder, which contains alum in any form or shape, shall securely affix, or cause to be securely affixed, to every box, can, or package containing such baking powder or like mixture or compound, a label, upon the outside and face of which is distinctly printed in legible type, no smaller than "brevier heavy gothic caps," the name and residence of the manufacturer, and the following words: "This baking powder contains alum." Any person violating the provisions of this section shall be deemed guilty of a misdemeanor, and shall, for each offense, be punished by a fine not less than twenty-five ($25) or more than one hundred ($100) dollars and costs, or by imprisonment in the county jail not to exceed thirty days.

Sec. 3. The having in possession by any person or firm of any of the articles or substances hereinbefore described, and not labeled, as provided by section two (2) of this act, shall be considered *prima facie* evidence that the same is kept by such person or firm in violation of the provisions of this act, and the State dairy and food commissioner, his assistants, experts, and chemists, or any one thereof, are hereby authorized to seize upon and take possession of such articles or substances, and upon the order of any court which has jurisdiction under this act, he shall sell the same, giving full notice of the time of such sale, and of the fact that such compound or substances contain alum, and the proceeds of such sale shall be placed to the credit of the State dairy and food commissioner's fund.

Sec. 4. The district and municipal courts and justices of the peace of this State shall have jurisdiction of all cases arising under this act, and their jurisdiction is hereby extended so as to enable them to enforce penalties imposed by any or all of the sections hereof.

Sec. 5. In all prosecutions under this act, the costs thereof shall be paid in the manner now provided by law, and such fine shall be placed to the credit of the State dairy and food commissioner's fund.

Sec. 8. Every person who manufactures for sale, or offers or exposes for sale, as cider vinegar, any vinegar not the legitimate product of pure apple juice, known as apple cider, or vinegar not made exclusively of said apple cider, or vinegar into which foreign substances, drugs, or acids have been introduced, as may appear by proper tests, shall be deemed guilty of a misdemeanor, and for each offense be punishable by fine of not less than twenty-five, or more than one hundred dollars and costs.

Sec. 9. Every person who manufactures for sale or offers for sale any vinegar, found upon proper tests to contain any preparation of lead, copper, sulphuric acid, or other ingredient injurious to health, shall be deemed guilty of a misdemeanor, and for such offense shall be punished by a fine of not less than ten (10) dollars nor more than one hundred (100) dollars and costs.

SEC. 10. No person, by himself, his servant, or agent, or as the servant or agent of any other person, shall sell, exchange, deliver, or have in his custody or possession, with intent to sell or exchange, or expose or offer for sale or exchange, any adulterated vinegar, or label, brand, or sell as cider vinegar, or as apple vinegar, any vinegar not the legitimate product of pure apple juice, or not made exclusively from apple cider.

SEC. 11. All vinegar shall have an acidity equivalent to the presence of not less than four and one-half per cent by weight of absolute acetic acid, and in case of cider vinegar shall contain in addition not less than two per cent by weight of cider vinegar solids upon full evaporation over boiling water, and if any vinegar contains any artificial coloring matter, or less than the above acidity, or, in the case of cider vinegar, if it contains less than the above amount of acidity or of cider vinegar solids, it shall be deemed to be adulterated within the meaning of this act. All manufacturers of vinegar in the State of Minnesota, and all persons who reduce or rebarrel vinegar in this State, and all persons who handle vinegar in lots of one barrel or more, are hereby required to stencil or mark in black figures at least one inch in length, on the head of each barrel of vinegar bought or sold by them, the kind of vinegar contained in each package or barrel, together with the name of the manufacturer and location of the factory where the same is made, and the standard strength of the vinegar contained in the package or barrel, which latter shall be denoted by the number of grains of pure bicarbonate of potash required to neutralize one fluid ounce of vinegar. And any neglect so to mark or stencil each package or barrel, or any false marking of packages or barrels, shall be deemed a misdemeanor, and shall be punished by a fine of not less than twenty-five (25) dollars nor more than one hundred (100) dollars and costs.

SEC. 12. Whoever violates any of the provisions of this act shall be deemed guilty of a misdemeanor and shall be punished by a fine of not less than ten (10) dollars nor more than fifty (50) dollars and costs.

SEC. 13. Whoever adulterates, for the purpose of sale, lard with cotton-seed oil, or other vegetable oils, or terra alba or any substance injurious to health, or whoever barters or gives away or sells, or has in possession with intent to sell, any substance intended for food, which has been adulterated with cotton-seed oil, terra alba, or any other substance injurious to health, shall be deemed guilty of a misdemeanor and shall be punished by a fine of not less than twenty-five dollars ($25) or more than one hundred dollars ($100) and costs for each offense.

SEC. 14. The having in possession of any adulterated lard, by any dealer or trader, shall for the purpose of this act be deemed *prima facie* evidence of intent to sell the same.

SEC. 15. No person shall within this State manufacture, brew, distill, have or offer for sale, or sell any spirituous or fermented or malt liquors containing any substance or ingredient not normal or healthful to exist in spirituous, fermented, or malt liquors, or which may be deleterious or detrimental to health when such liquors are used as a beverage; and any person violating any of the provisions of this act shall be deemed guilty of a misdemeanor, and upon conviction thereof shall be fined not less than twenty-five dollars ($25) or more than one hundred dollars ($100) and costs for the first offense, and by a fine of not less than fifty dollars ($50) or more than one hundred dollars ($100) and costs, or imprisonment of not less than thirty or more than ninety days, or by both such fine and imprisonment for each subsequent offense.

SEC. 16. It shall be the duty of the State dairy and food commissioner and his assistants, experts, and chemists by him appointed to enforce the provisions of this act. The said commissioner is hereby authorized and empowered to employ such experts and chemists as may be deemed by him necessary for the proper enforcement of this law, their compensation to be fixed by the commissioner. All charges, accounts, and expenses authorized by this act shall be paid by the State treasurer upon a warrant drawn by the State auditor.

SEC. 17. The said commissioner and assistant commissioner, and such experts and chemists as they shall duly authorize for the purpose, shall have access, ingress, and egress to all places of business, factories, and buildings where the same is manufactured or kept for sale, cases or vessels used in the manufacture and sale of any spirituous, fermented, or malt liquors, or any imitation thereof, or any of the substances or articles mentioned in this act. They shall also have power and authority to open any package, car, or vessel containing such articles which may be manufactured, sold, or exposed for sale in violation of the provisions of this act, and may inspect the contents therein, and may take samples therefrom for analysis. All clerks, bookkeepers, express agents, railroad officials, employés, or common carriers shall render to them all the assistance in their power, when so requested, in tracing, finding or discovering the presence of any prohibited article named in this act. Any refusal or neglect on the part of such clerks, bookkeepers, express agents, railroad officials, employés, or common carriers to render such friendly aid shall be deemed a misdemeanor and be punished by a fine not less than fifty dollars ($50) or more than one hundred dollars ($100) for each and every offense.

SEC. 18. The salary of the chemists shall not exceed two thousand dollars ($2,000) annually.

SEC. 19. This act shall take effect and be in force from and after August 1st, A. D. 1889.

Approved April 24th, 1889.

Approved as amended April 20th, 1891.

NEW HAMPSHIRE.

AN ACT to prevent the sale of adulterated foods, drugs, and other articles

SECTION 1. No person shall sell or offer for sale any adulterated drug or substance to be used in the manner of medicine taken internally or applied externally, or any adulterated article of food or substance to be used in the manner of food or drink.

SEC. 2. If any drug or substance used for medicine sold under a name recognized by the United States Pharmacopœia, or under a name not recognized in that work, but found in some other pharmacopœia or other standard work of materia medica, differs materially from the standard of strength, quality, or purity laid down in such work, or contains less of the active principle than is contained in the genuine article, weight for weight, or falls below the professed standard under which it is sold, it shall be deemed to be adulterated within the meaning of this act.

SEC. 3. If any food or substance to be eaten or used in the manner of food or drink contains a less quantity of any valuable constituent that is contained in the genuine article, weight for weight, or contains any substance foreign to the well-known article under whose name it is sold, or is colored, coated, polished, or powdered, whereby damage is concealed, or contains any added poisonous ingredient, or consists wholly or partly of any decomposed, putrid, or diseased substance, whether manufactured or not, or has become offensive or injured from age or improper care, it shall be deemed to be adulterated within the meaning of this act.

SEC. 4. Whoever fraudulently adulterates for the purpose of sale any article of food, drink, drug, or medicine, or knowingly sells any fraudulently adulterated article of food or drink, drug or medicine, or any kind of diseased or unwholesome provisions, as defined in this act, shall be imprisoned not exceeding one year or be fined not exceeding four hundred dollars, to be recovered by indictment for use of the county in which the offence was committed.

SEC. 5. The State board of health shall take cognizance of the interests of the public health relating to the sale of drugs and foods, and the adulteration of the same, and shall make all necessary investigations and inquiries in reference thereto, and the analytical work required under the provisions of this act shall be made by the United States Experimental Station and New Hampshire College of Agriculture and the Mechanic Arts,

SEC. 6. Every person offering or exposing for sale any drug or article of food within the meaning of this act shall furnish to any analyst or other officer duly appointed for the purpose, who shall apply to him for the same and tender him its value in money, a sample sufficient for the purpose of the analysis of any such drug or article of food which is in his possession.

SEC. 7. Any person who has reason to doubt the purity or genuineness of any article of food which he has purchased may send at his own expense a sealed sample of it to the State board of health for inspection. If upon examination the article appears to be adulterated, said board of health may obtain a certified sample of it by whatever way seems best to them, and should this sample prove to be adulterated the board shall begin proceedings at once against the vendor of the article.

SEC. 8. Whoever hinders, obstructs, or in any way interferes with any inspector, analyst, or other officer appointed hereunder in the performance of his duty, shall be punished by fine not exceeding fifty dollars for the first offence and one hundred dollars for each subsequent offence.

SEC. 9. Before commencing the analysis of any sample the analyst shall reserve a portion, which shall be sealed, and in case of a complaint against any person part of the reserved portion of the sample alleged to be adulterated shall, upon application, be delivered to the defendant or his attorney, and part of the reserved portion of the sample shall be delivered to the secretary of the State board of health.

SEC. 10. The State board of health shall adopt such measures as it may deem necessary to facilitate the enforcement of this act, and for the collecting and examining of drugs and foods, articles of clothing, fabrics, wall paper, or anything containing poisonous pigments or substances whereby the health of any person wearing or using the same may be injured.

SEC. 11. Said board of health shall report annually to the governor and council the number and kinds of samples examined, together with the results of such examination, the number of prosecutions made under this act, and an itemized account of all money expended in carrying out the provisions thereof.

SEC. 12. All acts and parts of acts inconsistent with this act are hereby repealed, and this act shall take effect upon its passage.

Approved April 7, 1891.

NEW JERSEY.

OLEOMARGARINE, FOOD, AND DRUGS.

AN ACT to prevent deception in the sale of oleomargarine, butterine, or any imitation of dairy products, and to preserve the public health.

1. *Be it enacted by the senate and general assembly of the State of New Jersey,* That no person shall offer or expose for sale, or sell, or have in possession for the purposes of sale, any oleomargarine or butterine or suine, or any substance in imitation or semblance of natural butter or cheese, or any substance that is rendered, made, manufactured, or compounded out of any animal or vegetable or mineral fat or oil not produced from pure milk or cream from pure milk, unless contained in or sold out of or in tubs, pails, firkins, vessels, or other packages marked and labeled as required by section three of this act.

2. That no person shall offer or expose for sale or sell, or have in possession for the purposes of sale, any mixture or compound of natural butter or cheese with oleomargarine, butterine, suine, or any animal or vegetable or mineral fat or oil, or any substance not the product of pure milk or cream from pure milk, except such mixture or compound shall be sold out of or in or contained in tubs, firkins, pails, vessels or packages marked or labeled as required by section three of this act.

3. That no oleomargarine, butterine, or suine, or any substance or compound or mixture in imitation or semblance of natural butter or cheese, or any substance that

is rendered, made, manufactured, or compounded out of animal or vegetable or mineral fat or oil not the product of pure milk or cream from pure milk, shall be sold or exposed or offered for sale, or held in possession for the purposes of sale, except when contained in tubs, pails, boxes, firkins, vessels, or other packages that are marked or labeled as follows, to wit, every such tub, pail, box, firkin, or other vessel or package shall have painted on the outside thereof and midway between the top and bottom thereof, a stripe or band, at least three inches wide, and extending completely around said vessel or package, and said stripe or band shall be painted with black paint; every such vessel or package shall have legibly branded and burnt in, by means of a branding or burning iron, on the outside of the cover and on the outside of said vessel or package, in two places as nearly opposite each other as possible, the words "oleomargarine," "butterine," "suine," or "imitation butter," or "imitation cheese," as the case may be, and said name or title shall be composed of Roman letters at least one-half an inch high and at least one-quarter of an inch broad, and said name or title shall be at least ten inches long; and every such tub, pail, box, firkin, or other vessel or package shall bear a label or shall have branded on it a mark giving the name and address of the maker of the contents thereof, and the name and location of the manufactory.

4. That no person shall sell any oleomargarine, butterine, suine, or any substance in imitation or semblance of natural butter or cheese, or any substance that is rendered, made, manufactured, or compounded out of any animal or vegetable or mineral fat or oil not produced from pure milk, or the cream from pure milk, at retail or in quantities less than the original tub, firkin, or other package, unless he shall first inform the purchaser that the substance is not natural butter or cheese, but is imitation butter or cheese, and at the time of sale and with each sale he shall give to the purchaser a card or notice printed on which shall be the name of the substance sold and the name and address of the seller or vendor, and said notice or card shall be at least six inches long, and at least four inches wide, and the printing thereon shall be in letters at least of the size known as two-line English, and said notice or card shall be printed in black and in the English language.

5. That no person shall offer or expose for sale, or sell, or have in possession for the purposes of sale, any oleomargarine, butterine, suine, or any substance in imitation of natural butter or cheese, or any substance that is rendered, made, manufactured, or compounded out of any animal or vegetable or mineral fat or oil not produced from pure milk or cream from pure milk, that is colored, stained, or mixed with annatto or any other coloring matter or substance.

6. That for the purposes of this act the terms "natural butter," or "natural butter or cheese," shall be taken to mean the product or products usually known by these names, and which are made and manufactured exclusively from milk or cream, or both, with salt or salt and rennet, and with or without coloring matter or sage; and the terms "oleomargarine," "butterine," "suine," or "substance in imitation or semblance of natural butter or cheese," shall be to mean any substance that is rendered, made, manufactured, or compounded out of any animal or vegetable or mineral oil or fat, not the product of pure milk or the cream from pure milk; also, any compound or mixture of natural butter or cheese, or milk or cream, with any of these substances not milk or cream.

7. That the possession by any person who is either manufacturer, merchant, broker, wholesale or retail dealer, or a hotel, inn, restaurant, or boarding-house keeper, of any oleaginous substance, mixture, or compound whatever as defined by this act, not natural butter, that is not contained in a tub, box, pail, or vessel, plainly marked and branded in accordance with the provisions of section three of this act, shall be prima facie evidence of intent to sell the same.

8. That no person shall in any way or manner erase, cancel, or obliterate, deface, or cover over or remove either the band or stripe of paint, or the brands required by section three of this act to be placed on the tub, box, pail, or vessel containing any loeaginous substance, mixture, or compound as defined by this act.

9. That every person who shall violate any of the provisions of this act shall be liable to a penalty of one hundred dollars for the first offense and two hundred dollars for each second or subsequent offense.

10. That every district court in any city, and every justice of the peace in any county, and any recorder in any city, is hereby empowered on oath or affirmation made according to law that any person or persons has or have violated any provision of this act, to issue process at the suit of the commissioner herein named as plaintiff for the use of the State of New Jersey, either in the manner of a summons or warrant, against the person or persons so charged, which process shall, when in the nature of a warrant, be returnable forthwith, and when in the nature of a summons, shall be returnable in not less than one nor more than ten entire days; such process shall state what provision of the law is alleged to have been violated by the defendant or defendants; and on the return of such process, or at any time to which the trial shall have been adjourned, the said court, justice of the peace, or recorder shall proceed to hear testimony and to determine and give judgment in the matter, without the filing of any pleadings, for the plaintiff, for the recovery of such penalty, with costs, or for the defendant; and the said court, justice of the peace, or recorder shall, if judgment be rendered for the plaintiff, forthwith issue execution against the goods and chattels and person of the defendant or defendants; and the said court, justice of the peace, or recorder is further empowered to cause any such defendant who may refuse or neglect to pay the amount of the judgment rendered against him, and all the costs and charges incident thereto, unless an appeal is granted, to be committed to the county jail for any period not exceeding ninety days.

11. That the officers to serve and execute all process under this act shall be the officers authorized to serve and execute process in said courts, and before such magistrates and officers as aforesaid, including the constables of such counties and all police officers of such cities.

12. That said district court, justice of the peace, or recorder shall have power to adjourn the hearing or trial in any case, from time to time, not exceeding thirty days from the return of the summons or warrant, and to bail the person so charged in such sum as he may deem proper for his appearance at such time and place as said trial or hearing shall be adjourned to, and in default of bail to commit the person so charged to the common jail of said county, to be there detained until the trial or hearing of the charge.

13. That either the complainant or defendant, upon paying all costs incurred and by filing with said district court, justice, or recorder, within ten days after trial before him, a written notice of his or her intention to appeal from the decision of said court, justice, or recorder, may appeal to the next court of general quarter sessions of the peace of the county in which said complaint may have been determined, and said court of general quarter sessions shall proceed and try the same and make such adjudications as are herein provided in case of such trial before said district court, justice, or recorder.

14. That all penalties imposed under this act shall be, immediately on receipt, paid into the treasury of this State by the commissioner.

15. That the State board of health shall appoint a commissioner, who shall be known as the State dairy commissioner, who shall be a citizen of this State, and who shall hold his office for the term of three years and until his successor shall be appointed, and said commissioner shall be paid a salary of two thousand dollars per annum and his traveling and other expenses, payable by the treasurer of this State on warrant of the comptroller, in quarterly payments; and said commissioner shall be appointed within fifteen days after the passage of this act, and shall be charged with the enforcement of the various provisions thereof; and said commissioner may be removed for just cause by the appointing power conferred by the act: *Provided*, That charges shall be first made in writing and he be given time to reply thereto; and the said commissioner shall make annual reports to the legislature not later than the fifteenth day of January in each year, and also to the State board of health at its

annual meeting; and said commissioner is hereby authorized and empowered to appoint or employ such assistants, chemists, agents, clerks, and counsel as may be deemed necessary for the proper enforcement of this act, their compensation to be fixed by the commissioner.

16. That the said commissioner shall be authorized to expend for the purposes of this act an amount not exceeding ten thousand dollars in any one year, and all expenses shall be paid by the treasurer of this State on warrant of the comptroller, upon presentation of properly certified accounts made by said commissioner, but such expenses shall not exceed in any one year the amount stated in this section.

17. That the said commissioner, and assistants, and clerks, and agents, as shall be duly commissioned so to do by the commissioner, shall have full and free access, ingress and egress, to all places of business, factories, farms, buildings, hotels, restaurants, boarding houses, carriages, cars, vessels, and cans used in the manufacture and sale of any dairy products, or any imitation thereof; they shall also have the power to open any package, can, or vessel, containing such articles which may be manufactured, sold, or exposed for sale in violation of the provisions of this act, if they have reason to believe it is being violated, and may inspect the contents therein, and may take therefrom samples for analysis.

18. That this act and each section thereof is declared to be enacted to prevent deception in the sale of oleomargarine, butterine, or any imitation of any dairy product, and to preserve the public health.

19. That an act entitled "An act for the protection of dairymen, and to prevent deception in sales of butter," approved February twenty-first, one thousand eight hundred and eighty-four, and an act entitled "An act to prohibit the manufacture and sale of impure and imitation dairy products," approved May fifth, one thousand eight hundred and eighty-four, and all acts and parts of acts inconsistent or in conflict with this act, be and the same are hereby repealed.

20. That this act shall take effect immediately.

Approved March 22, 1886.

CHAP. CL. LAWS OF 1887.

A SUPPLEMENT to an act entitled "An act to prevent deception in the sale of oleomargarine, butterine, or any imitation of dairy products, and to preserve the public health," approved March twenty-second, one thousand eight hundred and eighty-six.

1. *Be it enacted by the senate and general assembly of the State of New Jersey,* That nothing in said act shall be so construed as to permit the sale or the offering or exposing for sale, or the having in possession for the purposes of sale of any oleomargarine or butterine, or any substance in imitation of natural butter, that is, colored, stained, or mixed with annatto or any other coloring matter or substance.

2. That section four of said act be and the same is hereby amended so as to read as follows:

(4. That no person shall sell any oleomargarine, butterine, suine, or any substance in imitation or semblance of natural butter or cheese, or any substance that is rendered, made, manufactured, or compounded out of any animal or vegetable or mineral fat or oil, not produced from pure milk or the cream from pure milk, at retail or in quantities less than the original tub, firkin, or other package, unless he shall first inform the purchaser that the substance is not natural butter or cheese, but is imitation butter or cheese, and at the time of sale and with each sale he shall give to the purchaser a card or notice printed on which shall be the name of the substance sold and the name and address of the seller or vender, and nothing else shall be printed thereon unless it be the weight of the parcel; and said notice or card shall be at least six inches long and at least four inches wide, and the printing thereon shall be in letters at least of the size known as two-line English, and said notice or card shall be printed in black and in the English language, upon white paper, plainly and legibly, and shall be either upon the outside of the outer wrapper in which the

substance is delivered to the purchaser or upon a separate card or paper attached thereto; in either case the notice shall be so placed that no part thereof shall be concealed from view.)

3. That the State dairy commissioner is hereby directed and empowered to aid in the enforcement of the provisions of an act entitled "An act to prevent the adulteration of food or drugs," approved March twenty-fifth, one thousand eight hundred and eighty-one, and said commissioner and his assistants and agents are hereby clothed with the same powers as are conferred on inspectors or officers by the provisions of said act, and the expenses of such enforcement shall be paid out of the appropriation made for the purposes of the act to which this is a supplement.

4. That the State dairy commissioner may appoint the chemist or chemists, analyst or analysts required by the provisions of this act or the act to which this is a supplement, and shall fix the compensation to be paid such chemists or analysts.

5. That the conviction in prosecutions under the act to which this is a supplement shall be in the following or similar form:

STATE OF NEW JERSEY, } ss.
    County of A, }

Be it remembered, That on this —— day of ——, at —— in said county, C. D., defendant, was, by the district court of the city of J (or by the recorder, or as the case is), convicted of violating the —— section of 'An act to prevent deception in the sale of oleomargarine, butterine, or any imitation of dairy products, and to preserve the public health," approved March twenty-second, one thousand eight hundred and eighty-six, in a summary proceeding at the suit of A. B., State dairy commissioner, who sues for the use and benefit of the State of New Jersey, plaintiff, upon a complaint made by E. F.; and further, that the witnesses in said proceeding who testified for the plaintiff were (name them); and the witnesses who testified for the defendant (name them); wherefore the said court (or the recorder, or as the case is) doth hereby give judgment that the plaintiff recover of the defendant one hundred dollars penalty, and —— dollars costs of the proceeding.

The said conviction shall be signed by the judge of the district court, recorder, or other magistrate before whom the conviction is had; in case of the infliction of a penalty of two hundred dollars, the conviction shall contain a statement that it appeared that the defendant had been previously convicted of violating the said act; when an appeal is taken there shall be sent to the appellate court a copy of the complaint, summons, conviction, or judgment and notice of appeal; the costs in prosecutions under the act to which this is a supplement shall be the same as costs in the district courts in actions on contract.

6. That this act shall take effect on May first, one thousand eight hundred and eighty-seven.

Approved April 21, 1887.

MILK.

CHAP. LXXXII. LAWS OF 1882.

AN ACT to prevent the adulteration and to regulate the sale of milk.

1. *Be it enacted by the senate and general assembly of the State of New Jersey,* That every person who shall sell, or who shall offer or expose for sale, or who shall transport or carry, or who shall have in possession with intent to sell or offer for sale, any milk from which the cream or any part thereof has been removed, shall distinctly, durably, and permanently solder a label or tag of metal in a conspicuous place upon the outside of every can, vessel, or package containing such milk, and such metal label or tag shall have the words "skimmed milk" stamped, indented, or engraved thereon in letters not less than two inches in height, and such milk shall only be sold or shipped in or retailed out of a can, vessel, or package so marked.

2. That every person who shall sell, or who shall offer for sale, or who shall transport or carry for the purposes of sale, or who shall have in possession with intent to sell or offer for sale, any impure, adulterated, or unwholesome milk, and every person who shall adulterate milk, or who shall keep cows for the production of milk in a crowded or unhealthy condition, or feed the same on food that produces impure, diseased, or unwholesome milk, or shall feed cows on distillery waste, usually called swill, or upon any substance in a state of putrefaction or rottenness, or upon any substance of an unwholesome nature, shall be liable to the penalties hereinafter provided for in this act.

3. That the addition of water or any other substance or thing is hereby declared an adulteration, and milk that is obtained from animals that are fed on distillery waste, usually called "swill," or upon any substance in a state of putrefaction or rottenness, or upon any substance of an unhealthful nature, or milk that has been exposed to or contaminated by the emanations, discharges, or exhalations from persons sick with any contagious disease by which the health or life of any person may be endangered or compromised, is hereby declared to be impure and unwholesome.

4. That in all prosecutions under this act, if the milk shall be shown upon analysis by a member of the council of public analysts of this State, or the chemist of the State experiment station, to contain more than 88 per cent of watery fluids, or to contain less than 12 per cent of milk solids, such milk shall be deemed for the purposes of this act to be adulterated.

[NOTE.—Supplement of February 24th, 1887, permits the analysis to be made by any chemist appointed by the State board of health.]

5. That every person who shall violate any of the provisions of this act shall be liable to a penalty of $50 for the first offense and $100 for a second or subsequent offense.

6. That justices of the peace and recorders shall have jurisdiction to try and punish all persons for violating the provisions of this act, and the penalties prescribed in section 5 of this act, for the violations of any of the provisions of this act, may be enforced before any justice of the peace or recorder in any county where the offense is committed or where the offender is first apprehended.

7. That said justice of the peace or recorder, upon receiving due proof, made before him by an affidavit of one or more persons of the violation of any of the provisions of said act by any person or persons, is hereby authorized and required by his warrant, under his hand and seal, directed to any constable or police officer of his county, to cause such person or persons to be arrested and brought before said justice or recorder, who shall hear and determine the guilt or innocence of the person or persons so charged, and upon conviction of said person or persons, the said justice or recorder is hereby authorized and required to impose upon the offender so convicted before him the penalties prescribed for such offenses; and if any person so convicted shall fail to pay the penalties so imposed, together with the costs of the prosecution, the said justice or recorder is hereby authorized and required to commit such offender to the common jail of said county for a period of not less than ten or more than sixty days: *Provided, however,* That an analysis of condemned milk shall be made by a member of the council of public analysts of this State, or the chemist of the State experimental station.

[NOTE.—Supplements provide for a jury trial when demanded and for an analysis by chemists appointed by the State board of health.

Sec. 8 provides that a certificate of analysis shall be received as *prima facia* evidence, but as this is not legal no such course should be taken.]

9. That the State board of health is hereby empowered and directed to appoint each year a competent person, who shall act as a State inspector of milk, at a salary of $800 per annum, payable by the treasurer of this State, by warrant of the comptroller, in quarterly payments, for the purposes of this act, and in addition thereto said inspector shall be paid his actual travelling expenses while in the performance

of his duties, and actual expenses of suits and costs of analysis brought by him under this act, payable by the treasurer of this State by warrant of the comptroller; said inspector shall act until removed by said board, or until his successor is appointed, and shall make such reports to said board at such time as it may direct; said inspector, having reason to believe the provisions of this act are being violated, shall have power to open any can, vessel, or package containing milk, whether sealed, locked, or otherwise, or whether in transit or otherwise; and if upon inspection he shall find such can, vessel, or package to contain any milk which has been adulterated, or from which the cream, or any part thereof, has been removed, or which is sold, offered, or exposed for sale, or held in possession with intent to sell or offer for sale, in violation of any section of this act, said inspector is empowered and directed to take a sample of the same for analysis and put into a can, vessel, or package, to be sealed in the presence of one or more witnesses, and sent to any member of the council of public analysis or the chemist of the State experiment station, and also to condemn the same and pour the contents of such can, vessel, or package upon the ground or return the same to the consignor, and if upon analysis such milk shall prove to be adulterated, shall bring suit against the person or party so violating the law: *Provided, however*, That if upon analysis it is proved that the condemned milk is unadulterated, the State shall be liable for the value of the article destroyed, which shall be paid by the treasurer of this State by warrant of the comptroller; and said inspector is empowered to employ one or more assistants, who shall have power to inspect milk as provided by this act, said assistants to be paid not more than five dollars per day for each and every day of actual service in performance of their duties, as provided [by this act, payable by the treasurer of this State, by warrant of the comptroller.

[NOTE.—A supplement provides that the analysis may be made by any chemist appointed by the State board of health.]

10. That all penalties imposed shall be paid into the treasury of this State, except in case the local board of health of any city, borough, town, or township shall prosecute the offender, in which case the penalties shall be paid into the treasury of the city, borough, town, or township so prosecuting: *Provided*, That in prosecutions by the executive office of any local board of health no expense shall be incurred to the State.

[NOTE.—Sec. 11 repeals all former laws.]

Approved March 14, 1882.

CHAP. XC. LAWS OF 1884.

A SUPPLEMENT to an act entitled "An act to prevent the adulteration and to regulate the sale of milk," approved March fourteenth, one thousand eight hundred and eighty-two.

1. *Be it enacted by the senate and general assembly of the State of New Jersey*, That any time previous to the hearing of a complaint against any person under the provisions of the aforesaid act, either party may appear before the justice or recorder and demand a trial by jury; whereupon the said justice or recorder shall issue a venire facias to summon a jury of twelve men qualified by law to act as jurors, to try said complaint.

2. That in case the said jury find such person or persons guilty, then the said justice or recorder shall proceed as though he had determined such complaint without a jury; and in case such jury shall find such person or persons not guilty, the said justice or recorder shall enter judgment in his, her, or their favor accordingly, with costs.

3. That either party upon paying all costs incurred and by filing with said justice or recorder within ten days after the trial before him a written notice of his or her intentions to appeal from the decision of said justice, or recorder, or jury, may appeal to the next court of general quarter sessions of the peace of the county in which such complaint was made and determined.

4. That either party on appeal may demand a trial by jury, and said court of general quarter sessions shall proceed and try the same and make such adjudications as are herein provided in case of such trial before said justice or recorder.

[NOTE.--Sec 5 repeals conflicting sections in previous laws.]

CHAP. CLXXXVI. LAWS OF 1886.

A SUPPLEMENT to an act entitled "An act to prevent the adulteration and to regulate the sale of milk," approved March fourteenth, one thousand eight hundred and eighty-two.

[NOTE.—By this act the State dairy commissioner is invested with the powers and duties of the milk inspector.]

CHAP. II. LAWS OF 1887.

A SUPPLEMENT to an act entitled "An act to prevent the adulteration and regulate the sale of milk," approved March fourteenth, one thousand eight hundred and eighty-two.

1. *Be it enacted by the senate and general assembly of the State of New Jersey,* That the analysis of milk required by the provisions of sections four, seven, eight, and nine of the act to which this is a supplement may be made by any chemist or chemists appointed or designated by the State board of health, the provisions of said act to the contrary notwithstanding.

Approved, February 24th, 1887.

CHAP. CLXXXV. LAWS OF 1885.

AN ACT to prohibit the sale of adulterated and skimmed milk in the cities in this State.

1. *Be it enacted by the senate and general assembly of the State of New Jersey,* That no milk which has been watered, adulterated, or changed in any respect by the addition of water, or other substance, or by the removal of cream, or any part thereof, shall be kept or offered for sale in any city of the first class in this State.

[NOTE.—Sec. 2 provides that persons violating this law are liable to the same penalties as provided in the laws given above.]

FOOD AND DRUGS.

AN ACT to prevent the adulteration of food or drugs. Approved March 25th, 1881.

[NOTE.—Sec. 1 amended by supplement, which is given below.]

2. That the term "food," as used in this act, shall include every article used for food or drink by man, and that the term "drug," as used in this act, shall include all medicines for internal or external use.

3. That any article shall be deemed to be adulterated, within the meaning of this act:

(a)—*In the case of drugs.*

First. If when sold under or by a name recognized in the United States pharmacopœia, it differs from the standard of strength, quality, or purity laid down therein;

Second. If when sold under or by a name not recognized in the United States pharmacopœia, but which is found in some other pharmacopœia, or other standard work on materia medica it differs materially from the standard of strength, quality, or purity laid down in such work;

Third. If its strength or purity fall below the professed standard under which it is sold;

(b)—*In the case of food or drink.*

First. If any substance or substances has or have been mixed with it, so as to reduce or lower, or injuriously affect, its quality or strength ;

Second. If any inferior or cheaper substance or substances have been substituted wholly or in part for the article ;

Third. If any valuable constituent of the article has been wholly or in part abstracted ;

Fourth. If it be an imitation of or be sold under the name of another article ;

Fifth. If it consist wholly or in part of a diseased or decomposed or putrid or rotten animal or vegetable substance, whether manufactured or not ; or, in case of milk, if it is the produce of a diseased animal ;

Sixth. If it be colored or coated, or polished, or powdered, whereby damage is concealded, or it is made to appear better than it really is, or of greater value ;

Seventh. If it contain any added poisonous ingredient or any ingredient which may render such article injurious to the health of a person consuming it : *Provided,* That the State board of health may, with the approval of the governor, from time to time declare certain articles or preparations to be exempt from the provisions of this act : *And provided further,* That the provisions of this act shall not apply to mixtures or compounds recognized as ordinary articles of food : *Provided,* That the same are not injurious to health and that the articles are distinctly labeled as a mixture.

4. That the State board of health shall, from time to time, fix the limits of variability permissible in any article of food, or drug, or compound the standard of which is not established by any national pharmacopœia.

[NOTE—Sec. 5 amended by supplement.]

6. That every person selling, or offering or exposing any article of food or drugs for sale, or delivering any article to purchasers, shall be bound to serve or supply any inspector appointed under this act, who shall apply to him for that purpose, and on his tendering the value of the same for a sample sufficient for the purpose of analysis of any article which is included in this act and which is in the possession of the person selling, under a penalty not exceeding fifty dollars for a first offence, and one hundred for a subsequent offence.

[NOTE.—Sec. 7 amended by supplement.]

8. That any acts or parts of acts inconsistent with the provisions of this act are hereby repealed.

A SUPPLEMENT to an act entitled "An act to prevent the adulteration of food or drugs, "approved March twenty-fifth, one thousand eight hundred and eighty-one.

1. *Be it enacted by the senate and general assembly of the State of New Jersey,* That section one of the act to which this is a supplement be amended so as to read as follows :

1. That no person shall manufacture, have, offer for sale, or sell any article of food or drugs which is adulterated within the meaning of this act, and any person violating any of the provisions of this act shall be liable to a penalty of fifty dollars for the first offence and one hundred dollars for a second or any subsequent offence.

2. That section 5 of the act to which this is a supplement be amended so as to read as follows :

5. That the State board shall take cognizance of the interest of the public health as it relates to the sale of foods and drugs, and the adulteration of the same, and make all necessary inquiries and investigations relating thereto ; it shall also have the appointment and supervision of public analysts and chemists or inspectors to serve for general service, or for such special service or length of time as it may deem necessary ; and the board of health shall from time to time meet and adopt such measures as it may deem necessary for the enforcement of this act and of the act to which it is

a supplement, and prepare rules and regulations with regard to the proper method of collecting and examining articles of food or drugs; and the analysts, chemists, or inspectors appointed may act singly or as associated in a council for such time as may be approved or authorized by said board.

3. That section seven of the act to which this is a supplement be amended so as to read as follows:

7. That any person violating any of the provisions of this act, and any person who shall hinder, impede, obstruct, or otherwise prevent any analyst, inspector, or prosecuting officer in the performance of his duty shall be liable to a penalty of fifty dollars for the first offence and one hundred dollars for a second or subsequent offence.

4. That every district court in any city, and every justice of the peace in any county, and any police justice or recorder in any city is hereby empowered, on oath or affirmation made according to law, that any person or persons has or have violated any provision of the act to which this is a supplement to issue process at the suit of any person, either in the manner of a summons or warrant, against the person or persons so charged, which process shall, when in the nature of a warrant, be returnable forthwith, and when in the nature of a summons shall be returnable in not less than one nor more than ten entire days; such process shall state what provision of the law is alleged to have been violated by the defendant or defendants, and on the return of such process at any time to which the trial shall have been adjourned the said court, justice of the peace, police justice, or recorder shall proceed to hear testimony and to determine and give judgment in the matter without the filing of any pleadings; and the said court, justice of the peace, police justice, or recorder shall, if judgment be rendered for the plaintiff, forthwith issue execution against the goods and chattels and person of the defendant or defendants; and the said court, justice of the peace, police justice, or recorder is further empowered to cause any such defendant who may refuse or neglect to pay the amount of the judgment rendered against him and all the costs and charges incident thereto, unless an appeal is granted, to be committed to the county jail for any period not exceeding ninety days; but no district court of any city, justice of the peace, police justice, or recorder shall have jurisdiction of any offence against the act to which this is a supplement which offence shall take place outside of the territorial jurisdiction of such district court, justice of the peace, police justice, or recorder, as such territorial jurisdiction is now established by law.

5. That the officers to serve and execute all process under this act shall be the officers authorized to serve and execute process in said courts and before such magistrates and officers as aforesaid, including the constables of such counties and all police officers of such cities.

6. That all penalties imposed under the act to which this is a supplement shall be disposed of as follows: In case the suit is brought by any officer appointed by the State board of health, the penalty shall be paid into the treasury of this State; in case the suit is brought by an officer of any local board of health or of any city, borough, town, or township, the penalty shall be paid into the treasury of said local board of health, city, borough, town, or township; in case of any suit not otherwise provided for, the penalty shall be paid to the person bringing the suit.

7. That the State board of health shall be authorized to expend annually, in addition to all sums already appropriated for such board, an amount not exceeding one thousand dollars for the purpose of including in its work the carrying out of the provision of this act and for the protection of the public health.

8. That any analyst or inspector appointed by the State board of health, and any inspector or other officer of any local board of health, shall have power to inspect any article of food or drugs, wherever exposed for sale, or offered, or held for sale, or whether in transit or otherwise; and if, upon inspection of such food or drugs the same shall be found adulterated within the meaning of this act or the act to which this act is a supplement, the said inspector, or other officers aforesaid, shall have power and may prohibit the sale or disposal of said articles until decision shall be

rendered by the court, justice of the peace, recorder, or police justice before whom the defendant may be brought.

9. That this act shall not be so construed as to interfere with the special provisions of an act, approved March fourth, eighteen hundred and eighty-two, entitled "An act to prevent the adulteration and to regulate the sale of milk."

10. That this act shall take effect immediately. Approved March 23, 1883.

CHAPTER CXXVI. LAWS OF 1887.

A SUPPLEMENT to an act entitled "An act to prevent the adulteration of food or drugs," approved March twenty-fifth, one thousand eight hundred and eighty-one.

1. *Be it enacted, by the senate and general assembly of the State of New Jersey,* That the State dairy commissioner is hereby directed and empowered to aid in the enforcement of the provisions of the act to which this is a supplement, and said commissioner and his assistants duly commissioned shall be, and are hereby, made inspectors under the act to which this act is a supplement. The expense of enforcing said act shall be paid out of the appropriation already made for the use of said dairy commissioner for the enforcement of the act of March twenty-second, one thousand eight hundred and eighty-six, entitled "An act to prevent deception in the sale of oleomargerine, butterine, or any imitation of dairy products, and to preserve the public health."

2. That this act take effect immediately.

Approved April 11th, 1887.

CHAPTER XXXVI.

A SUPPLEMENT to an act entitled "An act to prevent the adulteration of food or drugs," approved March twenty-fifth, one thousand eight hundred and eighty-one, and the several supplements thereto.

1. *Be it enacted by the senate and general assembly of the State of New Jersey,* That any person accused before any court for selling or offering for sale any article adulterated within the meaning of the act to which this is a supplement, and the supplements thereto, who shall prove that he procured such article under a warranty from any person or persons that reside within the State, in the form hereinafter set forth, that said article was pure and unadulterated within the meaning of said acts, said person shall be discharged from prosecution: *Provided,* That such proof in defense shall be filed in court prior to the trial of such case, and a copy thereof left with the attorney for the prosecutor of the case.

2. That no warranty shall be considered as within the meaning of this act unless in the form hereinafter given, and unless the article or articles warranted shall be specifically named and described in the body of said warranty; and no warranty shall be a defense if the person offering it shall have been notified, prior to the sale complained of, that the articles mentioned in said warranty are adulterated within the meaning of said acts.

3. That any person uttering or giving a false warranty, or swearing falsely in relation thereto, shall be guilty of a misdemeanor, and on conviction thereof shall be punished by a fine of not more than five hundred dollars, or imprisonment at hard labor for not more than one year, at the discretion of the court.

4. That the warranty herein provided for shall be in the form following, to wit:

Warranty.

It is hereby warranted that the following described article or articles ——— are pure and unadulterated within the meaning of the acts of the legislature of the State of New Jersey regulating the sale of food and drugs. (Signature.) ———.

Dated at ——— this —— day of ———, anno Domini ——.

5. That this act shall take effect immediately.

Approved March 5th, 1891.

Following are the rules of the New Jersey board of health for its in spectors and analysts :

DUTIES OF INSPECTORS.

1. The inspector is to buy samples of food or drugs, and to seal each sample in the presence of a witness.

2. The inspector must affix to each sample a label bearing a number, his initials, and the date of purchase.

3. Under no circumstance is the inspector to inform the analyst as to the source of the sample before the analysis shall have been completed and formally reported to the president or secretary of the State board of health.

4. Inspectors are to keep a record of each sample as follows :

    (1) Number of sample.

    (2) Date and time of purchase.

    (3) Name of witness to sealing.

    (4) Name and address of seller.

    (5) Name and address of producer, manufacturer, or wholesaler, when known, with marks on original package.

    (6) Name of analyst and date of sending.

    (7) How sent to analyst.

5. If the seller desires a portion of the sample, the inspector is to deliver it under seal. The duplicate sample left with seller should have a label containing the same marks as are affixed to the portion taken by the inspector.

6. The inspector is to deliver the sample to the analyst, taking his receipt for the same, or he may send it by registered mail, express, or special messenger.

DUTIES OF THE ANALYSTS.

1. The analyst is to analyze the samples immediately upon receipt thereof.

2. Samples, with the exception of milk and similar perishable articles, are to be divided by the analyst and a portion sealed up, and a copy of the original label affixed. These duplicates are to be sent to the secretary of the State board of health at the end of each month, and to be retained by him until demanded for another analysis, as provided for in section 3 of these rules.

3. Should the result obtained by any analyst be disputed in any case, an appeal may be made to the State board of health, through its secretary, by the defendant or person selling the sample, or his attorney, and said secretary shall then require another member of the committee of public analysts to repeat the analysis, using the duplicate sample for such purpose. But when an appeal shall be made a sum of money sufficient to cover the expenses of the second analysis shall be deposited with the president of the State board of health, which sum shall be paid over to the analyst designated by the president and secretary of the board to perform the second analysis, in case the analysis shall be found to agree with the first in all essential particulars.

4. In the case of all articles having a standard of purity fixed by any of the laws of the State, the certificate of the analyst should show the relation of the article in question to that standard.

5. Where standards of strength, purity, or quality are not fixed by law, the committee of analysts shall present to the State board of health such standard as in their judgment should be fixed.

6. Each analyst should keep a record book, in which should be entered notes as follows :

    (1) From whom the sample is received.

    (2) Date, time, and manner in which the sample was received.

    (3) Marks on package, sealed or not.

    (4) Results of analysis in detail.

This record should be produced at each meeting of the committee.

7. At the completion of the analysis a certificate in the form given below should be forwarded to the person from whom the sample was received, and a duplicate copy sent to the State board of health.

CERTIFICATE.

To whom it may concern :

I, ———, a member of the committee of public analysts appointed by the State board of health of New Jersey under provisions of an act entitled "An act to prevent the adulteration of food and drugs," approved March 25, 1881, do hereby certify that I received from ———, on the ——— day of ———, 188-, a sample of ———, sealed as required by the rules of said board, and bearing the following words, to wit:—-—

I carefully mixed said samples and have analyzed the same, and hereby certify and declare the results of my analyses to be as follows:———.

[Signature.] ——— ———.

EXCEPTIONS.

The following exceptions are adopted :

Mustard.—Compounds of mustard with rice flour, starch, or flour may be sold if each package is marked "Compound Mustard," and if not more than 25 per cent. of such substance is added to the mustard.

Coffee.—Compounds of coffee with chicory, rye, wheat, or other cereals may be sold if the package is marked "A Mixture," and if the label states the per cent. of coffee contained in said mixture.

Oleomargarine and other imitation dairy products may be sold if each package is marked with the name of the substance, and in all respects fulfils the terms of the special law as to these.

Sirups.—When mixed with glucose, sirup may be sold if the package is marked "A Mixture."

NEW YORK.

The New York State general law of 1881 for the prevention of the adulteration of food and drugs is as follows :

SECTION 1. No person shall, within this State, manufacture, have, offer for sale, or sell any article of food or drugs which is adulterated within the meaning of this act, and any person violating this provision shall be deemed guilty of a misdemeanor, and upon conviction thereof shall be punished by fine not exceeding fifty dollars for the first offense and not exceeding one hundred dollars for each subsequent offense.

2. The term "food," as used in this act, shall include every article used for food or drink by man. The term "drug," as used in this act, shall include all medicines for internal and external use.

3. An article shall be deemed to be adulterated within the meaning of this act:

(a) In the case of drugs.

(1) If, when sold under or by a name recognized in the United States Pharmacopœia, it differs from the standard of strength, quality, or purity laid down therein.

(2) If, when sold under or by a name not recognized in the United States Pharmacopœia, but which is found in some other pharmacopœia or other standard work on materia medica, it differs materially from the standard of strength, quality, or purity laid down in such work.

(3) If its strength or purity fall below the professed standard under which it is sold.

(*b*) In the case of food or drink.

    (1) If any substance or substances has or have been mixed with it so as to reduce or lower or injuriously affect its quality or strength.

    (2) If any inferior or cheaper substance or substances have been substituted wholly or in part for the article.

    (3) If any valuable constituent of the article has been wholly or in part abstracted.

    (4) If it be an imitation of, or be sold under the name of, another article.

    (5) If it consists wholly or in part of a diseased or decomposed, or putrid or rotten, animal or vegetable substance, whether manufactured or not, or, in the case of milk, if it is the produce of a diseased animal.

    (6) If it be colored, or coated, or polished, or powdered, whereby damage is concealed, or it is made to appear better than it really is, or of greater value.

    (7) If it contain any added poisonous ingredient, or any ingredient which may render such article injurious to the health of the person consuming it: *Provided*, That the State board of health may, with the approval of the governor, from time to time declare certain articles or preparations to be exempt from the provisions of this act: *And provided further*, That the provisions of this act shall not apply to mixtures or compounds recognized as ordinary articles of food, provided that the same are not injurious to health and that the articles are distinctly labeled as a mixture, stating the components of the mixture.

4. It shall be the duty of the State board of health to prepare and publish from time to time lists of the articles, mixtures, or compounds declared to be exempt from the provisions of this act in accordance with the preceding section. The State board of health shall also from time to time fix the limits of variability permissible in any article of food or drug or compound, the standard of which is not established by any national pharmacopœia.

5. The State board of health shall take cognizance of the interests of the public health as it relates to the sale of food and drugs and the adulteration of the same, and make all necessary investigations and inquiries relating thereto. It shall also have the supervision of the appointment of public analysts and chemists, and upon its recommendation whenever it shall deem any such officers incompetent the appointment of any and every such officer shall be revoked and be held to be void and of no effect. Within thirty days after the passage of this act the State board of health shall meet and adopt such measures as may seem necessary to facilitate the enforcement of this act, and prepare rules and regulations with regard to the proper methods of collecting and examining articles of food or drugs, and for the appointment of the necessary inspectors and analysts; and the State board of health shall be authorized to expend, in addition to all sums already appropriated for said board, an amount not exceeding ten thousand dollars for the purpose of carrying out the provisions of this act. And the sum of ten thousand dollars is hereby appropriated, out of any moneys in the treasury not otherwise appropriated, for the purposes in this section provided.

6. Every person selling or offering or exposing any article of food or drugs for sale, or delivering any article to purchasers, shall be bound to serve or supply any public analyst or other agent of the State or local board of health appointed under this act, who shall apply to him for that purpose, and on his tendering the value of the same, with a sample sufficient for the purpose of analysis of any article which is included in this act, and which is in the possession of the person selling, under a penalty not exceeding $50 for a first offense and $100 for a second and subsequent offense.

7. Any violation of the provisions of this act shall be treated and punished as a misdemeanor; and whoever shall impede, obstruct, hinder, or otherwise prevent any analyst, inspector, or prosecuting officer in the performance of his duty shall be guilty of a misdemeanor, and shall be liable to indictment and punishment therefor.

8. Any acts or parts of acts inconsistent with the provisions of this act are hereby repealed.

9. All the regulations and declarations of the State board of health made under this act from time to time, and promulgated, shall be printed in the statutes at large.

10. This act shall take effect at the expiration of ninety days after it shall become a law.

Amendment of April 29, 1885.

SECTION 1. The title of chapter 407 of the laws of 1881, entitled "An act to prevent the adulteration of food and drugs," is hereby amended to read as follows: "An act to prevent the adulteration of food, drugs, and spirituous, fermented, or malt liquors in the State of New York."

* * * * * * *

3. Section 2 is hereby amended to read as follows:

"2. The term food as used in this act shall include every article of food or drink by man, including teas, coffees, and spirituous, fermented, and malt liquors. The term drug as used in this act shall include all medicines for internal or external use."

* * * * * * *

5. Section 5 is hereby amended to read as follows:

"5. The State board of health shall take cognizance of the interests of the public health as relates to the sale of food, drugs, spirituous, fermented, and malt liquors, and the adulteration thereof, and make all necessary inquiries relating thereto. It shall have the supervision of the appointment of public analysts and chemists, and upon its recommendation, whenever it shall deem any such officers incompetent, the appointment of any and every such officer shall be revoked and be held to be void and of no effect. Within thirty days after the passage of this act, and from time to time thereafter as it may deem expedient, the said board of health shall meet and adopt such measures, not provided for by this act, as may seem necessary to facilitate the enforcement of this act, and for the purpose of making an examination or analysis of spirituous, fermented, or malt liquors sold or exposed for sale in any store or place of business not herein otherwise provided for, and prepare rules and regulations with regard to the proper methods of collecting and examining articles of food, drugs, spirituous, fermented, or malt liquors, and for the appointment of the necessary inspectors and analysts. The said board shall at least once in the calendar year cause samples to be procured, in public market or otherwise, of the spirituous, fermented, or malt liquors distilled, brewed, manufactured, or offered for sale in each and every brewery or distillery located in this State, and a test, sample, or analysis thereof to be made by a chemist or analyst duly appointed by said board of health. The samples shall be kept in vessels and in a condition necessary and adequate to obtain a proper test and analysis of the liquors contained therein. The vessels containing such samples shall be properly labeled and numbered by the secretary of said board of health, who shall also prepare and keep an accurate and proper list of the names of the distillers, brewers, or vendors, and opposite each name shall appear the number which is written or printed upon the label attached to the vessel containing the sample of the liquor manufactured, brewed, distilled, or sold. Such lists, numbers, and labels shall be exclusively for the information of the said board of health, and shall not be disclosed or published unless upon discovery of some deleterious substance prior to the completion of the analysis, except when required in evidence in a court of justice. The samples when listed and numbered shall be delivered to the chemist, analyst, or other officer of said board of health, and shall be designated and known to such chemist, analyst, or officer only by its number, and by no other mark or designation. The result of the analysis or investigation shall thereupon, and within a convenient time, be reported by the officer conducting the same to the secretary of said State board of health, setting forth explicitly the nature of any deleterious substance, compound, or adulteration which may be detrimental to public health and which has been found upon analysis in such samples, and stating the number of the samples in which said substance was found. Upon such examination or analysis the brewer, distiller, or vendor in whose sample of spirituous, fermented, or malt liquor such deleterious substances, compounds, or adulterations shall be found, shall be deemed to have violated the provisions of this act, and shall be punishable as prescribed in section 7 of this act."

*   *   *   *   *   *   ,

7. Section 7 of said chapter 407 of the laws of 1881 is hereby amended to read as follows:

"7. Upon discovering that any person has violated any of the provisions of this act the State board of health shall immediately communicate the facts to the district attorney of the county in which the person accused of such violation resides or carries on business, and the said district attorney, upon receiving such communication or notification, shall forthwith commence proceeding for indictment and trial of the accused as prescribed by law in cases of misdemeanor."

8. The State board of health shall be authorized to expend, in addition to the sums already appropriated for said board, an amount not exceeding $3,000 for the purpose of carrying out the provisions of this act in relation to spirituous, fermented, or malt liquors. And the sum of $3,000 is hereby appropriated, out of any moneys in the treasury not otherwise appropriated and expended, for the purposes of this act.

9. This act shall take effect immediately.

OHIO.

[Senate bill No. 110.]

AN ACT to create the office of dairy and food commissioner.

Be it enacted by the general assembly of the State of Ohio, That there is hereby created the office of dairy and food commissioner of the State of Ohio. Said commissioner shall be appointed by the governor, by and with the consent of the senate; he shall be known as the "Ohio dairy and food commissioner;" his term of office shall be for two years, and until his successor is appointed and qualified; his salary shall be fifteen hundred dollars per year, and his necessary and reasonable expenses incurred in the discharge of his official duties under this act, to be paid at the end of each calendar month, on presentation of vouchers properly itemized and certified by him to be correct. Said expenses to be paid out of the general revenue fund, but not [to] exceed $600 in any one year.

SEC. 2. It shall be the duty of said commissioner or assistant commissioner to inspect any article of butter, cheese, lard, syrup, or other article of food or drinks made or offered for sale in the State of Ohio as an article of food or drink, and to prosecute or cause to be prosecuted any person or persons, firm or firms, corporation or corporations, engaged in the manufacture or sale of any adulterated article or articles of food or drink, or adulterated in violation of or contrary to any laws of the State of Ohio.

SEC. 3. The said commissioner, or any assistant commissioner, shall have power, in the performance of their duty, to enter into any creamery, factory, store, salesroom, drug store or laboratory, or place where they have reason to believe food or drink are made, prepared, sold or offered for sale, and to examine their books, and to open any cask, tub, jar, bottle or package, containing or supposed to contain any article of food or drink, and examine or cause to be examined and analyzed the contents thereof, and it shall be the duty of any prosecuting attorney in any county of the State, when called upon by said commissioner or assistant commissioner, to render him any legal assistance in his power to execute the laws, and to assist in the prosecution of cases arising under provisions of this act.

SEC. 4. Said commissioner may, with the consent and advice of the governor, appoint not more than two assistant commissioners, whose salaries shall be one thousand dollars each, per annum, and their necessary and reasonable expenses incurred in the discharge of their official duties, payable in time and manner like that of the commissioner and on itemized vouchers approved by the said commissioner. The said commissioner shall have power, with the advice and consent of the governor, to appoint three expert chemists, to be of acknowledged standing, ability, and integrity, to examine and analyze samples of food and drink, or of drugs or medicines submitted to them by the commissioner or assistant commissioner. The compensation of said expert chemists shall be for the actual number of determinations or examinations required and made, and shall not exceed for each determination or examination two-thirds the price, usually paid experts, for a single determination or examination of a similar kind. The compensation of said expert chemist shall be paid at the end of each quarter of the calender year, on itemized vouchers certified to by said commissioner, which said amount of expenses shall not exceed, in any one year for the three expert chemists combined, the sum of one thousand dollars, the sum to be paid out of the general revenue fund.

SEC. 5. All fines assessed or collected under prosecution, begun or caused to be begun by said commissioner or assistant commissioners, shall be paid into the State treasury.

SEC. 6. Said commissioner shall be furnished a suitable office in the department of the State board of agriculture within [the] State capitol building, and shall make an annual report to the governor, containing an itemized statement of all expenses incurred and fines collected, with such statistics as he may regard of value; and said report shall be published each year as a supplement to the annual agricultural report, and two thousand copies thereof shall be published separately, in pamphlet form.

SEC. 7. This act shall take effect and be in force from and after its passage.

DANIEL J. RYAN,
Speaker pro tem. of the House of Representatives.
ROB'T P. KENNEDY,
President of the Senate.

Passed May 8, 1886.

[Amended H. B. No. 185.]

AN ACT to prevent adulteration of and deception in the sale of dairy products, and supplementary to Chapter II, Title I, Part 4, of the Revised Statutes.

Be it enacted by the general assembly of the State of Ohio, That no person shall sell, exchange, expose or offer for sale or exchange, any substance purporting, appearing, or represented to be butter or cheese, or having the semblance of either butter or cheese, which substance is not made wholly from pure milk or cream, salt and harmless coloring matter, unless it be done under its true name, and each vessel, package, roll, or parcel of such substance has distinctly and durably painted, stamped, stenciled, or marked thereon the true name of such substance in ordinary bold-faced capital letters, not less than five-line pica in size, and also the name of each article or ingredient used or entering into the composition of such substance, in ordinary bold-faced letters, not less than pica in size, or sell or dispose of in any manner to another any such substance without delivering with each amount sold or disposed of a label on which is plainly or legibly printed in ordinary bold-faced capital letters not less than five-line pica in size, the true name of such substance, and also the name of such articles, used and entering into the composition of such substance in ordinary bold-faced letters, not less than pica size, if the same be not made wholly from pure milk or cream, salt and harmless coloring matter.

SEC. 2. No person or persons shall manufacture out of any oleaginous substance or substances, or any compound of the same other than that produced from unadulterated milk or cream, salt and harmless coloring matter, any article designed to be sold as butter or cheese made from pure milk or cream, salt and harmless coloring matter.

Nothing in this section shall prevent the use of pure skimmed milk in the manufacture of cheese.

SEC. 3. No person or persons shall manufacture, mix, compound with or add to natural or pure milk, cream, butter, or cheese, any animal fats, animal, mineral, or vegetable oils, nor shall any person or persons manufacture any oleaginous or other substance not produced from pure milk or cream, salt and harmless coloring matter, or have the same in his possession, or offer or expose the same for sale or exchange with intent to sell or in any manner dispose of the same as and for butter and cheese made from unadulterated milk or cream, salt and harmless coloring matter, nor shall any substance or compound so made be sold or disposed of to anyone as and for butter or cheese made from pure milk or cream, salt and harmless coloring matter.

SEC. 4. No person or persons shall sell, exchange, expose or offer for sale or exchange, dispose of or have in his possession any substance or article made in imitation or resemblance of, or as a substitute for, any dairy products which is falsely branded, stenciled, labeled, or marked as to the place where made, the name or cream value thereof, its composition or ingredients, or in any other respect.

SEC. 5. No person or persons shall sell, exchange, expose or offer for sale or exchange, dispose of or have in his possession any dairy products which are falsely branded, stenciled, labeled, or marked as to the place where made, date of manufacture, the name or cream value thereof, composition or ingredients, or in any other respect; and cheese made wholly from skimmed milk shall have branded on the box or can "made from skimmed milk."

SEC. 6. Every person in this State who shall deal in, keep for sale, expose or offer for sale or exchange, any substance other than butter or cheese made wholly from pure milk or cream, salt and harmless coloring matter, which appears to be, resembles or is made in imitation of, or as a substitute for butter or cheese, shall keep a card not less in size than eight by ten inches, in a conspicuous and visible place, where the same may be easily seen and read in the store, room, stand, booth, wagon, or place where such substance is, on which card shall be printed in bold, black, Roman letters, not less in size than eight-line pica, the true name of such substance, with the words "imitation butter, or imitation cheese, sold here."

SEC. 7. Every proprietor, keeper, or manager, or person in charge of any hotel, boarding house, restaurant, eating house, lunch counter, or lunch room, who therein sells, uses, or disposes of any substance which appears to be, resembles, or is made in or as an imitation of, or is made as a substitute for "butter or cheese," under whatsoever name, and which substance is not wholly made from pure milk or cream, salt and harmless coloring matter, shall display and keep a card in a conspicuous place, where the same may be easily seen and read in the dining, eating, restaurant, and lunch room, and place where such substance is sold, used, or disposed of, which card shall be in size not less than eight by ten inches, upon which shall be printed in plain, bold, black letters, not less in size than eight-line pica, the true name of such substance, and also the words "imitation butter, or imitation cheese, sold and used here," and such proprietor, keeper, manager, or person in charge shall not sell, furnish, or dispose of such substance as and for "butter or cheese" made from pure milk or cream, salt and harmless coloring matter, when butter or cheese is asked for.

SEC. 8. No person or persons shall pack, box, inclose, ship, or consign any substance as butter or cheese made from pure milk or cream, salt and harmless coloring matter, in such a manner as to conceal an inferior article by placing a finer grade of butter or cheese upon the surface of the same.

SEC. 9. No person or persons shall sell to any person, or deliver or carry or cause to be carried to any cheese or butter factory to be manufactured, any milk diluted with water or in any way adulterated, or from which any cream has been taken, or milk commonly known as "skimmed milk," or milk from which [the] part known as "strippings" has been withheld with the intent to defraud, or keeps or renders any false account of the quantity or weight of milk furnished at or to any factory for manufacture or sold to any manufacturer.

SEC. 10. No person or persons shall sell, exchange, or offer for sale or exchange, any unclean, impure, unhealthy, unwholesome milk, or sell, exchange, or offer for sale or exchange as " pure milk," milk diluted with water, or milk known as skimmed milk.

SEC. 11. No person or persons shall sell, exchange, expose or offer for sale or exchange, have in his possession or dispose of in any manner, any milk which is falsely branded, labeled, marked, or represented as to grade, quantity, or place where produced or procured.

SEC. 12. No person shall keep cows for the production of milk for any purpose, in a cramped or unhealthy condition, or feed them on unhealthy food, or upon food that produces impure, unhealthy, or unwholesome milk.

SEC. 13. No person shall manufacture, sell, exchange, expose or offer for sale or exchange, any condensed milk, unless the package, can, or vessel containing the same shall be distinctly labeled, stamped, or marked with its true name, brand, by whom and under what name made ; and no condensed milk shall be made, exchanged, exposed, or offered for sale or exchange, unless the same be made from pure, clean, healthy, fresh, unadulterated, and wholesome milk, from which the cream has not been removed, or unless the proportion of milk solids contained in the condensed milk shall be in amount the equivalent of 12 percentum of milk solids in crude milk, and of such solids, 25 percentum shall be fat.

SEC. 14. No butter or cheese not made wholly from pure milk or cream, salt, and harmless coloring matter, shall be used in any of the charitable or penal institutions of the State.

SEC. 15. Any person, or persons violating any of the provisions or sections of this act shall, upon conviction thereof, be fined not less than fifty or more than two hundred dollars for the first offense, or for each subsequent offense not less than one hundred dollars or more than five hundred dollars, and be imprisoned not less than ten days or more than ninety days, or both.

SEC. 16. One-half of all fines collected under any of the provisions of this act shall be paid over to the person or persons furnishing information under which conviction is procured.

SEC. 17. That section 7089 of the Revised Statutes and acts of April 13, 1881, vol. 78, page 130, and April 26, 1881, vol. 78, page 198, amendatory and supplementary of section 7090, and the act to prevent the manufacture and sale as butter of oleomargarine and other similar substances, passed April 27, 1885, vol. 82, page 159, are hereby repealed.

SEC. 18. This act shall take effect on its passage.

JOHN C. ENTREKIN,
Speaker of the House of Representatives.
ROBT. P. KENNEDY,
President of the Senate.

Passed May 17, 1886.

ADULTERATION OF FOOD.

[House Bill No. 18.]

AN ACT to provide against the adulteration of food and drugs.

Be it enacted by the general assembly of the State of Ohio, That no person shall, within this State, manufacture for sale, offer for sale, or sell any drug or article of food which is adulterated, within the meaning of this act.

SEC. 2. * * * The term "food," as used herein, shall include all articles used for food or drink by man, whether simple, mixed, or compound.

SEC. 3. An article shall be deemed to be adulterated within the meaning of this act : * * *

(a) In the case of drugs ; (1) if, when sold under or by a name recognized in the United States Pharmacopœia, it differs from the standard of strength, quality or purity laid down therein; (2) if, when sold under or by a name not recognized in the United States Pharmacopœia, but which is found in some other pharmacopœia, or other standard work on materia medica, it differs materially from the standard of strength, quality, or purity laid down in such work; (3) if its strength, quality, or purity falls below the professed standard under which it is sold.

(b) In the case of food: (1) If any substance or substances have been mixed with it, so as to lower or depreciate or injuriously affect its quality, strength, or purity; (2) if any inferior or cheaper substance or substances have been substituted wholly or in part for it; (3) if any valuable or necessary constituent or ingredient has been wholly or in part extracted from it; (4) if it is an imitation of, or is sold under the name of another article; (5) if it consists wholly, or in part, of a diseased, decomposed, putrid, infected, tainted, or rotten animal or vegetable substance or article, whether manufactured or not —or, in the case of milk, if it is the produce of a diseased animal; (6) if it is colored, coated, polished, or powdered, whereby damage or inferiority is concealed, or if by any means it is made to appear better or of greater value than it really is; (7) if it contains any added substance or ingredient which is poisonous or injurous to health; provided, that the provisions of this act shall not apply to mixtures or compounds recognized as ordinary articles or ingredients of articles of food, if *each and every package sold or offered for sale* be distinctly labeled as mixtures or compounds, *with the name and per cent. of each ingredient therein, and are not injurious to health.*

SEC. 4. Every person manufacturing, offering or exposing for sale. or delivering to a purchaser any * * * article of food included in the provisions of this act, shall furnish to any person interested, or demanding the same, who shall apply to him for the purpose, and shall tender him the value of the same, a sample sufficient for the analysis of any such * * * article of food which is in his possession.

SEC. 5. Whoever refuses to comply, upon demand, with the requirements of section 4, and whoever violates any of the provisions of this act, shall be guilty of a misdemeanor, and upon conviction shall be fined not exceeding one hundred nor less than twenty-five dollars, or imprisoned not exceeding one hundred nor less than thirty days, or both. And any person found guilty of manufacturing, offering for sale, or selling an adulterated article of food * * * under the provisions of this act, shall be adjudged to pay, in addition to the penalties hereinbefore provided for, all necessary costs and expenses incurred in inspecting and analyzing such adulterated articles of which said person may have been found guilty of manufacturing, selling, or offering for sale.

SEC. 6. This act shall take effect and be in force in forty days from and after its passage.

A. D. MARSH,
Speaker of the House of Representatives.
ELMER WHITE,
President pro tem. of the Senate.

Passed March 20, 1884.

[House Bill No. 887.]

AN ACT to prevent fraud in canning fruit and vegetables.

Be it enacted by the general assembly of the State of Ohio, That it shall hereafter be unlawful in this State for any packer or dealer in preserved or canned fruits and vegetables, or other articles of food, to offer such canned articles for sale after January 1, 1886, with the exception of goods brought from foreign countries or packed prior to the passage of this act, unless such articles bear a mark to indicate the grade or quality, together with the name and address of such firm, person, or corporation that pack the same, or dealer who sells the same.

SEC. 2. That all soaked goods, or goods put up from products dried before canning, shall be plainly marked by an adhesive label, having on its face the word " soaked " in letters not less in size than two-line pica of solid and legible type; and all cans, jugs, or other packages containing maple syrup or molasses, shall be plainly marked by an adhesive label, having on its face the name and address of the person, firm, or corporation who made or prepared the same, together with the name and quality of the goods, in letters of the size provided in this section.

SEC. 3. Any person, firm, or corporation who shall falsely stamp or label such cans or jars containing preserved fruit or food of any kind, or knowingly permit such false stamping or labeling, and any person, firm, or corporation who shall violate any of the provisions of this act, shall be deemed guilty of a misdemeanor, and punished with a fine not less than $50 in the case of vendors, and in the case of manufacturers, and those falsely or fraudulently stamping or labeling such cans or jars, a fine of not less than $500 nor more than $1,000; and it shall be the duty of any board of health in this State, cognizant of any violation of this act, to prosecute any person, firm, or corporation which it has reason to believe has violated any of the provisions of this act, and after deducting the costs of trial and conviction, to retain for the use of said board the balance of the fine or fines recovered.

SEC. 4. This act shall take effect January 1, 1886.

A. D. MARSH,
Speaker of the House of Representatives.
ELMER WHITE,
President pro tem. of the Senate.

Passed April 29, 1885.

ADULTERATION OF LIQUORS.

Section 7082 of the Revised Statutes provides that: "Whoever adulterates, for the purpose of sale, any spirituous, alcoholic, or malt liquors, used or intended for drink or medical or mechanical purposes, with cocculus indicus, vitriol, grains of paradise, opium, alum, capsicum, copperas, laurel water, logwood, Brazil wood, cochineal, sugar of lead, aloes, glucose, tannic acid, or any other substances which is poisonous or injurious to health, or with any substance not a necessary ingredient in the manufacture thereof; and whoever sells or offers or keeps for sale any such liquors so adulterated shall be fined in any sum not less than twenty nor more than one hundred dollars, or be imprisoned not less than twenty nor more than sixty days, or both, at the discretion of the court. And any person guilty of violating any of the provisions of this section shall be adjudged to pay, in addition to the penalties hereinbefore provided for, all necessary costs and expenses incurred in inspecting and analyzing any such adulterated liquors, of which said party may have been guilty of adulterating or selling, or keeping for sale, or offering for sale."

Passed March 25, 1882.

MANUFACTURING OR SELLING POISONED LIQUORS.

Section 7083 of the Revised Statutes provides that: "Whoever uses any active poison in the manufacture or preparation of any intoxicating liquor, or sells in any quantity any intoxicating liquor so manufactured or prepared, shall be imprisoned in the penitentiary not more than five years nor less than one year." [54 v. 183.]

ADULTERATION OF WINE.

Section 7081 of the Revised Statutes provides against the adulteration of native wines, as follows: "Whoever adulterates any wine made or juices expressed from grapes grown within the State of Ohio, by mixing therewith any drugs, chemicals, cider, whisky, or other liquor, and whoever sells, or offers to sell, any such adulterated wine or grape juice, knowing the same to be adulterated, shall be fined in any sum not more than three hundred nor less than fifty dollars." [62 v. 179.]

ADULTERATION OF CANDY.

[Senate bill No. 123.]

AN ACT to provide against the adulteration of candy.

Be it enacted by the general assembly of the State of Ohio, That no person shall manufacture for sale, or sell or offer to sell, any candy adulterated by the admixture of terra alba, berytes, talo, or other mineral substance, or poisonous colors or flavors, or other ingredients deleterious or detrimental to health.

SEC. 2. Every person manufacturing candy, or offering or exposing the same for sale, shall furnish to any person interested or demanding the same, who shall apply to him for that purpose and shall tender him the value of the same, a sample sufficient for the analysis thereof.

SEC. 3. Whoever refuses to comply, upon demand, with the requirements of section 2, and whoever violates any of the provisions of this act, shall be guilty of a misdemeanor, and upon conviction shall be fined not exceeding one hundred dollars nor less than twenty-five dollars, or imprisoned not exceeding one hundred nor less than thirty days, or both ; and he shall be adjudged to pay, in addition, all necessary costs and expenses incurred in the inspecting and analyzing such adulterated candy, and the same shall be forfeited and destroyed under the direction of the court.

SEC. 4. This act shall take effect upon its passage.

DANIEL J. RYAN,
Speaker pro tem. of the House of Representatives.
ROBT. P. KENNEDY,
President of the Senate.

Passed May 8, 1886.

[House bill No. 26.]

AN ACT to amend section[s] 1 and 2 of an act entitled "An act to prevent the adulteration of vinegar," passed March 21, 1887 (Ohio laws 84, 216), and to repeal section 3 of said act.

Be it enacted by the general assembly of the State of Ohio, That sections 1 and 2 of an act entitled "An act to prevent the adulteration of vinegar," passed March 21, 1887, be amended so as to read as follows :

"SEC. 1. That no person shall manufacture for sale, or knowingly offer or expose for sale as cider, apple, or orchard vinegar any vinegar not the legitimate product of pure apple juice known as apple cider, or vinegar not made exclusively of said apple cider, or vinegar into which foreign substances, drugs, or acids have been introduced as may appear by proper test, and upon said test shall contain not less than two per cent. by weight of cider vinegar solids upon full evaporation over boiling water.

"SEC. 2. No person shall manufacture for sale, or knowingly offer for sale, or have in his possession with intent to sell any vinegar found upon proper test to contain any preparation of lead, copper, sulphuric acid, or other ingredients injurious to health *or containing artificial coloring matter.*

"SEC. 4. Every person making or manufacturing cider vinegar, who is not a domestic manufacturer of cider or cider vinegar, shall brand on each head of the cask, barrel, or keg containing such vinegar the name and residence of the manufacturer, the date when same was manufactured, and the words "Cider Vinegar." And no vinegar shall be branded "Fruit Vinegar" unless the same be made wholly from apples, grapes, or other fruit.

"SEC. 5. Whoever violates any of the provisions of this act shall, upon conviction, be fined not less than fifty dollars nor more than one hundred dollars, or imprisoned not less than thirty days nor more than one hundred days, or both; and shall be adjudged to pay in addition all necessary costs and expenses incurred in inspecting and analyzing such vinegar. And all vinegar not in accordance with this act shall be subject to forfeiture and spoliation."

SEC. 2. Sections 1, 2, and 3 of an act passed March 21, 1887 (O. L., 84, p. 216), be, and the same are hereby, repealed.

SEC. 3. This act shall take effect and be in force from and after its passage.

ELBERT L. LAMPSON,
Speaker of the House of Representatives.
WM. C. LYON,
President of the Senate.

Passed April 14, 1888.

[Senate bill No. 59.]

AN ACT to amend sections [section?] 3718a of the Revised Statutes of Ohio.

Be it enacted by the general assembly of the State of Ohio, That section 3718a of the Revised Statutes of Ohio be, and the same is hereby, amended to read as follows:

SEC. 3718a. Any justice of the peace, within his county and city, police judge or mayor of any city or village, within his city or village, shall have jurisdiction in case of violation of the laws, to prevent adulteration of food and drink, the adulteration and deception in the sale of dairy products, and drugs and medicines, and any violation of the law for the prevention of cruelty to animals, or under section sixty-nine hundred and eighty-four of the Revised Statutes or section sixty-nine hundred and eighty-four *a* thereof as herein enacted. If such prosecutions be before a justice of the peace, and a trial by jury be not waived, the said justice shall issue a venire to any constable of the county, containing the names of sixteen electors of the county to serve as jurors to try such case and make due return thereof. Each party shall be entitled to two peremptory challenges, and shall be subject to the same challenges as jurors are subject to in criminal cases in the court of common pleas. If the venire of sixteen names be exhausted without obtaining the required number to fill the panel, the justice may direct the constable to summon any of the bystanders to act as jurors: *Provided,* That in all cases prosecuted under the provision of this section no costs shall be required to be advanced or paid by the person or persons authorized under the law to prosecute such cases: *And provided further,* That in all cases brought under the provision of this section, if the defendant be acquitted, or if convicted, and committed in default of paying fine and costs, the costs of each case shall be certified under oath to the county auditor, who, after correcting the same, shall issue [a] warrant on the county treasurer in favor of the person to whom such costs and fees shall be paid.

SEC. 2. The original section 3718a is hereby repealed.

SEC. 3. This act shall take [effect] from and after its passage.

ELBERT L. LAMPSON,
Speaker of the House of Representatives.
WM. C. LYON,
President of the Senate.

Passed April 3, 1888.

[House bill No. 407.]

AN ACT to regulate the sale of milk.

Be it enacted by the general assembly of the State of Ohio, That whoever, by himself or by his servant or agent, or as the servant or agent of any other person, sells, exchanges, or delivers, or has in his custody or possession with intent to sell or exchange, or exposes or offers for sale or exchange, adulterated milk, or milk to which water or any foreign substance has been added, or milk from diseased or sick cows, shall, for a first offense, be punished by a fine of not less than fifty nor more two hundred dollars; for a second offense, by fine of not less than one hundred dollars nor more than three hundred dollars, or by imprisonment in the workhouse for not less than thirty nor more than sixty days; and for a subsequent offense, by a fine of fifty dollars and by imprisonment in the workhouse of not less than sixty nor more than ninety days.

SEC. 2. Whoever, by himself or by his servant or agent or as the servant or agent of any other person, sells, exchanges, or delivers, or has in his custody or possession, with intent to sell or exchange, or exposes or offers for sale as pure milk any milk from which the cream or part thereof has been removed, shall be punished by the penalties provided in the preceding section.

SEC. 3. No dealer in milk, and no servant or agent of such a dealer, shall sell exchange, or deliver, or have in his custody or possession, with intent to sell, exchange, or deliver, milk from which the cream or part thereof has been removed, unless in a conspicuous place, above the center, upon the outside of every vessel, can, or package from which or in which such milk is sold, the words "skimmed milk" are distinctly marked in uncondensed gothic letters not less than one inch in length. Whoever violates the provisions of this section shall be punished by the penalties provided in section 1.

SEC. 4. In all prosecutions under this chapter, if the milk is shown upon analysis to contain more than eighty-seven per cent of watery fluid or to contain not less than twelve and one-half per cent solids, not less than one-fourth of which must be fat, it shall be deemed, for the purpose of this chapter, to be adulterated, and not of good standard quality, except during the months of May and June, when milk containing less than twelve per cent of milk solid shall be deemed to be not of good standard quality.

SEC. 5. This act shall take effect and be in force from and after its passage.

ELBERT L. LAMPSON,
Speaker of the House of Representatives.
THEO. F. DAVIS,
President pro tem. of the Senate.

Passed April 10, 1889.

[Senate bill No. 34.]

AN ACT to amend sections 6 and 7 of an act passed May 17, 1886 (O. L., pp. 178, 179, and 180, vol. 83), amended March 21, 1887 (pp. 182, 183, vol. 84, O. L.), to prevent adulteration and deception in the sale of dairy products.

Be it enacted by the general assembly of the State of Ohio, That sections 6 and 7 of the above-named act, passed May 17, 1886, amended March 21, 1837, be amended so as to read as follows:

SEC. 6. Every person in this State who shall deal in, keep for sale, expose, or offer for sale or exchange any substance other than butter or cheese made wholly from pure milk or cream, salt, and harmless coloring matter, which appears to be, resembles, or is made in imitation of, or as a substitute for butter or cheese, shall keep a card not less in size than ten by fourteen inches, in a conspicuous and visible place where the same may be easily seen and read in the store, room, stand, booth, wagon, or place where such substance is, on which card shall be printed, on a white ground, in bold, black, Roman letters, not less in size than twelve-line pica, the words "oleomargarine" or "imitation cheese" (as the case may be) "sold here," and said card shall not contain any other words than the ones above prescribed; and no person shall sell any oleomargarine, suine, imitation cheese, or other imitation dairy product, at retail or in any quantity less than the original package, tub, or firkin, unless he shall first inform the purchaser that the substance is not butter or cheese, but an imitation of the same.

SEC. 7. Every proprietor, keeper, or manager, or person in charge of any hotel, boarding house, restaurant, eating house, lunch counter, or lunch room, who therein sells, uses, or disposes of any substance which appears to be, resembles, or is made in or as an imitation of, or is made as a substitute for butter or cheese, under whatsoever name, and which substance is not wholly made from pure milk or cream, salt, and harmless coloring matter, shall display and keep a card in a conspicuous place, where the same may be easily seen and read in the dining, eating, restaurant, and lunch room, and place where such substance is sold, used, or disposed of, which card shall be white and in size not less than ten by fourteen inches, upon which shall be printed in plain, bold, black, Roman letters, not less in size than twelve-line pica, the words "oleomargarine sold and used here," or "imitation cheese sold and used here" (as the case may be), and said card shall not contain any other words than the ones above described, and such proprietor, keeper, manager, or person in charge shall not sell, furnish, or dispose of such substance as and for "butter and cheese," made from pure milk or cream, salt, and harmless coloring matter, when butter or cheese is asked for.

SEC. 2. That sections 6 and 7 of the above-named act, as amended March 21, 1887, be, and the same are hereby, repealed.

SEC. 3. This act shall take effect on its passage.

ELBERT L. LAMPSON,
Speaker of the House of Representatives.
WM. C. LYON,
President of the Senate.

Passed March 8, 1888.

[House bill No. 525.]

AN ACT to define pure wines, wines, compounded wines, and adulterated wines, and to regulate the manufacture and sale of compounded wines, and to prohibit the manufacture or sale of adulterated wines within the State of Ohio.

Be it enacted by the general assembly of the State of Ohio, That all liquors denominated as wine containing alcohol, "except such as shall be produced by the natural fermentation of pure, undried grape juice," or compounded with distilled spirits, or by both methods, whether denominated as wine, or by any other name whatsoever, in the nature of articles for use as beverages, or for compounding with other liquors intended for such use, and all compounds of the same with pure wine, and all preserved fruit juices compounded with substances not produced from undried fruit, in character of, or intended for use as beverages, and all wines (including all grades and kinds) which contain, or in the production or manufacture of which, any glucose, or uncrystallized grape or starch sugar, or cider, or pomace of grapes out of which the juice has been pressed or extracted, known as grape cheese, has been used, and all wines, imitation of wines, or other beverages produced from fruit into which carbonic acid gas has been artificially injected, or which shall contain any alum, baryta, salts, caustic lime, carbonate of soda, carbonate of potash, carbonic acid, salts of lead, salicylic acid or any other antiseptic, coloring matter (other than produced from undried fruit or pure sugar), essence of ether or any foreign substance whatsoever, which is injurious to health, shall be denominated as adulterated wine, and any person or persons who shall manufacture, or cause the same to be done, with intent to sell, or shall sell or offer to sell any of such wine or beverage, shall be guilty of a misdemeanor, and shall be punished by a fine of not less than two hundred dollars or more than one thousand dollars, or be imprisoned in the county jail for a term of not less than thirty days or more than six months, or by both such fine and imprisonment, in the discretion of the court, and shall be liable to a penalty of one dollar for each gallon thereof sold, offered for sale, or manufactured with intent to sell, and such wine or beverage shall be deemed a public nuisance and forfeited to the State, and shall be summarily seized and destroyed by any health officer, marshal, constable, or sheriff within whose jurisdiction the same shall be found, and the reasonable expense of such seizure and destruction, not exceeding the amount paid for similar services, shall be a county charge, and paid out of the county treasury in the same manner as costs in criminal cases, where the State fails to convict, are now allowed and paid out of such treasury.

Sec. 2. For the purpose of this act the words "pure wine" shall be understood to mean the fermented juice of the undried grapes, without the addition thereto of water, sugar, or any foreign substance whatever; and all such wines shall be known as "pure wine," and may be stamped, branded, labeled, designated, and sold as "pure wine," and the name and kind of wine, and that of the locality where such wine is made, and of the manufacturer, may also be added; and it shall be unlawful to affix any stamp, brand, or label containing the words "pure wine" (either alone or with other words) on any vessel, package, bottle, or other receptacle containing any substance other than pure wine as in this section defined, or to prepare or use on any vessel, package, bottle, or other receptacle containing any liquid, any imitation or counterfeit of such stamp, label, or brand, or any stamp, label, or brand of such form and appearance as to be calculated to mislead or deceive any person, or cause to be supposed that the contents thereof be pure wine, or to use any vessel, package, bottle, or other receptacle having such stamp, brand, or label affixed thereon, except for pure wine as in this section defined; and if the name of the manufacturer is added, then only of such manufacturer's make, providing the same is pure wine.

Sec. 3. For the further purpose of this act the word "wine" shall be understood to mean the fermented juice of undried grapes: *Provided, however,* That the addition of pure white or crystallized sugar to perfect the wine, or the using of the necessary things to clarify and refine the wine which are not injurious to health, shall not be construed as adulterations, but such wines shall contain at least seventy-five per cent of pure grape juice, and shall not contain any artificial flavoring whatever; and all such "wine" shall be known as "wine," and may be stamped, branded, labeled, and sold as "wine," in the same manner as is provided in section two of this act in case of pure wine, except the words in this case shall be "wine" without the prefix "pure," and all the provisions of said section two, as far as applicable, shall govern the manufacture and sale of "wine" as in this section defined.

Sec. 4. For the further purpose of this act, should any person or persons manufacture or cause the same to be done, with intent to sell, or offer to sell, any wine which contains less than the seventy-five per cent of pure undried grape-juice, and is otherwise pure, such wine shall be known as compounded wine and shall be branded, marked, labeled, and sold as compounded wine or sweet wine, and upon each and every package, barrel, or other receptacle of such wine which shall contain more than three gallons there shall be stamped upon both ends of such package, barrel, or other receptacle, in black printed letters at least one inch high and of proper proportion, the words "compounded wine or sweet wine," and upon all packages or other receptacle which shall contain more than one quart and up to three gallons there shall be stamped upon each of said packages or receptacles, in plain printed black letters at least one-half inch high and of proper proportion, the words compounded wine or sweet wine, and upon all packages, bottles, or other receptacle of one quart or less there shall be placed a label securely pasted thereon, on which label the words "compounded wine" or "sweet wine" shall be plainly printed in black letters at least one-fourth of an inch high and of proper proportion. Should any number of such packages or other receptacle be inclosed in a larger package, as a box, barrel, case, or basket, such outside package shall also receive the stamp "compounded wine" or "sweet wine," the letters to be the size according to the amount of such wine contained in such outside packages.

Sec. 5. Any person or persons who shall sell or offer for sale, or manufacture or cause the same to be done, with intent to sell any wine stamped or labeled, or branded, or designated in any manner as "pure wine," either by including the word "pure" with "wine" alone or in connection with other words, which is not "pure wine" as in section two of this act defined, or any wine stamped, or labeled, or branded, or in any manner designated as "wine," but which is not wine as in section three of this act defined, or shall violate any provision of said sections two and three of this act, or shall sell or offer for sale, or manufacture, or cause the same to be done, with intent to sell any wine of the kind and character as described in the fourth section of this act, which shall not be stamped, marked, or labeled after the manner and mode therein prescribed, or which is falsely stamped, or marked, or labeled, such person or persons shall be guilty of a misdemeanor, and shall be punished by a fine of not less than one hundred dollars or more than one thousand dollars for each and every offense, or by imprisonment in the county jail not less than thirty days, or more than six months, or both fine and imprisonment, in the discretion of the court, and in addition thereto shall be liable to a penalty of one-half dollar for each gallon thereof sold, offered for sale, or manufactured with intent to sell or offer for sale. All penalties imposed by this act may be recovered with costs of action by any person in his own name, before any justice of the peace in the county where the offense was committed, where the amount does not exceed the jurisdiction of such justice; and such penalties may be recovered in the like manner in any court of record in the State, but on the recovery by the plaintiff in such case for a sum less than fifty dollars, the plaintiff shall only be entitled to costs to amount equal to the amount of such recovery. It shall be the duty of the prosecuting attorney of the respective counties of this State, and they are hereby required, to prosecute or commence action in the name of the State of Ohio for the recovery of the penalties allowed herein, upon receiving proper information thereof, and in actions brought by such prosecuting attorney, one half of the penalty recovered shall belong to and be paid over to the person or persons giving the information upon which the action is brought, and the other one-half shall be paid to the treasurer of the county in which such action is brought, within thirty days from the time of its collection, and such money shall be placed to the credit of the poor fund of the town, city, or township in which the cause of action arose, after paying therefrom a reasonable attorney fee to the prosecuting attorney prosecuting such suit, to be fixed and allowed by the court trying such cause. All judgments recovered in pursuance of the provisions of this act, with interest thereon, may be collected and enforced by the same means and in the same manner as judgments in other cases. Two or more penalties may be included in the same action.

Sec. 6. The provisions of this act shall not apply to medicated wines such as are put up and sold for medicinal purposes only; nor to currant wine or other wines made from fruits, other than grapes, which are plainly labeled, or branded, or designated and sold, or offered for sale under names including the word wine, but also expressing distinctly the fruit from which they are made, as "gooseberry wine," "elderberry wine," or the like.

Sec. 7. This act shall take effect and be in force from and after September first next following its passage.

ELBERT L. LAMPSON,
Speaker of the House of Representatives.
WM. C. LYON,
President of the Senate.

Passed March 14, 1889.

[House Bill No. 70.]

AN ACT to prevent deception in the sale of dairy products and to preserve the public health.

Be it enacted by the general assembly of the State of Ohio, That no person, by himself or his agent, or his employé, shall render or manufacture for sale out of any animal or vegetable oils, not produced from unadulterated milk or cream from the same, any article in imitation or semblance of natural butter or cheese produced from pure unadulterated milk or cream from the same, nor compound with, or add to milk, cream, or butter any acids or other deleterious substance, or animal fats or animal or vegetable oils not produced from milk or cream, so as to produce any article or substance, or any human food, in imitation or semblance of natural butter or cheese, nor shall sell, keep for sale, or offer for sale any article, substance, or compound made, manufactured, or produced in violation of the provisions of this section, whether such article, substance, or compound shall be made or produced in this State or elsewhere.

SEC. 2. For the purpose of this act the terms "natural butter and cheese," "natural butter or cheese produced from pure unadulterated milk or cream from the same, butter and cheese made from unadulterated milk or cream, butter, or cheese, nor product of the dairy," and butter or cheese shall be understood to mean the products usually known by the terms butter and cheese, and which butter is manufactured exclusively from pure milk or cream or both, with salt and with or without any harmless coloring matter, and which cheese is manufactured exclusively from pure milk or cream or both, with salt and rennet, and with or without any harmless coloring matter or sage. It is further provided that nothing in this act shall be construed to prohibit the manufacture or sale of oleomargarine, in a separate and distinct form, *and in such manner as will advise the consumer of its real character*, free from any coloring matter or other ingredient causing it *to look like or to appear to be butter, as above defined.*

SEC. 3. Whoever violates the provisions of this act shall be guilty of a misdemeanor, and be punished by a fine of not less than one hundred dollars nor more than five hundred, or not less than six months nor more than one year's imprisonment, for the first offense, and by imprisonment for one year for each subsequent offense.

SEC. 4. This act shall take effect from and after the first day of May, 1890.

A. C. ROBESON,
Speaker pro tem. of the House of Representatives.
WILLIAM V. MARQUIS,
President of the Senate.

Passed March 7, 1890.

OREGON.

AN ACT to prevent the production and sales of unwholesome foods and to regulate sales of adulterated foods, drinks, and medicines.

Be it enacted by the legislative assembly of the State of Oregon, It shall be unlawful for any person or persons to sell or exchange, or expose for sale or exchange, any unwholesome, unclean, tainted, or diseased foods of any kind whatever.

SEC. 2. No person or persons shall sell or exchange, or expose for sale or exchange, or have in his or their possession for sale or exchange, any adulterated food, drink, or medicine, unless the same shall be plainly marked so as to establish its true character and distinguish it from pure articles of foods, drinks, or medicines; and in any public dining or eating room where adulterated foods or drinks are used, the bill of fare shall state the fact in the same sized type as is used in printing the body of said bill of fare, or if no bill of fare is used, then and in that case printed notice thereof shall be posted in a conspicuous place in said dining or eating room so as to be easily seen by anyone entering such room, in which notice shall be stated in large letters the fact that adulterated foods and drinks are being used for foods or for foods and drinks.

SEC. 3. When cows are kept by any person for dairy purposes, either for butter or cheese, or for the production of milk or cream for sale, and are confined in stables, such cows so confined shall be allowed at least eight hundred cubic feet each of air, and such cows so stabled shall not be confined facing each other, unless there shall be an air-tight partition between such cows at least four feet in height, and all stables where such cows are kept shall be well ventilated and kept in a good healthy [healthful] condition.

SEC. 4. Whosoever violates any of the provisions of this act shall be guilty of a misdemeanor, and upon conviction thereof shall be punished by a fine of not less than twenty-five dollars nor more than one hundred dollars, or by imprisonment in the county jail not less than thirty days nor more than six months.

SEC. 5. If any person or persons shall have purchased foods, drinks, or medicines, believing them to be pure and unadulterated, which shall prove by analyses to be adulterated, such person or persons shall not be deemed guilty under this act: *Pro-*

vided, That such person or persons pay to the food commissioner the price of any analysis or analyses that said commissioner shall have paid to determine the quality of such foods, drinks, or medicines, as the case may be, and who shall, after being informed of such adulteration, at once mark the same as required by section 2 of this act.

SEC. 6. An article of food or drink or medicine is deemed to be adulterated within the meaning of this act, when:

(1) Any substance or substances have been mixed with it so as to reduce or lower or injuriously affect its quality or strength.

(2) If any inferior or cheaper substance or substances have been substituted wholly or in part for it.

(3) If any valuable constituent has been wholly or in part abstracted from it.

(4) If it is an imitation of or is sold under the name of another article.

(5) If it consists wholly or in part of a diseased, decomposed, putrid, or rotten animal or vegetable substance, whether manufactured or not, or in the case of milk, if it is the manufactured product of a diseased animal.

(6) If it is colored, coated, polished, or powdered, whereby damage is concealed, or if it is made to appear better or of greater value than it really is: *Provided, however,* That salt and annetto or butter color, in which annetto is the principal ingredient, shall not be considered an adulteration when used in dairy products.

(7) If it contains any added * poisonous ingredient which may render it injurious to the health of a person consuming it.

SEC. 7. The legislative assembly at each regular session thereof, when assembled in joint convention, shall elect a commissioner who shall be known as the Oregon State food commissioner, who shall hold his office for the term of two years, or until his successor is elected and qualified, who shall qualify within thirty days from the time of his election by taking and filing an oath to faithfully perform the duties of said office with the secretary of State, and shall receive for his salary the sum of ten hundred dollars per year and his actual traveling expenses and expenses incurred in the discharge of the duties of his said office, and said commissioner shall be elected as aforesaid at any time before the final adjournment of the present legislature.

The said commissioner shall establish his office in the city of Portland, in this State, and shall, upon complaint being made by any citizen of the State of Oregon, or without it, if in his opinion necessary, examine into any case of violation or of supposed violation of the provisions of this act or any of them.

SEC. 8. It shall be the duty of the chemist of the State Agricultural College to correctly analyze any and all substances the said commissioner may send him for the purpose of carrying out the provisions of this act.

SEC. 9. The said commissioner, and such experts and chemists or agents as he shall duly authorize for the purpose, shall have access to, egress and ingress to all places of business, factories, stores, farm buildings, carriages, cars, vessels, and implements used in the manufacture, production, or sale of any foods, drinks, or medicines; and, they shall also have power and authority to open any package, case, or vessel containing such articles which may be manufactured, sold, or exposed for sale.

SEC. 10. Said commissioner shall keep a full and correct account of all business done by him or his experts, chemists, or agents, and report the same to the legislature.

SEC. 11. The doing of anything prohibited being done and the not doing of anything directed to be done by this act shall be presumptive evidence of wilful intent to violate the different sections thereof.

SEC. 12. In all prosecutions under this act the fine or fines collected shall go to the common school fund in the county where the suit of action is instituted.

SEC. 13. In all prosecutions under the provisions of this act relating to the sale of diseased foods or that which is unclean, impure, or unhealthy; milk drawn from

---

*Added should have been left out.

cows for fifteen days next before and five days next after parturition, or from cows fed on brewers' grains, commonly called "brewers' waste of malt," shall be deemed and declared unclean, impure, and unwholesome milk: *Provided further,* That anyone who shall use the box or boxes or cans used by any creamery or dairyman for the purpose of selling the butter of any other creamery or dairyman shall be subject to any or all fines provided for in this act.

SEC. 14. Chapter XXXVI of the miscellaneous laws of the State of Oregon, as compiled and annotated by W. Lair Hill, is hereby repealed.

Approved February 25, 1889.

PENNSYLVANIA.

LIQUORS.

237. It shall be unlawful for any person or persons to make use of any active poison or deleterious drugs in any quantity or quantities in the manufacture or preparation by process of rectifying, or otherwise, of any intoxicating malt or alcoholic liquors, or for any person or persons to knowingly sell such poisoned or drugged liquors in any quantity or quantities; and any person so offending shall be deemed guilty of a misdemeanor.

238. It shall be the duty of any person or persons engaged in the manufacture or sale of intoxicating malt or alcoholic liquors, or in rectifying or preparing the same in any way, to brand on each barrel, cask, or vessel containing the same, the name or names of the person or persons manufacturing, rectifying, or preparing the same, and also the words, "containing no deleterious drugs or added poison," and shall also certify the same fact or facts to the purchaser over his, her, or their own proper signature.

239. If any barrel, cask, or other vessel containing any such drugged or poisoned liquor shall be found in the possession of any person or persons designated in sections one and two it shall be deemed *prima facie* evidence of a violation of the provisions of this act.

240. Any suspected article or specimen of intoxicating malt or alcoholic liquor shall be subject to analysis by some competent person to perform the same under the direction of the court before which the case is tried, and such analysis duly certified under oath shall be deemed legal evidence in any court in this State: *Provided,* That upon any preliminary examination before any justice of the peace, mayor, or other magistrate, or competent authority, for the purpose of binding over, such officer under the inspection aforesaid to be made and make such order as may be necessary to preserve the evidence of the offence until the trial of the offender.

241. Any person offending against any of the provisions of this act shall be deemed guilty of a misdemeanor, and on conviction thereof shall be sentenced to pay a fine, not exceeding five hundred dollars, and to undergo an imprisonment not exceeding twelve months, or both, or either, in the discretion of the court.

242. In all actions for the sale of any spirituous, vinous, or malt liquors, or any admixture thereof, it shall be competent for the defendant, in every such case, to prove that such liquors or admixture thereof were impure, vitiated, or adulterated; and proof thereof being made, shall amount to a good and legal defence to the whole of the plaintiff's demand.

243. [Special provision for Allegheny County practically identical with the above.]

244. Any and all persons engaged in the business of brewing or manufacture of ale, beer, or other malt liquors, or in the fermentation, distillation, or manufacture of any vinous or spirituous liquors, be and they are hereby prohibited making use, in or about such business, or in any such process of brewing, fermentation, distillation, or manufacture, of any poisonous or deleterious drugs or chemicals, or any impure or injurious materials, or such as are prejudicial to the public health, or the health of any person drinking or making use of such malt, vinous, or spirituous liquors.

245. [The violation of the first section of this act is declared to be a misdemeanor, punishable by a fine of one thousand dollars and by an imprisonment of not more than one year.]

FOOD ADULTERATION.

200. If any person or persons shall adulterate or mix any improper and unwholesome ingredient in any flour of which bread shall be made as aforesaid, every such person or persons, being thereof legally convicted before any magistrate or justice of the city, borough, or county where such bread shall be so made, sold, or exposed to sale, who is hereby authorized and empowered to hear, try, and determine the same, shall forfeit and pay the sum of five pounds for every such offense.

201. Relates to forestalling the market.

202. It shall not be lawful for any butcher or other person to expose for sale any tainted or unwholesome meat or fish, or any veal less than three weeks old when killed in any of the market houses or other places for vending meat in any of the cities or boroughs in the several counties of this Commonwealth, under a penalty of ten dollars for each offence, to be recovered as other penalties are recoverable before any alderman or justice of the peace; one-half of said penalty to go to the informer and the other half for the benefit of the poor.

203. If any person shall sell or expose for sale the flesh of any diseased animals, or any other unwholesome flesh, knowing the same to be diseased or unwholesome, or sell or expose for sale unwholesome bread, drink, or liquor knowing the same to be unwholesome; or shall adulterate for the purpose of sale, or sell any flour, meal, or other article of foods, any wine, beer, spirits of any kind, or other liquor intended for drinking, knowing the same to be adulterated; or shall adulterate for sale, or shall sell, knowing the same to be adulterated, any drugs or medicines, such person so offending shall be guilty of a misdemeanor, and upon conviction be sentenced to pay a fine not exceeding one hundred dollars or undergo an imprisonment not exceeding six months, or both, or either, at the discretion of the court.

204. If any person shall manufacture for sale, or sell or offer to sell any candy or confectionery adulterated by the mixture of terra alba, barytes, talc, or other mineral substances, or by poisonous colors or flavors, or other ingredients, deleterious or detrimental to health, knowing the same to be so adulterated, such person so offending shall be guilty of a misdemeanor, and upon conviction be sentenced to pay a fine not exceeding one hundred dollars nor less than fifty dollars and the candy or confectionery so adulterated shall be forfeited and destroyed by the order of the court.

205. If any candy or confectionery adulterated in violation of the first section of this act shall be found in the possession of any manufacturer, or merchant, or dealer, it shall be deemed *prima facie* evidence that the same is offered for sale and that the person having it in possession knew that the same was so adulterated.

206. No action shall be maintained or recovery had in any case for the value of any candy or confectionery which may have been adulterated as specified in the first section of this act, and it shall be competent for the defendant in every such case to prove that the candy or confectionery was so adulterated, and proof thereof being so made shall amount to a good and legal defense to the whole of the plaintiff's claim therefor.

207. Relates to sale of oysters during June, July, and August, which it prohibits.

DAIRY PRODUCTS.

216. Any person or persons who shall knowingly sell or exchange any impure, adulterated, or unwholesome milk shall be deemed guilty of a misdemeanor, and on conviction shall be punished by a fine of not less than twenty dollars for each and every offense; and if the fine be not paid, shall be imprisoned for not less than fifteen days, or until said fine shall be paid.

217. Any person who shall adulterate milk with the view of offering the same for

sale or exchange, shall be deemed guilty of misdemeanor, and on conviction shall be punished by a fine of not less than ten dollars for each and every offence; and if the fine be not paid, shall be imprisoned for not less than eight days, or until said fine is paid.

220. The addition of water or of ice to milk is hereby declared an adulteration; any milk obtained from animals fed on distillery waste, or any substance in a state of putrefaction, is hereby declared to be impure and unwholesome.

223. Whoever, by himself, or by his servant or agent, or as the servant or agent of any other person, sells, exchanges, or delivers, or has in his custody or possession, with intent to sell or exchange, or exposes or offers for sale as pure milk any milk from which the cream or any part thereof has been removed shall, for such offense, be punished by penalty provided in section 222.*

230. No person, firm, or corporate body shall manufacture out of any oleaginous substance or any compound of the same, other than the product from unadultered milk or of cream from the same, any article designed to take the place of butter or cheese produced from pure unadulterated milk or cream from the same, or of any imitation or adulterated butter or cheese, nor shall sell or offer for sale, or have in his, her, or their possession with intent to sell the same as an article of food.

231. Every sale of such article or substance, which is prohibited by the first section of this act, made after this act shall take effect, is hereby declared to be unlawful and void and no action shall be maintained in any of the courts of this State to recover upon any contract for the sale of any such article or substance.

232. Every person, company, firm, or corporate body who shall manufacture, sell, or offer or expose for sale, or have in his, her, or their possession with intent to sell, any substance, the manufacture and sale of which is prohibited by the first section of this act, shall, for every such offense, forfeit and pay the sum of one hundred dollars, which shall be recovered with costs by any person suing in the name of the Commonwealth as debts of like amount are by law recoverable; one-half of which sum, when so recovered, shall be paid to the proper county treasurer for the use of the county in which suit is brought, and the other half to the person or persons at whose instance such a suit shall or may be commenced and prosecuted to recovery.

233. Every person who violates the provisions of the first section of this act shall be deemed guilty of a misdemeanor, and, upon conviction, shall be punished by a fine of not less than one hundred dollars, nor more than three hundred dollars, or by imprisonment in the county jail for not less than ten nor more than thirty days, or both, such fine and imprisonment for the first offense, and imprisonment for one year for every subsequent offense.

ACTION OF THE COURTS.

This act was declared constitutional by the Supreme Court, January 3, 1887. The act regulating the manufacture and sale of oleomargarine, hereby repealed, was that of 24 May, 1883. P. L., 43, P. D., 239.

The act of May 21, 1885, P. L., 22, prohibiting the manufacture and sale of oleomargarine, or the keeping the same with intent to sell, falls within the police power of the State, which may be prescribed to be the power vested in the legislature by the Constitution to make, ordain, and establish all manner of wholesome and reasonable laws, statutes, and ordinances, either with penalties or without, not repugnant to the Constitution, as they shall judge to be for the good and welfare of the Commonwealth, and the people of the same.

The test of the reasonableness of a police regulation prohibiting the making and vending of a particular article of food, is not alone whether it is in part unwholesome or injurious. If an article of food is of such a character that few persons will eat it, knowing its real character, if at the same time it is of such nature that it can be imposed upon the public as an article of food which is in common use, and against which there is no prejudice; and in addition to this, there is probable ground for believing that the only way to prevent the public being defrauded into purchasing the counterfeit article from the genuine is to prohibit altogether the manufacture and sale of the former, then such a prohibition may stand as a reasonable police regulation, although the article prohibited is in fact innocuous, and although its production might be found beneficial to the public, if in buying it they could distinguish

*Fine of not less than $20 or more than $100.

it from the production of which it is the imitation. The fact that scientific experts may pronounce a manufactured article intended for human food to be wholesome, and in a pure state good for food, does not render it incompetent for the legislature to prohibit the manufacture and sale of the article, if in the judgment of the legislature, and not of the courts, it be necessary to the protection of the lives, health, and property of the citizens, and to the preservation of good order and the public morals. The act of 21 May, 1885, is not in conflict with amendment XIV of the Constitution of the United States. Powell v. Commonwealth, 114 Pa. St., 265. See dissenting opinion of Justice Gordon, in same case.

VIRGINIA.

EXTRACTS FROM REVISED STATUTES, CODE 1887.

SEC. 3811. Selling unsound provisions, how punished : If any person knowingly sell any diseased, corrupted, or unwholesome provisions, whether meat or drink, without making the same known to the buyer, he shall be confined in jail not exceeding six months, and fined not exceeding one hundred dollars.

SEC. 3812. Adulterating food, drink, or medicine, how punished : If any person fraudulently or knowingly adulterate, for the purpose of sale, any drug or medicine, or any article of food or drink, with any substance that may be injurious to health, or with barytes or any substance intended to increase the weight or quantity of such food or drink, he shall be confined in jail not exceeding one year, and fined not exceeding five hundred dollars ; and the adulterated articles shall be forfeited and destroyed.

Virginia also has a law regulating the sale of oleomargarine.

WISCONSIN.

DAIRY AND FOOD COMMISSIONER.

[CHAPTER 452, Laws of 1889.]

SEC. 1. The office of dairy and food commissioner for the State of Wisconsin is hereby created. Such commissioner shall be appointed by the governor, by and with the advice and consent of the senate, and his term of office shall be for two years from the date of his appointment and until his successor is appointed and qualified; provided, that the term of office of the commissioner first appointed under this act shall expire on the first Monday in February, 1891, and vacancies occurring in the office for any cause shall be filled by appointment for the balance of the unexpired term. The salary of the commissioner shall be twenty-five hundred dollars per annum and his necessary and actual expenses incurred in the discharge of his official duties.

SEC. 2. Such commissioner may, with the consent and advice of the governor, appoint two assistants, each of acknowledged standing, ability, and integrity, one of whom shall be an expert in the matter of dairy products, and the other of whom shall be a practical analytical chemist. The salaries of such assistants shall not exceed eighteen hundred dollars each per annum and their necessary and actual expenses incurred in the discharge of their official duties.

SEC. 3. It shall be the duty of the commissioner to enforce all laws that now exist, or that may hereafter be enacted in this State, regarding the production, manufacture, or sale of dairy products, or the adulteration of any article of food or drink or of any drug ; and personally or by his assistants to inspect any article of milk, butter, cheese, lard, syrup, coffee, or tea, or other article of food or drink or drug, made or offered for sale within this State which he may suspect or have reason to believe to be impure, unhealthful, adulterated, or counterfeit, and to prosecute, or cause to be prosecuted, any person or persons, firm or firms, corporation or corporations, engaged in the manufacture or sale of any adulterated or counterfeit article or articles of food or drink or drug, contrary to the laws of this State.

SEC. 4. Said commissioner or any assistant shall have power in the performance of his official duties to enter into any creamery, factory, store, salesroom, or other place or building where he has reason to believe that any food or drink or drug is made, prepared, sold, or offered for sale, and to open any cask, tub, package, or receptacle of any kind containing, or supposed to contain, any such article, and to examine or cause to be examined and analyzed the contents thereof, and the commissioner or any of his assistants may seize or take any article of food or drink or drug for analysis, but if the person from whom such sample is taken shall request him to do so he shall at the same time, and in the presence of the person from whom such property is taken, securely seal up two samples of the article seized or taken, the one of which shall be for examination or analysis under the direction of the commissioner, and the other of which shall be delivered to the person from whom the articles were taken. And any person who shall obstruct the commissioner or any of his assistants by refusing to allow him entrance to any place which he desires to enter in the discharge of his official duty, or who refuses to deliver to him a sample of any article of food or drink or drug made, sold, offered, or exposed for sale by such person, when the same is requested and when the value thereof is tendered, shall be deemed guilty of a misdemeanor punishable by a fine of not exceeding twenty-five dollars for the first offense and not exceeding five hundred dollars or less than fifty dollars for each subsequent offense.

SEC. 5. It shall be the duty of the district attorney in any county of the State, when called upon by the commissioner or any of his assistants, to render any legal assistance in his power to execute the laws, and to prosecute cases arising under the provisions of this act, and all fines and assessments collected in any prosecution begun or caused to be begun by said commissioner or his assistants shall be paid into the State treasury.

SEC. 6. With the consent of the governor, the State board of health may submit to the commissioner, or to any of his assistants, samples of water or of food or drink or drugs for examination or analysis, and receive special reports showing the result of such examinations or analysis. And the governor may also authorize the commissioner or his assistants, when not otherwise employed in the duties of their offices, to render such assistance in the farmers' institutes, dairy and farmers' conventions, and the agricultural department of the university, as shall by the authorities be deemed advisable.

SEC. 7. The salaries of the commissioner and his assistants shall be paid out of the State treasury in the same manner as the salaries of other officers are paid, and their official expenses shall be paid at the end of each calendar month upon bills duly itemized and approved by the governor, and the amount necessary to pay such salaries and expenses is hereby appropriated annually.

SEC. 8. The commissioner may, under the direction of the governor, fit up a laboratory, with sufficient apparatus for making the analysis contemplated in this act, and for such purpose the sum of fifteen hundred dollars, or so much thereof as may be necessary, is hereby appropriated, and for the purpose of providing materials and for other necessary expenses connected with the making of such analyses there is also hereby appropriated so much as may be necessary, not exceeding six hundred dollars annually. The appropriations provided for in this section shall be drawn from the State treasury upon the certificates of the governor.

SEC. 9. Said commissioner shall be furnished a suitable office in the capitol, at Madison, and shall make an annual report to the governor, which shall contain an itemized account of all expenses incurred and fines collected, with such statistics and other information as he may regard of value, and with the consent of the governor, not exceeding twenty thousand copies thereof, limited to three hundred pages, may be published annually as other official reports are published, and of which five thousand copies shall be bound in cloth.

SEC. 10. All acts and parts of acts conflicting with this act are hereby repealed.

SEC. 11. This act shall take effect and be in force from and after its passage and publication.

Approved April 16, 1889.

[NOTE TO SECTION 4, SUPRA.—If there is contradictory evidence concerning the sufficiency of the seal of a sample, and the credibility of the witnesses for the prosecution is submitted to the jury the defendant is not injured. If there is evidence that a few drops of carbolic acid was added to a sample of milk, and it is submitted to the jury as a question of fact whether this would change the character of the milk, make the analysis impossible or difficult, or in any way injuriously affect the sample for the purpose of analysis, the defendant has no cause of complaint. *Commonwealth* v. *Spear*, 143 Mass., 172.

It is observed of a similar statute that it is intended to secure a fair examination and analysis, by providing the defendant with the means of making an analysis of a portion of the same specimen which the State has analyzed. If the sample is not saved, or not saved in proper condition, he has no means of showing that his evidence, if any he has as to the quality of the milk, applies to that with reference to which the government witnesses testify. It can not be said that a portion reserved is sealed, within the meaning of the statute, when wax is merely placed on the top of the cork, and not extended over the mouth of the bottle and thus making it airtight, if it is shown that the character of the milk will be affected by the air. *Commonwealth* v. *Lockhardt*, 144 Mass., 132.

Where the article analyzed has not been taken under the statute, the competency of evidence is to be determined by the common law, and the testimony of any person who had sufficient skill to analyze it, and who had analyzed some which had proven to have been sold by the defendant, is admissible. *Commonwealth* v. *Holt*, 146 Mass., 38.]

PURE MILK, STANDARD OF.

[Chapter 425, Laws of 1889.]

SEC. 1. Any person who shall sell or offer for sale or furnish or deliver, or have in his possession, with intent to sell or offer for sale or furnish or deliver to any creamery, cheese factory, corporation, person or persons whatsoever, as pure, wholesome and unskimmed, any unmerchantable, adulterated, impure or unwholesome milk, shall, upon conviction thereof, be punished by a fine of not less than ten nor more than one hundred dollars for each and every offense.

SEC. 2. In all prosecutions or other proceedings under this or any other law of this State relating to the sale or furnishing of milk, if it shall be proven that the milk sold or offered for sale, or furnished or delivered, or had in possession with intent to sell or offer for sale, or to furnish or deliver as aforesaid, as pure, wholesome and unskimmed, contain less than three per centum of pure butter fat, when subjected to chemical analysis or other satisfactory test, or that it has been diluted or any part of its cream abstracted, or that it or any part of it was drawn from cows known to the person complained of to have been within fifteen days before or four days after parturition, or to have any disease or ulcers or other running sores, then and in either case the said milk shall be held, deemed, and adjudged to have been unmerchantable and adulterated, impure or unwholesome, as the case may be.

SEC. 3. All acts and parts of acts conflicting with or contrary to the provisions of this act are hereby repealed.

SEC. 4. This act shall take effect and be in force from and after its passage and publication.

Approved April 16, 1889.

[NOTE—VALIDITY.—A New York law (chapter 183, of 1885; chapter 202, of 1884) provides that "no person or persons shall sell, supply or bring to be manufactured, to any butter or cheese manufactory, any milk diluted with water, or any unclean, impure, unhealthy, adulterated or unwholesome milk." *Held*, a valid exercise of legislative power. *People* v. *West*, 106 N. Y., 293.

A statute is not invalid because it fixes an arbitrary standard for pure or unadulterated milk, though it is drawn from healthy cows, and is sold in its natural state. *In People* v. *Cipperly*, 37 Hun. (N. Y.), 324, it was held otherwise, one judge dissenting.

On appeal this case was reversed, without opinion, on the grounds given in the dissenting opinion : 101 N. Y., 634. The supreme court of New Hampshire say on this question : Practically it makes no difference whether milk is diluted after it is drawn from the cow, or whether it is made watery by giving her such food as will produce milk of an inferior quality, or whether the dilution, regarded by legislature as excessive, arises from the nature of a particular animal, or a particular breed of cattle. The sale of such milk to unsuspecting consumers, for a price in excess of its value, is a fraud, which the statute was designed to suppress. It is a valid exercise by the legislature of the police power for the prevention of fraud and protection of the public health, and such as is constitutional. *State* v. *Campbell*, 13 Atl. Rep., 585.]

[CONSTRUCTION—INDICTMENT.—The New York law does not make fraudulent intent a necessary ingredient of the offense, and it would not be a reasonable construction of it to apply it to a dairyman who owns and conducts a butter or cheese factory for the manufacture of those articles from milk furnished exclusively by himself, from his own cows. If the defendant is such a person, these facts are matter of defense, and their existence need not be negatived on the face of the indictment. *People* v. *West*, 106 N. Y., 293.

Under a Massachusetts law imposing a penalty for selling or offering to sell "adulterated milk, or milk to which any foreign substance has been added," it is immaterial whether the substance added is injurious or not. The indictment need not allege the quantity of such substance. *Commonwealth* v. *Schaffner*, 16 Northeast. Rep., 280.

Under an act which prohibits the sale of milk which is not of a good, standard quality, the fact that the milk was delivered under a contract to furnish the person who bought it with the milk of one dairy is not a defense if that furnished was not of such quality. The contract would be held to contemplate milk which should be bought and sold. *Commonwealth* v. *Holt*, 14 Northeast. Rep., 930.

Where one is charged with having in his possession, with intent to sell, milk which is not of a good, standard quality, the fact that he was upon a wagon which had his name painted on it, and that therein were cans of milk, and that a sample was given from one of them to one employed by the milk inspector for analysis, is competent evidence to go to the jury upon the question of his intent. *Commonwealth* v. *Rowell*, 15 Northeast. Rep., 154.]

[EFFECT OF THE ACT OF 1889 UPON PREVIOUS LAWS.—It seems reasonably clear that section 1, of chapter 425, Laws of 1889, *supra*, supersedes section 1, of chapter 157, laws of 1887, as to the offense of selling diluted, impure, and unclean milk. Both the acts referred to cover the provisions of section 4607, Revised Statutes, and hence that section is not in force.]

PROOF OF ADULTERATION, HOW MADE.

[Section 2, of Chapter 157, of the Laws of 1887, as amended by chapter 344, Laws of 1889.]

SEC. 1. Proof of adulterations and skimming may be made with such standard tests and lacometers as are used to determine the quality of milk, or by chemical analysis.

SEC. 2. This act shall take effect and be in force from and after its passage and publication.

Approved April 10, 1889.

[NOTE.—This act supersedes chapter 361, Laws of 1885, so far as the last-mentioned act is valid. The act of 1885 prohibited the manufacture out of any oleaginous substances, or any compound of the same, other than that produced from unadulterated milk, or cream of the same, any article designed to take the place of butter or cheese, produced from pure, unadulterated milk, or cream of the same, and the offering of the same for sale or selling it as an article of food, without providing, as does the act of 1889, that the sale or offering for sale such an article must be made as and for butter or cheese, the product of the dairy. See, to the effect that such a clause is unconstitutional, *People* v. *Arensberg*, 103 N. Y., 388.

NOTE—ORIGIN.—This section, except as to the penalty, is a copy of a part of section 8, chapter 183, laws of New York, 1885.

VALIDITY.—Section 7, chapter 183, Laws of New York, 1885, "prohibits: 1st. The manufacture out of any animal fat, or animal or vegetable oils, not produced from unadulterated milk or cream from the same, of any product in imitation or semblance or designed to take the place of natural butter produced from milk, etc. 2d. Mixing, compounding with, or adding to milk, cream, or butter, any acids or other deleterious substances, or animal fats, etc., with design or intent to produce any article in imitation or semblance of natural butter. 3d. Selling, or keeping or offering for sale any article manufactured in violation of the provisions of this section." *Held*, that if butter made from animal fat or oil is as wholesome and nutritious and suitable for food as dairy butter, the producers of butter made from animal fat or oils have no constitutional right to resort to devices for the purpose of making their product resemble in appearance the more expensive article known as dairy butter. It is competent for the legislature to enact laws to prevent the simulated article being put upon the market in such a form and manner as to be calculated to deceive. The statute is intended to reach a designed and purposed imitation of dairy butter in manufacturing the product which is not such butter, and not a resemblance in qualities inherent in the articles and common to both kinds of butter. *People* v. *Arensberg*, 105 N. Y., 123.

A State may lawfully prohibit the manufacture out of oleaginous substances, or out of any of its compounds other than that produced from unadulterated milk or cream from such milk, of an article designed to take the place of butter or cheese produced from unadulterated milk. It may also prohibit the manufacture, or sale, or the offering for sale, of any imitation or adulterated butter or cheese, or the having of it in possession with intent to sell the same as an article of food. *Powell* v. *Pennsylvania*, 127 U. S., 678.

Though it may be severe to punish those who unintentionally sell the article prohibited, the legislature has power to so provide in order that the much larger number may be protected. *State* v. *Newton*, 14 Atl. Rep., 604.

The supreme court of New Jersey has held that a statute enacted for a purpose similar to that which caused the passage of this act is not invalid because it prohibits the sale of oleomargarine brought to that State from other States and not intended for further transportation. The act produces only an indirect and incidental effect upon interstate commerce. *State* v. *Newton*, 14 Atl. Rep., 604.]

ADULTERATED HONEY MUST BE MARKED.

[Part of chapter 40, Laws of 1881.]

SEC. 2. Every person, company, or corporation who shall sell or offer for sale, honey, or any imitation of honey, which is adulterated with glucose, or any other substance, shall mark the package or parcel with the words "adulterated honey," as required by section one of this act.

[NOTE.—Section 1, of chapter 40, Laws of 1881, related to the manufacture of imitation butter, and provided that each firkin, tub, package or parcel thereof, should be marked on top of same in letters not less than one-half inch in length, and breadth in proportion, and in such manner that it may be plainly seen. As applied to butter the said section was repealed by chapter 361, Laws of 1885. Section 3, of the act of 1881, related to imitation cheese. It was also repealed by the act of 1885.]

SEC. 4. Any person found guilty of any violation of this act shall, for each offense, be punished by imprisonment in the county jail, not less than ten days nor more than six months, or by a fine of not less than ten dollars nor more than one hundred dollars, or both, in the discretion of the court.

SEC. 5. One-half of all fines imposed by the enforcement of this act shall be paid to the person who informs against and prosecutes such offender to conviction.

SEC. 6. All acts or parts of acts conflicting with the provisions of this act are hereby repealed.

SEC. 7. This act shall take effect and be in force from and after its passage and publication.

Approved March 3, 1881.

PENALTY FOR THE SALE OF UNWHOLESOME PROVISIONS.

[Section 4599, Revised Statutes.]

SEC. 4599. Any person who shall knowingly sell any kind of diseased, corrupt, or unwholesome provisions, whether for meat or drink, without making the same fully known to the buyer, shall be punished by imprisonment in the county jail not more than six months or by fine not exceeding one hundred dollars.

ADULTERATION OF FOOD, LIQUORS, AND CANDIES.

[Section 4600, Revised Statutes.)

SEC. 4600. Any person who shall fraudulenty adulterate, for the purpose of sale, any substance intended for food, or any wine, spirits, malt liquors, or other spirituous liquors, or any other fluid, intended for drinking, or any candy or sweetmeat, with substance, coloring matter, or anything poisonous, deleterious or injurious to health, or who shall knowingly manufacture, sell, or offer for sale any such adulterated food, liquor, candy, or sweetmeat, shall be punished by imprisonment in the county jail not more than six months or by fine not exceeding one hundred dollars, and any article so adulterated shall be forfeited and destroyed.

NOTE.—See chapter 248, laws of 1879, *infra*, which appears to supersede this section in part.

ADULTERATION OF FOOD AND DRUGS—DECEPTIVE LABELING OF.

[Chapter 248, laws of 1879.]

SEC. 1. No person shall mix, color, stain, powder, order or permit any other person to mix, color, stain, or powder any article of food with any ingredient or material so as to render the article injurious to health, with intent that the same may be sold in that condition. And any person that shall sell any such article so mixed, colored, stained, or powdered shall be subjected to a penalty in each case not exceeding a fine of fifty dollars for the first offense, and for a second offense shall be punished by imprisonment in the State prison for a period not exceeding one year, with hard labor.

SEC. 2. No person shall, except for the purpose of compounding as hereinafter described, mix, color, stain, or powder, or permit any other person to mix, color, stain, or powder, any drug with any ingredient or material so as to affect injuriously the quality or potency of such drug, with intent that the same may be sold in that condition. And any person who shall sell any such drug so mixed, colored, stained, or powdered shall be liable to the same penalty or punishment in each case, respectively, as in the preceding section for a first and subsequent offense: *Provided,* That no person shall be liable to be convicted under the foregoing sections of this act, in respect to the sale of any article of food or of any drug, if he shows to the satisfaction of the justice or court before whom he is charged that he did not know of the article or drug sold by him being so mixed, colored, stained, or powdered, as in that section mentioned, and that he could not, with reasonable diligence, have obtained that knowledge ; or that such mixing, coloring, staining, or powdering was required for the production, extraction, preparation, preservation, consumption, or transportation as an article of commerce in a State fit for carriage ; or where the drug or food is supplied in the State required by the specification of the patent in force; or that the food or drug was unavoidably mixed with some extraneous matter in process of collection or preparation.

SEC. 3. Every person who shall compound or put up for sale any food, drug, or liquor in casks, boxes, bottles, or packages with any label, mark, or device whatever so as and with intent to mislead or deceive as to the true name, nature, kind, and quality thereof, shall be liable to a penalty of not to exceed five hundred dollars for the first offense, and for every offense after the first offense shall be punished by imprisonment in the State prison for not less than one year nor more than ten years.

SEC. 4. The term "food" as herein used shall include every article used for food or drink by man other than drugs. The term "drug" shall include medicine for internal or external use.

SEC. 5. This act shall take effect and be in force from and after the first day of July, after its passage and publication.

Approved, March 5, 1879.

DRUGS AND MEDICINES.

[Section 4601, Revised Statutes.]

SEC. 4601. Any person who shall fraudulently adulterate for the purpose of sale any drug or medicine in such a manner as to render the same injurious to health shall be punished by imprisonment in the county jail not more than one year or by fine not exceeding three hundred dollars.

NOTE.—See chapter 248, laws of 1879, *supra*.

COLORING GRAIN.

[Section 4606, Revised Statutes.]

SEC. 4606. Any person who shall fumigate any barley, wheat, or other grain by the use of sulphur or other substance, or shall in any way, or by the use of any chemical, material, or process, affect the color or healthfulness of such grain, or who shall sell or offer for sale any such grain, knowing that the same has been so fumigated, or the color or healthfulness thereof so affected, shall be punished by imprisonment in the county jail not more than one month or by fine not exceeding fifty dollars.

ANALYSIS OF FOOD, DRUGS, AND DRINK.

[Chapter 252, laws of 1880.]

SEC. 1. The governor of the State shall appoint one of the professors of the State University of sufficient competence, knowledge, skill, and experience as State analyst, whose duty it shall be to analyze all articles of food and drink, and all drugs and liquors manufactured, sold, or used within this State, when submitted to him as hereinafter provided. The term of office of such analyst shall be three years from his appointment, unless sooner removed by the appointing power, and his compensation shall not exceed two hundred dollars in addition to his annual salary as professor, and shall be paid by the board of regents of the State university from the university fund.

SEC. 2. The State board of health and vital statistics, medical officers of health, inspectors of weights and measures, boards of supervisors of any town, boards of trustees of any village, aldermen or common council of any city in this State, or a majority of said corporate bodies, may, at the cost of their respective corporations, purchase a sample of any food, drugs, or liquors offered for sale in any town, village, or city in this State in violation of sections number one, two, and four of chapter two hundred and forty-eight of laws of A. D. 1879, or if they have good reasons to suspect the same to have been sold or put up for sale contrary to the provisions of said chapter two hundred and forty-eight may submit the same to the State analyst as hereinafter provided; and the said analyst shall, upon receiving such article duly submitted to him, forthwith analyse the same, and give a certified certificate to such person or officer submitting the same, wherein he shall fully specify the result of the analysis.

SEC. 3. Any person purchasing any article with the intention of submitting it to an analysis shall, after the purchase shall have been made and completed, forthwith notify the seller or his agent selling the same of his or their intention to have the same analyzed by the State analyst, and shall offer to accompany the seller or his agent with the article purchased to the town, village, or city clerk of the place in which the article was bought, and shall forthwith remove the article purchased to the office of said clerk, and in the presence of the seller or his agent, if pres-nt, divide said article in two parts, each to be marked, fastened, and sealed up in such a manner as its nature will permit. The said clerk shall forthwith forward one part to the State analyst by mail, express, or otherwise, as he shall elect, and shall retain the other part or package subject to the order of any court in which proceedings shall thereafter be taken. The certificate of the State analyst shall be held in all the courts of this State as prima facie evidence of the properties of the articles analyzed by him.

SEC. 4. If any person applying to purchase any article of food, drug, or liquor exposed for sale or on sale by retail on any premises in any town, village, or city in this State, and shall tender the price of the quantity which he shall want, for the purpose of analysing, not being more than shall be reasonably required, and the person exposing the same for sale shall refuse to sell the same, such person so refusing to sell shall be liable to a penalty not exceeding fifty dollars.

SEC. 5. The State analyst shall report to the State board of health and vital statistics the number of all the articles analysed, and shall specify the results thereof to said board annually, with full statement of all the articles analysed and by whom submitted.

SEC. 6. The State board of health and vital statistics may submit to the State analyst any samples of food, drugs, or drink for analysis as hereinbefore provided.

SEC. 7. This act shall take effect and be in force from and after its passage and publication.

Approved, March 15, 1880.

FRAUD IN DAIRY MANUFACTORIES.

[Section 1494 a, Revised Statutes.]

Any butter or cheese manufacturer who shall knowingly use, or allow any of his employés, or any other person, to use for his or their own individual benefit, any milk, or cream from the milk, brought to said butter or cheese manufacturer, without the consent of all the owners thereof, or any butter or cheese manufacturer who shall refuse or neglect to keep, or cause to be kept, a correct account (open to the inspection of any one furnishing milk to such manufacturer) of the amount of milk daily received, or of the number of pounds of butter, and the number and aggregate weight of cheese made each day, or of the number cut or otherwise disposed of, and the weight of each, shall, for each and every offense, forfeit and pay a sum not less than twenty-five dollars, nor more than one hundred dollars, to be recovered in an action in any court of competent jurisdiction, one-half for the benefit of the person or persons, firm or association, or their assigns, upon whom such fraud or neglect shall be committed, first having made complaint therefor, the remainder to the school fund.

LAW PASSED BY THE LEGISLATURE OF 1891.

[This act repeals Chap. 240, laws of 1887, as amended by Chap. 455, laws of 1889.]

SEC. 1. Chapter 455 of the laws of 1889 is hereby repealed.

SEC. 2. Every person who shall, at any cheese factory in the State, manufacture cheese, shall distinctly and durably stamp upon each and every such cheese, whether cheddar, twin, flat, or Young America, or by whatever name or style known, upon the sale thereof, in full-faced capital letters, the grade of the same, as " Wisconsin full cream," "standard," or "skimmed," as hereafter provided for in this act, together with the name of the city, village, or town where such factory shall be located.

SEC 3. Such cheese only as shall have been manufactured from pure and wholesome milk, and from which no portion of the butter fat shall have been removed by skimming or by any other process, and in the manufacture of which neither butter nor any substitute for butter or other animal or vegetable fats or oils have been used, nor any fat which has been extracted from milk in any form and returned for the purpose of filling the cheese, shall be stamped " Wisconsin full cream." All cheese manufactured as above required from pure and wholesome milk, but from which a portion of the fat has been removed, shall if it contain not less than thirty per centum of pure butter fat, be stamped or branded "standard." All cheese containing less than thirty per centum of pure butter fat shall be stamped or branded "skimmed."

SEC. 4. The stamp provided for in this act designating the grade of cheese shall be such as to produce an impression not less than three inches in width and five inches in length, and the words "Wisconsin full cream," "standard," or "skimmed," together with the name of the city, village, or town where the cheese shall have been manufactured, as provided for in the foregoing sections of this act, shall be in full-faced capital letters of as large a size as the space hereby provided for will permit, and the whole to be included within a plain heavy border. Ordinary "stamping ink," either red, green, purple, or violet in color, and of such composition as not to be easily removed or wholly obliterated by moisture, shall be used in stamping, as provided for in this act.

SEC. 5. Any manufacturer of cheese who shall sell or dispose of any cheese without being stamped as required by this act, or who shall falsely stamp the same, and any dealer or other person who shall remove such stamp from cheese, shall, upon conviction thereof, be fined not less than fifty nor more than one hundred dollars for the first offense, and for each subsequent offense not less than one hundred nor more than two hundred dollars, or be imprisoned in the county jail not less than thirty nor more than ninety days, or both, in the discretion of the court before whom such conviction may be had. One-half of all fines collected under the provisions of this act shall be paid to the person or persons furnishing the information upon which such conviction is procured.

SEC. 6. Nothing in this act shall be construed to apply to Edam, brickstein, pineapple, Limburger, Swiss, or hand cheese, or other cheese by whatever name or style known not made by the ordinary cheddar process.

SEC. 7. All acts or part of acts inconsistent with the provisions of this act are hereby repealed.

SEC. 8. This act shall take effect and be in force from and after its passage and publication.

There are three distinctive brands necessary under the law quoted.

No. 1.—Full Cream Cheese.

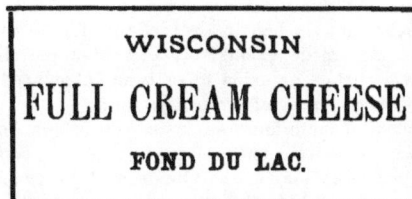

```
┌──────────────────────────────────────┐
│             WISCONSIN                 │
│                                       │
│    FULL CREAM CHEESE                  │
│                                       │
│            FOND DU LAC.               │
└──────────────────────────────────────┘
```

All cheese made by the cheddar process, and made from milk from which no fat has been taken, shall bear brand No. 1.

No. 2.—Standard Cheese.

```
STANDARD CHEESE.

FOND DU LAC, WIS.
```

All cheese made by the cheddar process, and made from milk from which any fat has been taken, but still leaving not less than 30 per cent of fat in the cheese, shall bear brand No. 2.

No. 3.—Skimmed Cheese.

```
SKIMMED CHEESE.

FOND DU LAC, WIS.
```

All cheese made by the cheddar process, and made from milk from which enough fat has been taken so that the cheese is left with less than 30 per cent. of fat, shall bear brand No. 3.

The law provides that the stamp or brand shall be not less than three by five inches and inclosed by a plain heavy border. The ink shall be indelible, so that it will not rub off. The brand or stamp is to be placed upon the bandage of the cheese. A rubber stamp costs about the same as a stencil and does much better work.

The name of the manufacturer can not be placed inside the border. If the maker wishes his name to appear it can be placed on the cheese anywhere except within the impression.

The law of 1889, which provided for marking the box, is repealed.

Rubber-stamp manufacturers are in possession of this law and you can be provided with stamps by any of them. The firm from which you buy your supplies can furnish you the necessary stamps.

Filling cheese with foreign fat is prohibited by chapter 424, Laws of 1889.

Enriching skim milk with butter is prohibited by chapter 264, Laws of 1891, also by chapter 165, Laws of 1891.

DEALERS AND MANUFACTURERS OF VINEGAR.

[Text and suggestions relating to the law passed by the legislature of 1891.]

SEC. 1. Every person who manufactures for sale or offers or exposes for sale, as cider vinegar, any vinegar not the legitimate product of pure apple juice, known as apple cider, or vinegar not made exclusively of said apple cider, or vinegar into which foreign substances, drugs, or acids have been introduced, as may appear by proper tests, shall be deemed guilty of a misdemeanor.

SEC. 2. Every person who manufactures for sale or offers for sale any vinegar, found, upon proper tests, to contain any preparation of lead, copper, sulphuric acid, or other ingredient injurious to health, shall be deemed guilty of a misdemeanor.

SEC. 3. No person, by himself, his servant, or agent, or as the servant or agent of any other person, shall sell, exchange, deliver, or have in his custody or possession, with intent to sell or exchange, or expose or offer for sale or exchange, any adulterated vinegar, nor shall he label, brand, or sell as cider vinegar, or as apple vinegar, any vinegar not the legitimate product of pure apple juice or not made exclusively from apple cider.

SEC. 4. All vinegar shall have an acidity equivalent to the presence of not less than four per cent by weight of absolute acetic acid, and, in the case of cider vinegar, shall contain in addition not less than two per cent by weight of cider vinegar solids upon full evaporation over boiling water at 212°; and if any vinegar contains any artificial coloring matter injurious to health or less than the above amount of acidity, or, in the case of cider vinegar, if it contains less than the above amount of acidity or of cider vinegar solids, it shall be deemed adulterated within the meaning of this act. All manufacturers of vinegar in the State of Wisconsin, and all persons who reduce or rebarrel vinegar in this State, and all persons who handle vinegar in lots of one barrel or more, are hereby required to stencil or mark in black figures at least one inch in length on the head of each barrel of vinegar bought or sold by them the standard strength of the vinegar contained in the package or barrel, which shall be denoted by the per centum of acetic acid. And any neglect so to mark or stencil each package or barrel or any false markings of packages or barrels shall be deemed a misdemeanor.

SEC. 5. Whoever violates any of the provisions of this act shall be deemed guilty of a misdemeanor, and shall be punished by a fine of not less than ten nor more than one hundred dollars and costs.

SEC. 6. This act shall take effect and be in force from and after its passage and publication.

Section 1 provides that any person who makes cider vinegar shall sell it as such.

Section 2 provides that no injurious ingredients shall be used in the manufacture of vinegar.

Section 3 provides that no person, or his agent, shall sell adulterated or spirit vinegar as cider vinegar.

Section 4 provides that all vinegar shall test not less than four per cent of acetic acid, and that cider vinegar shall contain not less than two per cent of solids, and that manufacturers and reducers, and persons who handle vinegar, shall brand upon head of barrel, in letters not less than one inch, the per centum of acetic acid, as follows:

ACETIC ACID 4 PER CENTUM.

Chapter 248, Laws of 1879, provides that no label, mark or device shall be upon any package or cask, which shall mislead or deceive as to the true contents.

The law relating to the branding of casks will be enforced on and after June 1, 1891.

ACT REPEALING CHAPTER 185, LAWS OF 1887.

SEC. 1. No person shall sell, exchange, expose, or offer for sale or exchange, or ship or consign, or have in his possession with intent to sell, ship, or consign, any substance purporting, appearing, or represented to be butter or cheese, or having the semblance of either butter or cheese, which substance is not made wholly and directly from pure milk or cream, salt, and harmless coloring matter, unless it be done under its true name, and each vessel, package, roll, or parcel of such substance has distinctly and durably painted, stamped, stenciled, or marked thereon the true name of such substance in ordinary bold-faced capital letters, not less than five-line pica in size, or sell or dispose of in any manner to another, any such substance in quantities less than the original package, without delivering with each amount sold or disposed of, a label, on which is plainly and legibly printed in ordinary bold-faced letters not less than five-line pica in size, the true name of each substance.

SEC. 2. No person or persons shall manufacture out of any oleaginous substance or substances, or any compound of the same other than that produced wholly, directly, and at the time of manufacture from unadulterated milk or cream, salt, and harmless coloring matter any article in imitation of or designed to be sold, shipped, or consigned as butter or cheese. Nothing in this section shall prevent the use of pure skimmed milk in the manufacture of cheese; but cheese made wholly or in part from skimmed milk should be plainly labeled "skimmed."

[This section repeals chapter 424, laws of 1889.]

SEC. 3. No person or persons shall manufacture, mix, compound with, or add to, natural or pure milk, cream, butter, or cheese, any animal fats, animal, mineral, or vegetable oils, or extraneous butter fat, or oil ; nor shall any person or persons manufacture any oleaginous or other substance not produced wholly and at the time from pure milk or cream, salt, and harmless coloring matter, or have the same in his possession with intent to offer or expose the same for sale, or exchange, or sell, consign, ship, or in any manner dispose of the same as and for butter or cheese, nor shall any substance or compound so made be sold or disposed of to anyone as and for butter or cheese.

SEC. 4. No person or persons shall sell, exchange, expose, or offer for sale or exchange, dispose of, ship or consign, or have in his possession any substance or article made in imitation or resemblance of any dairy product which is falsely branded, stenciled, labeled, or marked.

SEC. 5. Every person in this State who shall deal in, keep for sale, expose, or offer for sale or exchange, any substance other than butter or cheese, made wholly and directly from pure milk or cream, salt, and harmless coloring matter, which appears to be, resembles, or is made in imitation of, butter and cheese, shall keep a card not less in size than ten by fourteen inches, posted in a conspicuous and visible place, where the same may be easily seen and read in the storeroom, stand, booth, wagon, or place where such substance is so kept or exposed for sale, on which card shall be printed, on a white ground, in bold, black Roman letters, not less in size than twelve-line pica, the words "oleomargarine," "butterine," or "imitation cheese" (as the case may be), "sold here," and said card shall not contain any other words than the ones above prescribed ; and no person shall sell any oleomargarine, butterine, imitation cheese, or other imitation dairy product, at retail or in any quantity less than the original package, tub, or firkin, unless he shall first inform the purchaser that the substance is not butter or cheese, but an imitation of the same.

SEC. 6. Every proprietor, keeper, or manager, or person in charge of any hotel, boarding house, restaurant, eating house, lunch counter, or lunch room, who therein sells, uses or disposes of any substance which appears to be, resembles, or is made in imitation of butter or cheese, under whatsoever name, and which substance is not wholly and directly made from pure milk or cream, salt, and harmless coloring matter, shall display and keep a card posted in a conspicuous place, where the same may be easily seen and read, in the dining room, eating room, lunch room, restaurant, and place where such substance is sold, used, or disposed of, which card shall be white, and in size not less than ten by fourteen inches, upon which shall be printed in plain, black, Roman letters, not less in size than twelve-line pica, the words " oleomargarine used here," " butterine used here," or " imitation cheese used here" (as the case may be), and said card shall not contain any other words than the ones above prescribed, and such proprietor, keeper, manager, or person in charge shall not sell, furnish, or dispose of substance as and for " butter or cheese " made from pure milk or cream, salt, and harmless coloring matter, when butter or cheese is asked for.

SEC. 7. No butter or cheese not made wholly and directly from pure milk or cream, salt, and harmless coloring matter shall be used in any of the charitable or penal institutions of the State.

SEC. 8. Any person or persons violating any of the provisions or sections of this act, shall, upon conviction thereof, be fined not less than twenty-five nor more than fifty dollars for the first offense, or for each subsequent offense not less than fifty nor more than one hundred dollars, or be imprisoned in the county jail not less than ten or more than ninety days, or both.

Sec. 9. One-half of all the fines collected under the provisions of this act shall be paid to the person or persons furnishing information upon which conviction is procured.

Sec. 10. All acts or parts of acts contravening the provisions of this act are hereby repealed.

Sec. 11. This act shall take effect and be in force from and after its passage and publication.

ENGLAND.

The English law is as follows:

THE SALE OF FOOD AND DRUGS ACT.

AN ACT to repeal the adulteration of food acts, and to make better provision for the sale of food and drugs in a pure state. (11th August, 1875.)

Whereas it is desirable that the acts now in force relating to the adulteration of food should be repealed, and that the law regarding the sale of food and drugs in a pure and genuine condition should be amended:

Be it therefore enacted by the Queen's Most Excellent Majesty, by and with the advice and consent of the lords spiritual and temporal, and Commons, in this present Parliament assembled, and by the authority of the same, as follows:

(1) From the commencement of this act the statutes of the twenty-third and twenty-fourth Victoria, chapter eighty-four, of the thirty-first and thirty-second of Victoria, chapter one hundred and twenty-one, section twenty-four, of the thirty-third and thirty-fourth of Victoria, chapter twenty-six, section three, and of the thirty-fifth and thirty-sixth of Victoria, chapter seventy-four, shall be repealed, except in regard to any appointment made under them and not then determined, and in regard to any offense committed against them or any prosecution or other act commenced and not concluded or completed, and any payment of money then due in respect of any provision thereof.

(2) The term "food" shall include every article used for food or drink by man, other than drugs or water;

The term "drug" shall include medicine for internal or external use;

The term "county" shall include every county of a city or town not being a borough;

The term "justices" shall include any police and stipendiary magistrate invested with the powers of a justice of the peace in England, and any divisional justices in Ireland.

DESCRIPTION OF OFFENSES.

(3) No person shall mix, color, stain, or powder, or order or permit any other person to mix, color, stain, or powder, any article of food with any ingredient or material so as to render the article injurious to health, with intent that the same may be sold in that state; and no person shall sell any such article so mixed, colored, stained, or powdered, under a penalty in each case not exceeding fifty pounds for the first offense. Every offense, after a conviction for a first offense, shall be a misdemeanor, for which the person, on conviction, shall be imprisoned for a period not exceeding six months with hard labor.

(4) No person shall, except for the purpose of compounding as hereinafter described, mix, color, stain, or powder, or order or permit any other person to mix, color, stain, or powder any drug with any ingredient or material so as to affect injuriously the quality or potency of such drug, with intent that the same may be sold in that state, and no person shall sell any such drug so mixed, colored, stained, or powered under the same penalty in each case respectively as in the preceding section for a first and subsequent offense.

(5) *Provided*, That no person shall be liable to be convicted under either of the two last foregoing sections of this act in respect of the sale of any article of food, or of any drug, if he shows to the satisfaction of the justice or court before whom he is charged that he did not know of the article of food or drug sold by him being so mixed, colored, stained, or powdered, as in either of those sections mentioned, and that he could not with reasonable diligence have obtained that knowledge.

(6) No person shall sell to the prejudice of the purchaser any article of food or any drug which is not of the nature, substance, and quality of the article demanded by such purchaser, under a penalty not exceeding twenty pounds: provided, that an offense shall not be deemed to be committed under this section in the following cases; that is to say:

(*a*) Where any matter or ingredient not injurious to health has been added to the food or drug because the same is required for the production or preparation thereof as an article of commerce, in a state fit for carriage or consumption, and not fraudulently to increase the bulk, weight, or measure of the food or drug, or conceal the inferior quality thereof;

(*b*) Where the food or drug is compounded as in this act mentioned;

(*c*) Where the food or drug is unavoidably mixed with some extraneous matter in the process of collection or preparation.

(7) No person shall sell any compounded drug which is not composed of ingredients in accordance with the demand of the purchaser, under a penalty not exceeding twenty pounds.

(8) *Provided*, That no person shall be guilty of any such offense as aforesaid, in respect of the sale of an article of food or a drug mixed with any matter fraudulently to increase its bulk, weight, or measure, or conceal its inferior quality, if at the time of delivering such article or drug he shall supply to the person receiving the same a notice, by a label distinctly and legibly written or printed on or with the article or drug, to the effect that the same is mixed.

(9) No person shall, with the intent that the same may be sold in its altered state without notice, abstract from an article of food any part of it so as to affect injuriously its quality, substance, or nature, and no person shall sell any article so altered without making disclosure of the alteration, under penalty in each case not exceeding twenty pounds.

APPOINTMENT AND DUTIES OF ANALYSTS, AND PROCEEDINGS TO OBTAIN ANALYSIS.

(10) In the city of London and the liberties thereof, the commissioners of sewers of the city of London and the liberties thereof, and in all other parts of the metropolis the vestries and district boards acting in execution of the act for the better local management of the metropolis, the court of quarter sessions of every county, and the town council of every borough having a separate court of quarter sessions, or having under any general or local act of Parliament or otherwise a separate police establishment, may, as soon as convenient after the passing of this act, where no appointment has hitherto been made, and in all cases as and when vacancies occur, or when required so to do by the local government board, shall, for their respective city, districts, counties, or boroughs, appoint one or more persons possessing competent knowledge, skill, and experience, as analysts of all articles of food and drugs sold within the said city, metropolitan districts, counties or boroughs, and shall pay to such analysts such remuneration as shall be mutually agreed upon, and may remove him or them as they shall deem proper; but such appointments and removals shall at all times be subject to the approval of the local government board, who may require satisfactory proof of competency to be supplied to them, and may give their approval absolutely or with modifications as to the period of the appointment and removal, or otherwise: *Provided*, That no person shall hereafter be appointed an analyst for any place under this section who shall be engaged directly or indirectly in any trade or business connected with the sale of food or drugs in such place.

In Scotland the like powers shall be conferred and the like duties shall be imposed upon the commissioners of supply at their ordinary meetings for counties, and the commissioners or boards of police, or where there are no such commissioners or boards, upon the town councils for boroughs within their several jurisdictions; provided that one of Her Majesty's principal secretaries of state in Scotland shall be substituted for the local government board of England.

In Ireland the like powers and duties shall be conferred and imposed respectively upon the grand jury of every county and town council of every borough; provided that the local government board of Ireland shall be substituted for the local government board of England.

(11) The town council of any borough may agree that the analyst appointed by any neighboring borough or for the county in which the borough is situated, shall act for their borough during such time as the said council shall think proper, and shall make due provision for the payment of his remuneration, and if such analyst shall consent, he shall during such time be the analyst for such borough for the purposes of this act.

(12) Any purchaser of an article of food or of a drug in any place being a district, county, city, or borough where there is any analyst appointed under this or any act hereby repealed shall be entitled, on payment to such analyst of a sum not exceeding ten shillings and sixpence, or if there be no such analyst then acting for such place, to the analyst of another place, of such sum as may be agreed upon between such person and the analyst, to have such article analyzed by such analyst, and to receive from him a certificate of the result of his analysis.

(13) Any medical officer of health, inspector of nuisances or inspector of weights and measures, or any inspector of a market, or any police constable under the direction and at the cost of the local authority appointing such officer, inspector, or constable, or charged with the execution of this act, may procure any sample of food or drugs, and if he suspect the same to have been sold to him contrary to any provision of this act, shall submit the same to be analyzed by the analyst of the district or place for which he acts, or if there be no such analyst then acting for such place, to the analyst of another place, and such analyst shall, upon receiving payment, as is provided in the last section, with all convenient speed analyze the same and give a certificate to such officer, wherein he shall specify the result of the analysis.

(14) The person purchasing any article with the intention of submitting the same to analysis shall, after the purchase shall have been completed, forthwith notify to the seller or his agent selling the article his intention to have the same analyzed by the public analyst, and shall offer to divide the article into three parts, to be then and there separated, and each part to be marked and sealed or fastened up in such manner as its nature will permit, and shall, if required to do so, proceed accordingly, and shall deliver one of the parts to the seller or his agent.

He shall afterwards retain one of the said parts for future comparison, and submit the third part, if he deems it right to have the article analyzed, to the analyst.

(15) If the seller or his agent do not accept the offer of the purchaser to divide the article purchased in his presence, the analyst receiving the article for analysis shall divide the same into two parts, and shall seal or fasten up one of those parts and shall cause it to be delivered, either upon receipt of the sample or when he supplies his certificate to the purchaser, who shall retain the same for production in case proceedings shall afterwards be taken in the matter.

(16) If the analyst do not reside within two miles of the residence of the person requiring the article to be analyzed, such article may be forwarded to the analyst through the post-office as a registered letter, subject to any regulations which the Postmaster-General may make in reference to the carrying and delivery of such article, and the charge for the postage of such article shall be deemed one of the charges of this act or of the prosecution, as the case may be.

(17) If any such officer, inspector, or constable, as above described, shall apply to

purchase any article of food or any drug exposed to sale, or on sale by retail on any premises or in any shop or stores, and shall tender the price for the quantity which he shall require for the purpose of analysis, not being more than shall be reasonably requisite, and the person exposing the same for sale shall refuse to sell the same to such officer, inspector, or constable, such person shall be liable to a penalty not exceeding ten pounds.

(18) The certificate of the analysis shall be in the form set forth in the schedule hereto, or to the like effect.

(19) Every analyst appointed under any act hereby repealed or this act shall report quarterly to the authority appointing him the number of articles analyzed by him under this act during the foregoing quarter, and shall specify the result of each analysis and the sum paid to him in respect thereof, and such report shall be presented at the next meeting of the authority appointing such analyst, and every such authority shall annually transmit to the local government board, at such time and in such form as the board shall direct, a certified copy of such quarterly report.

PROCEEDINGS AGAINST OFFENDERS.

(20) When the analyst having analyzed any article shall have given his certificate of the result, from which it may appear that an offense against some one of the provisions of this act has been committed, the person causing the analysis to be made may take proceedings for the recovery of the penalty herein imposed for such offense, before any justices in petty sessions assembled having jurisdiction in the place where the article or drug sold was actually delivered to the purchaser, in a summary manner.

Every penalty imposed by this act shall be recovered in England in the manner described by the eleventh and twelfth of Victoria, chapter forty-three. In Ireland such penalties and proceedings shall be recoverable, and may be taken with respect to the police district of Dublin metropolis, subject and according to the provisions of any act regulating the powers and duties of justice of the peace for such district, or of the police of such district; and with respect to other parts of Ireland, before a justice or justices of the peace sitting in petty sessions, and subject and according to the provisions of "The petty sessions (Ireland) act, 1851," and any act amending the same.

Every penalty herein imposed may be reduced or mitigated according to the judgment of the justices.

(21) At the hearing of the information in such proceeding the production of the certificate of the analyst shall be sufficient evidence of the facts therein stated, unless the defendant shall require that the analyst shall be called as a witness, and the parts of the articles retained by the person who purchased the article shall be produced, and the defendant may, if he think fit, tender himself and his wife to be examined on his behalf, and he or she shall, if he so desire, be examined accordingly.

(22) The justice before whom any complaint may be made, or the court before whom any appeal may be heard, under this act may, upon the request of either party, in their discretion cause any article of food or drug to be sent to the commissioners of inland revenue, who shall thereupon direct the chemical officers of their department at Somerset House to make the analysis, and give a certificate to such justices of the result of the analysis; and the expenses of such analysis shall be paid by the complainant or the defendant as the justices may by order direct.

(23) Any person who has been convicted of any offense punishable by an act hereby repealed or by this act by any justices may appeal in England to the next general or quarter sessions of the peace which shall be held for the city, county, town, or place wherein such conviction shall have been made, provided that such person enter into a recognizance within three days next after such conviction, with two sufficient sureties, conditioned to try such appeal, and to be forthcoming to abide the judgment and determination of the court at such general or quarter sessions, and

to pay such costs as shall be by such court awarded; and the justices before whom such conviction shall be had are hereby empowered and required to take such recognizance; and the court at such general or quarter sessions are hereby required to hear and determine the matter of such appeal, and may award such costs to the party appealing or appealed against as they or he shall think proper.

In Ireland any person who has been convicted of an offense punishable by this act may appeal to the next court of quarter sessions to be held in the same division of the county where the conviction shall be made by any justice or justices in any petty sessions district, or to the recorder at his next sessions where the conviction shall be made by the divisional justices in the police district of Dublin metropolis, or to the recorder of any corporate or borough town (unless when any such sessions shall commence within ten days from the date of any such conviction, in which case, if the appellant sees fit, the appeal may be made to the next succeeding sessions to be held for such division or town), and it shall be lawful for such court of quarter sessions or recorder (as the case may be) to decide such appeal, if made in such form and manner and with such notices as are required by the said petty sessions acts respectively hereinbefore mentioned as to appeals against orders made by justices at petty sessions, and all the provisions of the said petty sessions acts respectively as to making appeals and as to executing the orders made or appeal, or the original orders where the appeals shall not be duly prosecuted, shall also apply to any appeal made under this act.

(24) In any prosecution under this act, where the fact of an article having been sold in a mixed state has been proved, if the defendant shall desire to rely upon any exception or provision contained in this act, it shall be incumbent upon him to prove the same.

(25) If the defendant in any prosecution under this act prove to the satisfaction of the justices or court that he had purchased the article in question as the same in nature, substance, and quality as that demanded of him by the prosecutor, and with a written warranty to that effect, that he had no reason to believe at the time when he sold it that the article was otherwise, and that he sold it in the same state as when he purchased it, he shall be discharged from the prosecution, but shall be liable to pay the costs incurred by the prosecution, unless he shall have given due notice to him that he will rely on the above defense.

(26) Every penalty imposed and recovered under this act shall be paid in the case of a prosecution by any officer, inspector, or constable of the authority who shall have appointed an analyst or agreed to the acting of an analyst within their district, to such officer, inspector, or constable, and shall be by him paid to the authority for whom he acts, and be applied toward the expense of executing this act, any statute to the contrary notwithstanding; but in the case of any other prosecution the same shall be paid and applied in England according to the law regulating the application of penalties for offenses punishable in a summary manner, and in Ireland in the manner directed by the fines act, Ireland, 1851, and the acts amending the same.

(27) Any person who shall forge, or shall utter, knowing it to be forged for the purposes of this act, any certificate or any writing purporting to contain a warranty, shall be guilty of a misdemeanor and be punishable on conviction by imprisonment for a term of not exceeding two years with hard labor.

Every person who shall willfully apply to an article of food, or a drug, in any proceedings under this act, a certificate or warranty given in relation to any other article or drug, shall be guilty of an offense under this act, and be liable to a penalty not exceeding twenty pounds.

Every person who shall give a false warranty in writing to any purchaser in respect of an article of food or a drug sold by him as principal or agent, shall be guilty of an offense under this act, and be liable to a penalty not exceeding twenty pounds.

And every person who shall willfully give a label with any article sold by him which shall falsely describe the article sold, shall be guilty of an offense under this act, and be liable to a penalty not exceeding twenty pounds.

(28) Nothing in this act contained shall affect the power of proceeding by indictment, or take away any other remedy against any offender under this act, or in any way interfere with contracts and bargains between individuals, and the rights and remedies belonging thereto.

Provided, That in any action brought by any person for a breach of contract on the sale of any article of food or of any drug, such person may recover alone or in addition to any other damages recoverable by him the amount of any penalty in which he may have been convicted under this act, together with the costs paid by him upon such conviction and those incurred by him in and about the defense thereto, if he prove that the article or drug the subject of such conviction was sold to him as and for an article or drug of the same nature, substance and quality as that which was demanded of him, and that he purchased it not knowing it to be otherwise, and afterwards sold it in the same state in which he had purchased it; the defendant in such action being nevertheless at liberty to prove that the conviction was wrongful, or that the amount of costs awarded or claimed was unreasonable.

EXPENSES OF EXECUTING THE ACT.

(29) The expenses of executing this act shall be borne, in the city of London and the liberties thereof, by the consolidated rates raised by the commissioners of sewers of the city of London and the liberties thereof, and in the rest of the metropolis by any rates or funds applicable to the purposes of the act for the better local management of the metropolis, and otherwise as regards England, in counties by the county rate, and in boroughs by the borough fund or rate.

And as regards Ireland, in counties by the grand jury cess, and in boroughs by the borough fund or rate; all such expenses payable in any county out of grand jury cess shall be paid by the treasurer of such county; and

The grand jury of any such county shall, at any assizes at which it is proved that any such expenses have been incurred or paid without previous application to presentment sessions, present to be raised off and paid by such county the moneys required to defray the same.

SPECIAL PROVISIONS AS TO TEA.

(30) From and after the first day of January, one thousand eight hundred and seventy-six, all tea imported as merchandise into, and landed at any port in Great Britain or Ireland, shall be subject to examination by persons to be appointed by the commissioners of customs, subject to the approval of the treasury, for the inspection and analysis thereof, for which purpose samples may, when deemed necessary by such inspectors, be taken, and with all convenient speed, be examined by the analysts to be so appointed; and if upon such analysis the same shall be found to be mixed with other substances or exhausted tea, the same shall not be delivered unless with the sanction of the said commissioners, and on such terms and conditions as they shall see fit to direct, either for home consumption or for use as ships' stores or for exportation; but if on such inspection and analysis, it shall appear that such tea is in the opinion of the analyst unfit for human food, the same shall be forfeited and destroyed, or otherwise disposed of in such manner as the said commissions may direct.

(31) Tea, to which the term "exhausted" is applied in this act, shall mean and include any tea which has been deprived of its proper quality, strength, or virtue, by steeping, infusion, decoction, or other means.

(32) For the purposes of this act, every liberty of a cinque port, not comprised within the jurisdiction of a borough, shall be part of the county in which it is situated, and subject to the jurisdiction of the justices of such county.

(33) In the application of this act to Scotland, the following provisions shall have effect:

(*a*) The term "misdemeanor" shall mean "a crime or offense."

(*b*) The term "defendant" shall mean "defender" and include "respondent."

(c) The term "information" shall include "complaint."

(d) This act shall be read and construed as if for the term "justices," wherever it occurs therein, the term "sheriff" were substituted.

(e) The term "sheriff" shall include "sheriff substitute."

(f) The term "borough" shall mean any royal burgh, and any burgh returning or contributing to return a member to Parliament.

(g) The expenses of executing this act shall be borne, in Scotland, in counties, by the county general assessment, and in burghs by the police assessment.

(h) This act shall be read and construed as if for the expression, "the local government board," wherever it occurs therein, the expression "one of her majesty's principal secretaries of state" were substituted.

(i) All penalties provided by this act to be recovered in a summary manner shall be recovered before the sheriff court, or at the option of the person seeking to recover the same in the police court, in any place where a sheriff officiates as a police magistrate under the provisions of "the summary procedure act, 1864," or of the police act in force for the time in any place in which a sheriff officiates as aforesaid, and all the jurisdiction, powers, and authorities necessary for this purpose are hereby conferred on sheriffs.

Every such penalty may be recovered at the instance of the procurator fiscal of the jurisdiction, or of the person who caused the analysis to be made from which it appeared that an offense had been committed against some one of the provisions of this act.

Every penalty imposed and recovered under this act shall be paid to the clerk of the court, and by him shall be accounted for and paid to the treasurer of the county general assessment, or the police assessment of the burgh, as the sheriff shall direct.

(j) Every penalty imposed by this act may be reduced or mitigated according to the judgment of the sheriff.

(k) It shall be competent to any person aggrieved by any conviction by a sheriff in any summary proceeding under this act to appeal against the same to the next circuit court, or where there are no circuit courts to the high court of justiciary at Edinburgh, in the manner prescribed by such provisions of the act of the twentieth year of the reign of King George the Second, chapter forty-three, and any acts amending the same, as relate to appeals in matters criminal, and by and under the rules, limitations, conditions, and restrictions contained in the said provisions.

(34) In the application of this act to Ireland the term "borough" shall mean any borough subject to the act of the session of the third and fourth years of the reign of Her present Majesty, chapter one hundred and eight, entitled "An act for the regulation of municipal corporations in Ireland."

The term "county" shall include a county of a city and a county of a town not being a borough.

The term "assizes" shall, with respect to the county of Dublin, mean "presenting term."

The term "treasurer of the county" shall include any person or persons or bank in any county performing duties analogous to those of the treasurer of the county in counties, and with respect to the county of Dublin, it shall mean the finance committee.

The term "police constable" shall mean, with respect to the police district of Dublin metropolis, constable of the Dublin metropolitan police, and with respect to any other part of Ireland, constable of the Royal Irish constabulary.

(35) This act shall commence on the first day of October, one thousand eight hundred and seventy-five.

(36) This act may be cited as "the sale of food and drugs act, 1875."

CANADA.

The Canadian law is as follows, in addition to which there is an elaborate act respecting the inspection of staple articles of Canadian produce:

CHAPTER 107.—An act respecting the adulteration of food, drugs, and agricultural fertilizers.

Her Majesty, by and with the advice and consent of the Senate and House of Commons of Canada, enacts as follows:

SHORT TITLE.

1. This act may be cited as "*The adulteration act.*"—48–49 V., c. 67, s. 1.

INTERPRETATIONS.

2. In this act, unless the context otherwise requires—

(*a*) The expression "food" includes every article used for food or drink by man or by cattle.

(*b*) The expression "drug" includes all medicines for internal or external use for man or for cattle.

(*c*) The expression "agricultural fertilizer" means and includes every substance imported, manufactured, prepared, or disposed of for fertilizing or manuring purposes which is sold at more than ten dollars per ton and which contains phosphoric acid or ammonia or its equivalent of nitrogen.

(*d*) The expression "officer" means any officer of inland revenue or any person authorized under this act or "*the fertilizers act*" to procure samples of articles of food, drugs, or agricultural fertilizers, and to submit them for analysis.

(*e*) Food shall be deemed to be "adulterated" within the meaning of this act—

(1) If any substance has been mixed with it so as to reduce or lower or injuriously affect its quality or strength.

(2) If any inferior or cheaper substance has been substituted, wholly or in part, for the article.

(3) If any valuable constituent of the article has been wholly or in part abstracted.

(4) If it is an imitation of, or is sold under the name of, another article.

(5, If it consists wholly or in part of a diseased or decomposed or putrid or rotten animal or vegetable substance, whether manufactured or not, or, in the case of milk or butter, if it is the produce of a diseased animal or of an animal fed upon unwholesome food.

(6) If it contains any added poisonous ingredient or any ingredient which may render such an article injurious to the health of a person consuming it.

(*f*) Every drug shall be deemed to be "adulterated" within the meaning of this act—

(1) If, when sold or offered or exposed for sale under or by a name recognized in the British or United States pharmacopœia, it differs from the standard of strength, quality, or purity laid down therein.

(2) If, when sold or offered or exposed for sale under or by a name not recognized in the British or United States pharmacopœia, but which is found in some other generally recognized pharmacopœia or other standard work on *materia medica*, it differs from the standard of strength, quality, or purity laid down in such work.

(3) If its strength or purity falls below the professed standard under which it is sold or offered or exposed for sale.

(*g*) Provided, that the foregoing definitions as to the adulteration of food and drugs shall not apply—

(1) If any matter or ingredient not injurious to health has been added to the food

or drug because the same is required for the production or preparation thereof as an article of commerce, in a state fit for carriage or consumption, and not fraudulently to increase the bulk, weight, or measure of the food or drug or to conceal the inferior quality thereof, if such articles are distinctly labeled as a mixture, in conspicuous characters, forming an inseparable part of the general label, which shall also bear the name and address of the manufacturer.

(2) If the food or drug is a proprietary medicine, or is the subject of a patent in force, and is supplied in the state required by the specification of the patent.

(3) If the food or drug is unavoidably mixed with some extraneous matter in the process of collection or preparation.

(4) If any articles of food not injurious to the health of the person consuming the same are mixed together and sold or offered for sale as a compound, and if such articles are distinctly labeled as a mixture, in conspicuous characters, forming an inseparable part of the general label, which shall also bear the name and address of the manufacturer.

(h) Every agricultural fertilizer shall be deemed to be "adulterated" within the meaning of this act if, when sold, offered, or exposed for sale, the chemical analysis thereof shows a deficiency of more than one per cent of any of the chemical substances, the percentages whereof are required to be specified in the certificate, by "the fertilizers act" required to be affixed to each barrel, box, sack, or package containing the same, or (if the agricultural fertilizer is in bulk) to be produced to the inspector; or if it contains less than the minimum percentage of such substances required by the said act to be contained in such fertilizer. (48–49 V., c. 67, s. 2.)

ANALYSIS.

3. The governor in council may appoint one or more persons possessing competent medical, chemical and microscopical knowledge as analysts of food, drugs, and agricultural fertilizers purchased, sold, or exposed or offered for sale within such territorial limits as are assigned to each of them respectively, and may also select from among the aforesaid analysts so appointed, or may appoint in addition thereto, a chief analyst, who shall be attached to the staff of the department of inland revenue at Ottawa.

(2) No analyst shall be appointed until he has undergone an examination before a special examining board appointed by the governor in council, and until he has obtained from such board a certificate setting forth that he is duly qualified to perform the duties attached to the office of analyst. (48–49 V., c. 67, s. 3; 49 V., c. 41, s. 1.)

4 The governor in council may cause such remuneration to be paid to such chief analyst and to such analysts as he deems proper, and such remuneration, whether by fees, or salary, or partly in one way, and partly in the other, may be paid to them out of any sums voted by Parliament for the purposes of this act. (48–49 V., c. 67, s. 4.)

5. The officers of inland revenue, the inspectors and deputy inspectors of weights and measures, and the inspectors and deputy inspectors acting under "the general inspection act," or any of them, shall, when required so to do by any regulation made in that behalf by the minister of inland revenue, procure and submit samples of food, drugs, or agricultural fertilizers suspected to be adulterated, to be analyzed by the analysts appointed under this act. (48–49 V., c. 67, s. 5.)

6. The council of any city, town, county, or village may appoint one or more inspectors of food, drugs, and agricultural fertilizers; and such inspectors shall, for the purposes of this act, have all the powers by this act vested in officers of inland revenue; and any such inspector may require any public analyst to analyze any samples of food, drugs, or agricultural fertilizers collected by him, if such samples have been collected in accordance with the requirements of this act.

(2) The said analyst shall, upon tender of his fees fixed for the analysis of such class of articles by the governor in council, forthwith analyze the same, and give the inspector a certificate of such analysis.

(3) Such inspector may prosecute any person manufacturing, selling, or offering or exposing for sale within the city, county, town, or village for which he is appointed inspector, any article of food, drug, or agricultural fertilizer which has been certified by any public analyst to have been adulterated within the meaning of this act.

(4) Notwithstanding any other provision of this act in respect of the disposition of penalties, all penalties imposed and recovered at the suit of any such inspector shall be paid into the revenue of the city, county, town, or village by the council of which such inspector was appointed, and may be distributed in such manner as the council of such city, county, town, or village by by-law directs. (48–49 V., c. 67, s. 6.)

7. Any officer may procure samples of food, drugs, or agricultural fertilizers which have not been declared exempt from the provisions of this act, from any person who has such articles in his possession for the purpose of sale, or who sells or exposes the same for sale; and he may procure such samples either by purchasing the same or by requiring the person in whose possession they are to show him and allow him to inspect all such articles in his possession, and the place or places in which such articles are stored, and to give him samples of such articles, on payment or tender of the value of such samples. (48–49 V., c. 67, s. 7.)

8. If the person who has such articles in his possession, or his agent or servant, refuses or fails to admit the officer, or refuses or omits to show all or any of the said articles in his possession, or the place in which any such articles are stored, or to permit the officers to inspect the same, or to give any samples thereof, or to furnish the officer with such light or assistance as he requires, when required so to do in pursuance of this act, he shall be liable to the same penalty as if he knowingly sold or exposed for sale adulterated articles knowing them to be adulterated. (48–49 V., c. 67, s. 8.)

9. The officer purchasing any article with the intention of submitting the same to be analyzed, shall, after the purchase has been completed, forthwith notify the seller or his agent selling the article of his intention to have the same analyzed by the public analyst, and shall, except in specific cases, respecting which provision is made by the governor in council, divide the article into three parts—to be then and there separated, and each part to be marked and sealed up, as its nature permits—and shall deliver one of the parts to the seller or his agent, if required by him so to do.

(2) He shall transmit another of such parts to the minister of inland revenue for submission to the chief anaylist in case of appeal, and shall submit the remaining part to the analyist for the district within which the samples were taken, unless otherwise directed by the minister of inland revenue. (48–49 V., c. 67, s. 9.)

10. The person from whom any sample is obtained under this act may require the officer obtaining it to annex to the vessel or package containing the part of the sample which he is hereby required to transmit to the minister of inland revenue the name and address of such person, and to secure, with a seal or seals belonging to him, the vessel or package containing such part of the sample, and the address annexed thereto, in such manner that the vessel or package can not be opened, or the name and address taken off, without breaking such seals; and the certificate of the chief analyst shall state the name and address of the person from whom the said sample was obtained, that the vessel or package was not open, and that the seals, securing to the vessel or package the name and address of such person, were not broken until such time as he opened the vessel or package for the purpose of making his analysis; and in such case no certificate shall be receivable in evidence, unless there is contained therein such statement as above, or a statement to the like effect. (48–49 V., c. 67, s. 10.)

11. When the officer has, by either of the means aforesaid, procured samples of the articles to be analyzed, he shall cause the same to be analyzed by one of the analysts appointed under this act, and if it appears to the analyst that the sample is adulterated within the meaning of this act, he shall certify in such fact, stating in such certificate, in the case of an article of food or a drug, whether such adulteration is of a nature injurious to the health of the person consuming the same; and the certificate so given shall be received as evidence in any proceedings taken against any person in

pursuance of this act, subject to the right of any person against whom proceedings are taken to require the attendance of the analyst, for the purposes of cross-examination. (48-49 V., c. 67, s. 11.)

12. If the vendor of the article respecting which such certificate is given deems himself aggrieved thereby, he may, within forty-eight hours of the receipt of the first notification of the intention of the officer or other purchaser to take proceedings against him (whether such notification is given by the purchaser or by the ordinary process of law), notify the said officer or purchaser in writing that he intends to appeal from the decision of the analyst to the judgment of the chief analyst; and in such case the officer or purchaser shall transmit such notification to the chief analyst, and the chief analyst shall, with all convenient speed, analyze the part of the sample transmitted to the minister of inland revenue for that purpose, and shall report thereon to the said minister; and the decision of such chief analyst shall be final, and his certificate thereof shall have the same effect as the certificate of the analyst in the next preceding section mentioned. (48-49 V., c. 67, s. 12.)

13. Every analyst appointed under this act shall report quarterly to the minister of inland revenue the number of articles of food, drugs, and agricultural fertilizers analyzed by him under this act during the preceding quarter, and shall specify the nature and kind of adulterations detected in such articles of food, drugs, and agricultural fertilizers; and all such reports, or a synopsis of them, and the names of the vendors or persons from whom obtained, and of the manufacturers when known, shall be printed and laid before Parliament as an appendix to the annual report of the said minister. (48-49 V., c. 67, s. 13.)

ADULTERATION.

14. No person shall manufacture, expose, or offer for sale, or sell any food, drug, or agricultural fertilizer which is adulterated within the meaning of this act. (48-49 V. c. 67, s. 14.)

15. If milk is sold, or offered or exposed for sale, after any valuable constituent of the article has been abstracted therefrom, or if water has been added thereto, or if it is the product of a diseased animal fed upon unwholesome food, it shall be deemed to have been adulterated in a manner injurious to health, and such sale, offer, or exposure for sale shall render the vendor liable to the penalty hereinafter provided in respect to the sale of adulterated food; except that skimmed milk may be sold as such if contained in cans bearing upon their exterior, within twelve inches of the tops of such vessels, the word "skimmed" in letters of not less than two inches in length, and served in measures also similarly marked; but any person supplying such skimmed milk, unless such quality of milk has been asked for by the purchaser, shall not be entitled to plead the provisions of this section as a defense to or in extenuation of any violation of this act.

(2) Nothing in this section shall be interpreted to permit or warrant the admixture of water with milk, or any other process than the removal of cream by skimming. (48-49 V., c. 67, s. 15.)

16. Vinegar sold, or offered or exposed for sale, shall be deemed to be adulterated in a manner injurious to health if any mineral acid has been added thereto or if it contains any soluble salt having copper or lead as a base thereof, whether such mineral acid or salt is added either during the process of manufacture or subsequently. (48-49 V., c. 67, s. 16.)

17. Alcoholic, fermented, or other potable liquors sold or offered or exposed for sale shall be deemed to have been adulterated in a manner injurious to health if they are found to contain any of the articles mentioned in the schedule of this act or any article hereafter added to such schedule by the governor in council. (48-49 V., c. 67, s. 17.)

18. The governor in council may from time to time declare certain articles or preparations exempt in whole or in part from the provisions of this act, and may add to the

schedule to this act any article or ingredient the addition of which is by him deemed necessary in the public interest; and every order in council in that behalf shall be published in the Canada Gazette, and shall take effect at the expiration of thirty days from the date of such publication.   (48–49 V., c. 67, s. 18.)

19. The governor in council shall, from time to time, cause to be prepared and published lists of the articles, mixtures, or compounds declared exempt from the provisions of this act, in accordance with the next preceding section, and shall also, from time to time, fix the limits of variability permissible in any article of food or drug or compound the standard of which is not established by any such pharmacopœia or standard work as is hereinbefore mentioned; and the orders in council fixing the same shall be published in the Canada Gazette and shall take effect at the expiration of thirty days after the publication thereof.   (48–49 V., c. 67, s. 19.)

20. Whenever any article or food, any drug, or any agricultural fertilizer is reported by any analyst as being adulterated within the meaning of this act, the minister of inland revenue may, if he thinks fit, order such article and all other articles of the same kind and quality, which were in the same place at the time the article analyzed was obtained, to be seized by any officer of customs or inland revenue and detained by him until an analysis of samples of the whole is made by the chief analyst.   (48–49 V., c. 67, s. 20.)

21. If the chief analyst reports to the minister of inland revenue that the whole or any part of such articles are adulterated, the minister may declare such article, or so much thereof as the chief analyst reports as being adulterated, to be forfeited to the Crown; and such articles shall thereupon be disposed of as the minister directs.   (48–49 V., c. 67, s. 21.)

PENALTIES.

22. Every person who wilfully adulterates any article of food or any drug, or orders any other person so to do, shall—

(a) If such adulteration is within the meaning of this act deemed to be injurious to health, for the first offense incur a penalty not exceeding fifty dollars and not less than ten dollars and costs, and for each subsequent offense a penalty not exceeding two hundred dollars and not less than fifty dollars and costs.

(b) If such adulteration is within the meaning of this act deemed not to be injurious to health, incur a penalty not exceeding thirty dollars and costs, and for each subsequent offense a penalty not exceeding one hundred dollars and not less than fifty dollars and costs.   (48–49 V., c. 67, s. 22.)

23. Every person who, by himself or his agent, sells, offers for sale, or exposes for sale any article of food or any drug which is adulterated within the meaning of this act shall—

(a) If such adulteration is within the meaning of this act deemed to be injurious to health, for a first offense incur a penalty not exceeding fifty dollars and costs, and for each subsequent offense a penalty not exceeding two hundred dollars and not less than fifty dollars and costs.

(b) If such adulteration is within the meaning of this act deemed not to be injurious to health, incur for each such offense a penalty not exceeding fifty dollars and not less than five dollars and costs.

(2) *Provided,* That if the person accused proves to the court before which the case is tried that he did not know of the article being adulterated, and shows that he could not, with reasonable diligence, have obtained that knowledge, he shall be subject only to the liability to forfeiture under the twenty-first section of this act.   (48–49 V., c. 67, s. 23.)

24. Every compounder or dealer in and every manufacturer of intoxicating liquors who has in his possession or in any part of the premises occupied by him as such any adulterated liquor, knowing it to be adulterated, or any deleterious ingredient specified in the schedule hereto, or added to such schedule by the governor in council, for

the possession of which he is unable to account to the satisfaction of the court before which the case is tried, shall be deemed knowingly to have exposed for sale adulterated food and shall incur for the first offense a penalty not exceeding one hundred dollars, and for each subsequent offense a penalty not exceeding four hundred dollars. (48–49 V., c. 67, s. 24.)

25. Every person who knowingly attaches to any article of food or any drug any label which falsely describes the article sold or offered or exposed for sale, shall incur a penalty not exceeding one hundred dollars and not less than twenty dollars and costs. (48–49 V., c. 67, s. 25.)

26. Every penalty imposed and recovered under this act shall, except as herein otherwise provided and except in the case of any suit, action, or prosecution brought or instituted under the provisions of the next following section, be paid over to the minister of finance and receiver-general, and shall form part of the consolidated revenue fund. (48–49 V., c. 67, s. 26.)

GENERAL PROVISIONS.

27. Nothing herein contained shall be held to preclude any person from submitting any sample of food, drug, or agricultural fertilizer for analysis to any public analyst, or from prosecuting the vendor thereof if such article is found to be adulterated, but the burden of proof of sale and of the fact that the sample was not tampered with after purchase shall be upon the person so submitting the same.

(2) Any public analyst shall analyze such sample on payment of the fee prescribed in respect of such article or class of article by the governor in council. (48–49 V., c. 67, s. 27.)

28. Any expenses incurred in analyzing any food, drug, or agricultural fertilizer, in pursuance of this act, shall, if the person from whom the sample is taken is convicted of having in his possession, selling, offering or exposing for sale adulterated food, drugs, or agricultural fertilizers, in violation of this act, be deemed to be a portion of the cost of the proceedings against him, and shall be paid by him accordingly; and in all other cases such expenses shall be paid as part of the expenses of the officer or of the person who procured the sample, as the case may be. (48–49 V., c. 67, s. 28.)

29. The governor in council may, from time to time, make such regulations as to him seem necessary for carrying the provisions of this act into effect. (48–49 V., c. 67, s. 29.

30. The provisions of "the inland revenue act," whether enacted with special reference to any particular business or trade or with general reference to the collection of the revenue, or the prevention, detection, or punishment of fraud or neglect in relation thereto, shall extend, apply, and be construed and shall have effect with reference to this act as if they had been enacted with special reference to the matters and things herein provided for.

(2) Every penalty imposed under this act may be enforced and dealt with as if imposed under the said act, and every compounder, and the apparatus used by him, and the place in which his business is carried on, and the articles made or compounded by him, or used in compounding any such article, shall be "subject to excise" under the said act. (48–49 V., c. 67, s. 30.)

SCHEDULE.

Cocculus indicus, chloride of sodium (otherwise common salt), copperas, opium, cayenne pepper, picric acid, Indian hemp, strychnine, tobacco, darnel seed, extract of logwood, salts of zinc, copper, or lead, alum, methyl alcohol and its derivatives, amyl alcohol, and any extract or compound of any of the above ingredients.

UNITED STATES.

[PUBLIC—No. 156.]

AN ACT to provide for the inspection of live cattle, hogs, and the carcasses and products thereof which are the subjects of interstate commerce, and for other purposes.

Be it enacted by the Senate and House of Representatives of the United States of America in Congress assembled, That the Secretary of Agriculture shall cause to be made a careful inspection of all cattle intended for export to foreign countries from the United States, at such times and places, and in such manner, as he may think proper, with a view to ascertain whether such cattle are free from disease; and for this purpose he may appoint inspectors, who shall be authorized to give an official certificate clearly stating the condition in which such animals are found, and no clearance shall be given to any vessel having on board cattle for exportation to a foreign country unless the owner or shipper of such cattle has a certificate from the inspector herein authorized to be appointed, stating that said cattle are sound and free from disease.

SEC. 2. That the Secretary of Agriculture shall also cause to be made a careful inspection of all live cattle the meat of which is intended for exportation to any foreign country, at such times and places, and in such manner, as he may think proper, with a view to ascertain whether said cattle are free from disease and their meat sound and wholesome, and may appoint inspectors, who shall be authorized to give an official certificate clearly stating the condition in which such cattle and meat are found, and no clearance shall be given to any vessel having on board any fresh beef for exportation to and sale in a foreign country from any port of the United States until the owner or shipper shall obtain from an inspector appointed under the provisions of this act such certificate.

SEC. 3. The Secretary of Agriculture shall cause to be inspected prior to their slaughter, all cattle, sheep, and hogs which are subjects of interstate commerce and which are about to be slaughtered at slaughterhouses, canning, salting, packing or rendering establishments in any State or Territory, the carcasses or products of which are to be transported and sold for human consumption in any other State or Territory, or the District of Columbia, and in addition to the aforesaid inspection, there may be made in all cases where the Secretary of Agriculture may deem necessary or expedient, under rules and regulations to be by him prescribed, a post-mortem examination of the carcasses of all cattle, sheep, and hogs about to be prepared for human consumption at any slaughterhouse, canning, salting, packing or rendering establishment in any State or Territory, or the District of Columbia, which are the subjects of interstate commerce.

SEC. 4. That said examination shall be made in the manner provided by rules and regulations to be prescribed by the Secretary of Agriculture, and after said examination the carcasses and products of all cattle, sheep, and swine found to be free of disease, and wholesome, sound, and fit for human food, shall be marked, stamped, or labeled for identification as may be provided by said rules and regulations of the Secretary of Agriculture.

Any person who shall forge, counterfeit, or knowingly and wrongfully alter, deface, or destroy any of the marks, stamps, or other devices provided for in the regulations of the Secretary of Agriculture, of any such carcasses or their products, or who shall forge, counterfeit, or knowingly and wrongfully alter, deface, or destroy any certificate provided for in said regulations, shall be deemed guilty of a misdemeanor, and on conviction thereof shall be punished by a fine not exceeding one thousand dollars, or imprisonment not exceeding one year, or by both said punishments in the discretion of the court.

SEC. 5. That it shall be unlawful for any person to transport from one State or Territory or the District of Columbia into any other State or Territory or the District of Columbia, or for any person to deliver to another for transportation from one State or Territory or the District of Columbia into another State or Territory or the District of Columbia the carcasses of any cattle, sheep, or swine, or the food products thereof, which have been examined in accordance with the provisions of sections three and four of this act, and which on said examination have been declared by the inspector making the same to be unsound or diseased. Any person violating the provisions of this section shall be deemed guilty of a misdemeanor and punished for each offense as provided in section four of this act.

SEC. 6. That the inspectors provided for in sections one and two of this act shall be authorized to give official certificates of the sound and wholesome condition of the cattle, sheep, and swine, their carcasses and products described in sections three and four of this act, and one copy of every certificate granted under the provisions of this act shall be filed in the Department of Agriculture, another copy shall be delivered to the owner or shipper, and when the cattle, sheep, and swine, or their carcasses and products are sent abroad, a third copy shall be delivered to the chief officer of the vessel on which the shipment shall be made.

SEC. 7. That none of the provisions of this act shall be so construed as to apply to any cattle, sheep, or swine slaughtered by any farmer, upon his farm, which may be transported from one State or Territory or the District of Columbia into another State or Territory or the District of Columbia: *Provided, however,* That if the carcasses of such cattle, sheep, or swine go to any packing or canning establishment and are intended for transportation to any other State or Territory or the District of Columbia as hereinbefore provided, they shall there be subject to the post-mortem examination provided for in sections three and four of this act.

Approved, March 3, 1891.

[PUBLIC—NO. 122.]

AN ACT to provide for the safe transport and humane treatment of export cattle from the United States to foreign countries, and for other purposes.

Be it enacted by the Senate and House of Representatives of the United States of America in Congress assembled, That the Secretary of Agriculture is hereby authorized to examine all vessels which are to carry export cattle from the ports of the United States to foreign countries, and to prescribe by rules and regulations or orders the accommodations which said vessels shall provide for export cattle, as to space, ventilation, fittings, food and water supply, and such other requirements as he may decide to be necessary for the safe and proper transportation and humane treatment of such animals.

SEC. 2. That whenever the owner, owners, or master of any vessel carrying export cattle shall wilfully violate or cause or permit to be violated any rule, regulation, or order made pursuant to the foregoing section, the vessel in respect of which such violation shall occur may be prohibited from again carrying cattle from any port of the United States for such length of time, not exceeding one year, as the Secretary of Agriculture may direct, and such vessel shall be refused clearance from any port of the United States accordingly.

Approved March 3, 1891.

[PUBLIC—NO. 247.]

AN ACT providing for an inspection of meats for exportation, prohibiting the importation of adulterated articles of food or drink, and authorizing the President to make proclamation in certain cases, and for other purposes.

Be it enacted by the Senate and House of Representatives of the United States of America in Congress assembled, That the Secretary of Agriculture may cause to be made a careful inspection of salted pork and bacon intended for exportation, with a view to determining whether the same is wholesome, sound, and fit for human food whenever the laws, regulations, or orders of the Government of any foreign country to which such pork or bacon is to be exported shall require inspection thereof relating to the importation thereof into such country, and also whenever any buyer, seller, or exporter of such meats intended for exportation shall request the inspection thereof.

Such inspection shall be made at the place where such meats are packed or boxed, and each package of such meats so inspected shall bear the marks, stamps, or other device for identification provided for in the last clause of this section : *Provided*, That an inspection of such meats may also be made at the place of exportation if an inspection has not been made at the place of packing, or if, in the opinion of the Secretary of Agriculture, a reinspection becomes necessary. One copy of any certificate issued by any such inspector shall be filed in the Department of Agriculture; another copy shall be attached to the invoice of each separate shipment of such meat, and a third copy shall be delivered to the consignor or shipper of such meat as evidence that packages of salted pork and bacon have been inspected in accordance with the provisions of this act and found to be wholesome, sound, and fit for human food; and for the identification of the same such marks, stamps, or other devices as the Secretary of Agriculture may by regulation prescribe shall be affixed to each of such packages.

Any person who shall forge, counterfeit or knowingly and wrongfully alter, deface, or destroy any of the marks, stamps, or other devices provided for in this section on any package of any such meats, or who shall forge, counterfeit, or knowingly and wrongfully alter, deface, or destroy any certificate in reference to meats provided for in this section, shall be deemed guilty of a misdemeanor, and on conviction thereof shall be punished by a fine not exceeding one thousand dollars or imprisonment not exceeding one year, or by both said punishments, in the discretion of the court.

SEC. 2. That it shall be unlawful to import into the United States any adulterated or unwholesome food or drug or any vinous, spirituous, or malt liquors, adulterated or mixed with any poisonous or noxious chemical drug or ingredient injurious to health. Any person who shall knowingly import into the United States any such adulterated food or drug, or drink, knowing or having reasons to believe the same to be adulterated, being the owner or the agent of the owner, or the consignor or consignee of the owner, or in privity with them, assisting in such unlawful act, shall be deemed guilty of a misdemeanor, and liable to prosecution therefor in the district court of the United States for the district into which such property is imported; and, on conviction, such person shall be fined in a sum not exceeding one thousand dollars for each separate shipment, and may be imprisoned by the court for a term not exceeding one year, or both, at the discretion of the court.

SEC. 3. That any article designed for consumption as human food or drink, and any other article of the classes or description mentioned in. this act, which shall be imported into the United States contrary to its provisions, shall be forfeited to the United States, and shall be proceeded against under the provisions of chapter eighteen of title thirteen of the Revised Statutes of the United States; and such imported property so declared forfeited may be destroyed or returned to the importer for exportation from the United States after the payment of all costs and expenses, under such regulations as the Secretary of the Treasury may prescribe; and the Secretary of the Treasury may cause such imported articles to be inspected or examined in order to ascertain whether the same have been so unlawfully imported.

SEC. 4. That whenever the President is satisfied that there is good reason to believe that any importation is being made, or is about to be made into the United States, from any foreign country, of any article used for human food or drink that is adulterated to an extent dangerous to the health or welfare of the people of the United States, or any of them, he may issue his proclamation suspending the importation of such articles from such country for such period of time as he may think necessary to prevent such importation ; and during such period it shall be unlawful to import into the United States from the countries designated in the proclamation of the President any of the articles the importation of which is so suspended.

SEC. 5. That whenever the President shall be satisfied that unjust discriminations are made by or under the authority of any foreign state against the importation to or sale in such foreign state of any product of the United States, he may direct that such products of such foreign state so discriminating against any product of the United States as he may deem proper shall be excluded from importation to the United States ; and in such cases he shall make proclamation of his direction in the premises, and therein name the time when such direction against importation shall take effect, and after such date the importation of the articles named in such proclamation shall be unlawful. The President may at any time revoke, modify, terminate, or renew any such direction as, in his opinion, the public interest may require.

SEC. 6. That the importation of neat cattle, sheep, and other ruminants, and swine, which are diseased or infected with any disease, or which shall have been exposed to such infection within sixty days next before their exportation, is hereby prohibited, and any person who shall knowingly violate the foreg .ing provision shall be deemed guilty of a misdemeanor, and shall, on conviction, be punished by a fine not exceeding five thousand dollars, or by imprisonment not exceeding three years, and any vessel or vehicle used in such unlawful importation with the knowledge of the master or owner of said vessel or vehicle that such importation is diseased or has been exposed to infection as herein described, shall be forfeited to the United States.

SEC. 7. That the Secretary of Agriculture be, and is hereby, authorized, at the expense of the owner, to place and retain in quarantine all neat cattle, sheep, and other ruminants, and all swine, imported into the United States, at such ports as he may designate for such purpose, and under such conditions as he may by regulation prescribe, respectively, for the several classes of animals above described ; and for this purpose he may have and maintain possession of all lands, buildings, animals, tools, fixtures, and appurtenances now in use for the quarantine of neat cattle, and hereafter purchase, construct, or rent as may be necessary, and he may appoint veterinary surgeons, inspectors, officers, and employés by him deemed necessary to maintain such quarantine, and provide for the execution of the other provisions of this act.

SEC. 8. That the importation of all animals described in this act into any port in the United States, except such as may be designated by the Secretary of Agriculture, with the approval of the Secretary of the Treasury, as quarantine stations, is hereby prohibited ; and the Secretary of Agriculture may cause to be slaughtered such of the animals named in this act as may be, under regulations prescribed by him, adjudged to be infected with any contagious disease or to have been exposed to infection so as to be dangerous to other animals ; and that the value of animals so slaughtered as being so exposed to infection, but not infected, may be ascertained by the agreement of the Secretary of Agriculture and owners thereof, if practicable ; otherwise, by the appraisal by two persons familiar with the character and value of such property, to be appointed by the Secretary of Agriculture, whose decision, if they agree, shall be final ; otherwise, the Secretary of Agriculture shall decide between them, and his decision shall be final ; and the amount of the value thus ascertained shall be paid to the owner thereof out of money in the Treasury appropriated for the use of the Bureau of Animal Industry ; but no payment shall be made for any animal imported in violation of the provisions of this act. If any animals subject to quarantine according to the provisions of this act are brought into any port of the United States where no quarantine station is established the collector of such port shall require the same to be conveyed by the vessel on which they are imported or are found to the nearest quarantine station, at the expense of the owner.

SEC. 9. That whenever, in the opinion of the President, it shall be necessary for the protection of animals in the United States against infections or contagious diseases, he may, by proclamation, suspend the importation of all or any class of animals for a limited time, and may change, modify, revoke, or renew such proclamation as the public good may require ; and during the time of such suspension the importation of any such animals shall be unlawful.

SEC. 10. That the Secretary of Agriculture shall cause careful inspection to be made by a suitable officer of all imported animals described in this act, to ascertain whether such animals are infected with contagious diseases or have been exposed to infection so as to be dangerous to other animals, which shall then either be placed in quarantine or dealt with according to the regulations of the Secretary of Agriculture; and all food, litter, manure, clothing, utensils, and other appliances that have been so related to such animals on board ship as to be judged liable to convey infection shall be dealt with according to the regulations of the Secretary of Agriculture; and the Secretary of Agriculture may cause inspection to be made of all animals described in this act intended for exportation, and provide for the disinfection of all vessels engaged in the transportation thereof, and of all barges or other vessels used in the conveyance of such animals intended for export to the ocean steamer or other vessels, and of all attendants and their clothing, and of all head ropes and other appliances used in such exportation, by such orders and regulations as he may prescribe; and if, upon such inspection, any such animals shall be adjudged, under the regulations of the Secretary of Agriculture, to be infected or to have been exposed to infection so as to be dangerous to other animals, they shall not be allowed to be placed upon any vessel for exportation; the expense of all the inspection and disinfection provided for in this section to be borne by the owners of the vessels on which such animals are exported.

Approved, August 30, 1890.

CIRCULARS OF INQUIRY.

U. S. Department of Agriculture,
Division of Chemistry,
Washington, D. C., April 10, 1891.

SIR: Congress having made it the duty of the Department of Agriculture to examine into and report upon the extent and character of the adulteration of food, drugs, and liquors, it has been determined to ask information bearing upon the subject from chemists, druggists, manufacturers and dealers in food and drug products, as supplemental to the extended analysis already made by the chemists of the Department. Wishing to be thoroughly accurate and absolutely impartial, the fullest information is desired, and anything you can furnish bearing on the subject will be duly appreciated and judiciously used. Inclosed you will find penalty envelope for reply.

H. W. WILEY, *Chemist.*

A. J. WEDDERBURN,
Special Agent.

ADULTERANTS OF FOODS, DRUGS, AND LIQUORS.

U. S. Department of Agriculture,
Division of Chemistry,
Washington, D. C., April 7, 1891.

The information desired is indicated by the following questions, to which full replies are earnestly requested:

1. What articles of food coming under your observation are adulterated?
2. What articles of drugs?
3. What articles of liquors?
4. What adulterants are used in any or all of the above articles?
5. Which, if any, of the adulterants are poisonous or injurious?
6. Which adulterants are noninjurious?
7. Are any beneficial?
8. Please furnish any other information bearing on the subject that will assist the Department to make an accurate and impartial report.

Date, ———.

173

NAMES OF STATE COMMISSIONERS.

H. K. Finseth, Commissioner. St. Paul, Minn.
Dr. C. W. Chancellor, Secretary, Baltimore, Md.
Dr. Benj. Lee, Secretary State Board of Health, 1532 Pine street, Philadelphia, Pa.
George W. McGuire, Commissioner, Trenton, N. J.
Edward Bethel, Commissioner, Columbus, Ohio.
Dr. Lewis Balch, Secretary Board of Health, Albany, N. Y.
Dr. S. W. Abbott, Secretary Board of Health, Boston, Mass.
W. W. Baker, Food Commissioner, Portland, Oregon.
H. C. Thom, Food Commissioner, Madison, Wis.
A. C. Tupper, Dairy Commissioner, Des Moines, Iowa.
   174

○

9 33 82